A Consumer's Guide to

Alternative
Health Care

Also by Virginia McCullough

*When The Wrong Thing Is Right: How to Overcome
Conventional Wisdom, Popular Opinion, and All the
Lies Your Parents Told You,* (with S. Bigelsen)
MasterMedia, 1994

Coping With Radiation Therapy: A Ray of Hope,
(with D. Cukier) Lowell House , 1993

Testing And Your Child, Plume Books, 1992

Touch: A Personal Workbook,
(with G. Risberg) Open Arms Press, 1991

TMJ Syndrome: The Overlooked Diagnosis,
(with A. R. Goldman) Contemporary Books, 1986

A Consumer's Guide to

Alternative
Health Care

Craig Clayton
and Virginia McCullough

ADAMS PUBLISHING
Holbrook, Massachusetts

Published by Adams Media Corporation
260 Center Street, Holbrook, MA 02343

ISBN: 1-55850-551-2

Printed in the United States of America.

J I H G F E D C B A

Library of Congress Cataloging-in-Publication Data
Clayton, Craig.
    A consumer's guide to alternative health care / Craig
Clayton and Virginia McCullough.
        p.   cm.
    Includes bibliographical references.
    ISBN 1-55850-551-2
    1. Alternative medicine—Popular works. 2. Consumer
education. I. McCullough, Virginia. II. Title.
    R733.C564   1995
    615-5—dc20   95-22376
                                                              CIP

This publication is designed to provide accurate and authoritative information with regard to the subject matter covered. It is sold with the understanding that the publisher is not engaged in rendering legal, accounting, or
other professional advice. If legal advice or other expert assistance is
required, the services of a competent professional person should be sought.
    — From a *Declaration of Principles* jointly adopted by a Committee of
                    the American Bar Association and a Committee of
                                Publishers and Associations

This book is available at quantity discounts for bulk purchases.
For information, call 1-800-872-5627.

Table of Contents

Acknowledgments

We would like to thank the many professional practitioners who helped make this book a reality. We owe a debt of gratitude to a number of people, and, unfortunately, can only name a few here. For their expertise in traditional Chinese medicine (TCM) and acupuncture, accolades must go to William Dunbar, D.N., and Robert Chelnick, M.Ac. The gifted massage therapist and reflexologist Larry Clemmons was generous with his insights into his field of expertise, as was nutritionist Elizabeth Pavka. Vermont herbalist Rosemary Gladstar was patient with our questions and generous with her in-depth knowledge.

Thanks also to literary agents Lyle Steele and Jim Kepler, and to editor Dan Weaver, who helped focus the book and move it along the path to publication. Additionally, a personal thanks to our friends Julia Schopick, Hal Wright, and Carol Wyant for their support during the whole process.

Chapter One

The World of Alternative Therapies

You have probably heard the terms: acupuncture, reflexology, Bach flower remedies, visualization, Ayurvedic body types, colonics, orthomolecular medicine, shark cartilage therapies, and so on. However, if you are like most people, you may not know what these terms mean, and more importantly, you don't know how these treatments and remedies work.

Sure, you know that these "alternative" healing systems and treatments exist, probably in your own community. You may have considered going to, or have already visited, a practitioner using one or more of the many nontraditional healing systems available today.

The number of people voting with their bodies and their dollars tells the story of a significant change in the world of health care. In 1992 alone, the so-called alternative health care practitioners accounted for over sixty million office visits. Alternative health care is now a fourteen-billion-dollar-a-year business and is growing rapidly.

Various media increasingly cover these myriad health care systems and treatments, but with condensed reporting that cannot do justice to new or reemerging tools and techniques of health care. Almost every week, one of the "magazine" television shows presents an alternative treatment, sometimes with an attitude of advocacy, but at other times with clear skepticism.

Media coverage can be helpful, but it can leave you even more confused about health care choices. Nevertheless, many people have decreasing faith in conventional medicine and increasing curiosity about certain alternative practitioners. You may have already noticed a growing emphasis on empowerment as an issue, that is, empowering average people to make informed decisions about their own health care. The information you receive might lead you to a health care treatment unknown to your parents. We have written this book to give you basic information to help you make choices about your own health care.

What Does "Alternative" Mean?

This revolution in health care has been called by many names, from nontraditional to holistic to unconventional. However, the term "alternative" is the one that appears to have lasted. The word simply means that there is a world of health care practitioners who collectively offer alternatives to the medical practices to which we are most accustomed. We chose to use this term because the other labels tend to confuse the concepts. For example, while acupuncture may be nontraditional to those in the West, it is a traditional and conventional treatment in most Asian countries. In fact, it has been evolving in that part of the world for nearly five thousand years.

In addition, during the last two decades, Americans have educated their conventional physicians about acupuncture, not the other way around. Consumers have chosen this noninvasive healing procedure, and many individual state governments have found ways to license practitioners. Acupuncture treatments may be reimbursed by insurance companies, depending on the setting in which they are performed. Some cities, such as

New York City and Portland, Oregon, have authorized publicly funded chemical dependency programs to use acupuncture as a painless, safe, and relatively inexpensive method to relieve the unpleasant withdrawal symptoms addicts experience.

For millions of people, even in this country, acupuncture is not "unconventional" treatment; rather, it is simply one alternative to Western medicine. We also decided against using the term "holistic" medicine because many of the treatment methods we describe in this book, such as massage or biofeedback, do not claim to be fully integrated treatments, although they are often mentioned as part of the holistic health care movement. Many treatments included in this book may best be described as individual pieces of a treatment plan. While they share a common view that the body cannot be treated as a separate entity from the mind, they may concentrate on only one aspect of health and healing. For example, massage therapists will not ordinarily claim that they can treat any and all illnesses. They know their treatment usually works best in conjunction with other therapies, or as a tool of prevention.

Greater recognition and acceptance of "alternative" methods was demonstrated by the National Institute of Health with the creation of its Office of Alternative Medicine. Established in 1991 and funded (with two million dollars) in 1992, this office received 452 grant applications and funded 30. In 1995 this budget was raised to 5 million dollars. Small grants, awarded to universities, clinics, and practitioners, cover a variety of treatments. For example, antioxidant vitamins are being studied to see if they enhance the ability of anticancer drugs to eradicate cancer cells. Guided imagery, also known as visualization, is being tested for its ability to boost the immune system and help the body resist or fight disease. Acupuncture is being tested with women as a treatment for depression. While not comprehensive, these studies represent the start of "official" acceptance of what already is a reality. As we've said, patients are voting with their dollars and their feet and seeking these treatments.

Sorting Through the Confusion

You have probably seen the ads and business cards—Mike Smith, Herbalist; Jill Jones, Polarity Therapy; Thomas Washington, Colonic Center of Averagetown; or, Cynthia Carlson, Aromatherapist. You see advertisements for chiropractic clinics that have nutritionists and acupuncturists on staff. An acupuncturist might offer "moxibustion." Naturopaths might offer acupressure and body work, and may be trained in homeopathic therapies. Just recently, you saw an ad for an Ayurvedic clinic near your home. You've just heard of that—isn't there a famous doctor who talks and writes about this system? Now you wonder what it is all about. And now, you hear that your family physician is referring patients for chelation therapy or guided imagery and during your last visit, yoga came up in the conversation as a way to get valuable exercise and relax your mind.

When you wander through your local bookstore, you see many books that offer self-help techniques, but you don't have the time—or the self-confidence—to concoct herbal formulations or treat your own allergies. And you certainly don't know where to begin to heal your back problems, but you do know your regular doctor's treatment plan hasn't worked. You're tired of taking pain medications that mask the symptoms and dull your senses. You're willing to try a different treatment, so you begin to ask questions and look for help.

While there are many things we can do for ourselves, most of us want some guidance, and we are confused by the variety of nutritional supplements and herbal or homeopathic formulations that line the shelves of health food stores. In the best health care settings, you can and should expect to be told about the ways in which you can help yourself. For example, you may have been told by an internist that you should watch your intake of fat. However, an alternative practitioner may recommend a specific diet, along with supplements, or he or she may refer you to a nutritionist who can help you help yourself.

You may think that your Western-trained doctor is too outer-directed, that is, he or she writes a prescription and gives you directions and then walks away. In general, alternative practitioners have a reputation for spending more time with their patients than the typical conventional medical doctor. Alternative practitioners also often ask more questions about you as a person, and these professionals may offer you a number of ways to solve your problem, rather than just treating the symptoms.

Our book is designed to help you sort through the new opportunities in self-empowering health care. The information we present about various healing systems will help you take charge of your own quest for health.

Some of the healers described in this book can serve as primary health care practitioners and can help you with preventive care. Others are usually consulted for help for specific problems. Like the family practitioner who refers patients to specialists, some of the health care professionals whose systems we describe should also be able to provide referrals to other practitioners.

We hope this book will serve to increase your confidence in your own knowledge when you visit an alternative health care practitioner. You'll know what to expect and have a basic idea of what this healing system is all about. You may wish to have more information than we can provide in a survey book such as this. That is why we have also included the names, addresses, and phone numbers for associations and organizations that can lead you to more information, and in some cases, provide referrals to practitioners and treatment centers. A reading list is included at the end of the book.

What We Include and Why

It's not easy to sort through the many health practices available in the United States today and determine which are efficacious and which are not. Therefore, we have had to make some difficult choices, especially in the area of mind/body healing. You will see entries for meditation and visualization, but we did not include past-life regression or faith healing. We didn't exclude them because we think they have no value but because (1) they are not tied to the health care world in any systematic way, and (2) certain spiritual and/or religious views are necessary for their practice. It is not necessary to have these views when one begins to practice, for example, yoga or meditation, or when choosing hypnotherapy or guided imagery.

This is not to say that belief, or at least confidence, is unimportant in some of the other systems. If acupuncture terrifies you or sounds just too weird, it is unlikely that you will believe the practitioner can help you. However, if you have an open mind, you may benefit from acupuncture even if you don't completely understand how it works. In fact, since acupuncture has been widely practiced in this country for only two decades, few Americans are fully aware of how this complex healing system works. But an open mind is usually enough to gain some benefit. Similarly, one can benefit from body work without fully comprehending the way joints and muscles move, or from herbal formulations without understanding their chemistry. Here too, a sense that the treatment may help you is usually enough with which to start.

We also include various therapies that are practiced by what we call "maverick" Western-trained physicians. For example, you'll see a section that includes, among other things, the work of Dr. Deepak Chopra, who is a widely known practitioner of Ayurvedic medicine combined with Western treatments. We also describe Dean Ornish's revolutionary treatment of heart disease and discuss the associations that support physicians who have expanded their therapies to include some unconventional methods. We also include a chapter on environmental medicine (clinical ecology) because some medical doctors who treat chemical sensitivity are shunned by their more conventional colleagues. We believe that as more of these mavericks work with the so-called alternative healers, all of us will benefit.

Throughout this book we refer to terms that describe the body's energy (Chi or Qi, for example); we also use expressions that occur frequently in alternative health care, all of which attempt to describe the body's inner wisdom and its innate ability to heal itself. Again and again, we saw many ways to say the same thing: We heal ourselves, and treatment is an aid, or an agent, that helps our bodies and minds be restored to greater health and well-being. While health care practitioners may be all over the map about the best ways to cure illness and maintain health, just about everybody agrees that ultimately, we become better because there is an inner drive to heal. All the treatments listed in this book recognize this and are by nature interactive. Therefore, all these philosophies encourage us to take responsibility for our own health and healing.

Choosing an Alternative Practitioner

You should choose alternative practitioners with as much care as you choose your family doctor. In describing each of the systems, we answer the following questions:

1. What is the philosophy behind the system or treatment?
2. How does one become a practitioner? Are there specific credentials a practitioner should have? (This area is more clear with some therapies than with others.)
3. What are some of the conditions known to respond favorably to this treatment or system of treatment?
4. Equally important, what conditions are not effectively treated with this healing system?
5. What should you watch out for when you visit a practitioner? Does he or she claim to heal everybody all the time? What kind of financial commitment is being demanded?
6. What can you expect when you visit the particular practitioner? How does acupuncture feel? What questions will a

homeopath ask you? What happens when you seek polarity therapy? How much time do treatments take? What follow-up care will usually be suggested?

7. What other types of therapies are compatible with this one? Will your chiropractor ask you to see a nutritionist to augment his or her care? Will your naturopath suggest acupuncture or hypnotherapy to help treat your nicotine addiction?

8. How can you find a practitioner and what referral sources are available?

Visiting any health care practitioner involves evaluating how comfortable you are with that person and the way his or her practice is set up. Some red flags should go up immediately if the practitioner claims to heal every condition all the time, or discourages you from seeing other practitioners, even your family doctor. Furthermore, just as we might reject Western doctors who have closed their minds to other healing systems, we should be cautious about undergoing treatment with a practitioner who criticizes all other health care philosophies.

Ask yourself if the practitioner listens to you and addresses your concerns and questions. Is he or she willing to provide you with information so that you can learn more about the philosophy or therapy? Will the practitioner help you in a reasonable period of time? We've heard of certain practitioners who ask for a long-term and very expensive commitment from a new patient. This isn't a reasonable demand, and an ethical practitioner should be able to work with you to develop a sensible and affordable treatment plan. This is especially important because some of these treatments are not covered by insurance policies.

We seldom return to medical doctors with whom we have no rapport. When we aren't compatible with a health care practitioner a barrier is created that may be insurmountable. Sometimes it's simply a clash of personalities. So, if you don't click with an alternative practitioner, we advise looking around for another person.

A Word About Insurance

There is a growing trend among insurers to cover alternative medical practices. Prudential Insurance, for instance, covers various treatments, including acupuncture for chronic pain control. American Western Life Insurance, through its Wellness Plan, covers herbal, food, and massage therapy for some ailments. At this time half a dozen states require private health insurers to cover acupuncture, and over forty states require some kind of coverage for chiropractic.

Even old-line Mutual of Omaha has been sending heart patients to Dr. Dean Ornish's drug-free, diet adjustment, life style adjustment centers. Blue Cross of Washington has initiated a pilot program in Seattle called Alterna Path covering both allopathic and alternative practitioners. The trend toward acceptance of these new and reemerging therapies continues to grow because of public demand sparked by the increasing awareness of the effectiveness of alternative medicine.

Getting the Most from this Book

Our goal for this book is simple: We have attempted to provide fundamental information about a wide range of alternative health care practitioners and their health care philosophies. This knowledge will enable you to choose the type of practitioner you believe may help you. No single book can provide all the details about the myriad treatment plans that may be offered, and as an informed consumer, you will have to make your own judgments. Our book is meant to be one tool among many that can help you on your path to wellness.

Each chapter is designed to stand alone, enabling you to get information about the particular healing system you are interested in pursuing without having to read the entire book. In addition, the resources and referral information at the end of each chapter may help you locate a practitioner in your city or town.

This book is not meant to be a substitute for seeking help from qualified health care professionals. We neither endorse nor recommend *any* specific treatment listed in this book for specific health problems you might have. When we discuss medical conditions sometimes treated with any one of these therapies, we are offering general background information only and are not advocating specific treatments or therapies for any major or minor illness or condition.

This is an exciting time in the health care world. We've never had so many choices, nor have we ever seen such rapid change. We hope our book helps you make the most of the smorgasbord of opportunity that characterizes our current world of health care.

Chapter Two

The Not-So-Unconventional Chiropractors and Osteopaths

Although chiropractic and osteopathy have similar roots, they have developed quite differently in this country, and each has a unique place in today's alternative health care arena. Today, most people view chiropractors as separate and distinct from traditional allopathic physicians; osteopaths, on the other hand, are usually seen as "regular" doctors, whose treatment techniques are often indistinguishable from their traditionally trained colleagues. This is true in some cases, but not accurate in others. To help you understand the distinction between the two philosophies, as well as their similarities, we discuss both in this chapter.

Chiropractic

When you enter the modern chiropractic office, you are usually entering a world in which a holistic philosophy of health care, healing, and prevention underlies both treatment and self-help techniques. For many people, chiropractic is the first alternative health care method sought, usually because traditional treatments haven't alleviated a specific condition (generally persistent neck, shoulder, or back pain). Nowadays, in addition to traditional chiropractic treatment, referred to as spinal adjustments or manipulation, you may receive acupuncture, massage therapy, nutritional counseling, homeopathic remedies, and so forth, in a chiropractic office. Depending on the size of the clinic and the qualifications of other practitioners on staff, you may even learn about light and sound therapies and aromatherapy. If these therapies aren't available in your chiropractor's office, it is likely that referrals can be readily made. Many chiropractors believe in an integrated team approach to healing and health maintenance; in recent decades, they have been among the most vocal proponents of this philosophy.

For a variety of reasons, some having to do with licensing and regulations affecting alternative health care, chiropractors have become diversified and their offices are often primary care health facilities. For example, in some states, acupuncture treatments may be covered by insurance only if they are performed by or under the supervision of a chiropractor. It is not unusual to find chiropractors who have taken additional training in order to become qualified acupuncturists or to competently prescribe homeopathic remedies.

What Is the Philosophy of Chiropractic?

Chiropractic is rooted in the belief that the spinal column is crucial—central—to optimal health. Indeed, the spinal column and its role in maintaining the health of the nervous system is key to a well-functioning body, and according to this philosophy, when the body is functioning efficiently, it is self-curing. While chiropractors maintain that a healthy skeletal system is the key to good health, few continue to claim (as the early chiropractors did) that all illnesses are the result of spinal abnormalities and can be treated with adjustments only. This expansion in knowledge and philosophy has resulted in the variety of treatments that some chiropractors now offer.

Although there is some evidence that spinal manipulation, the cornerstone of chiropractic treatment, was practiced by ancient Egyptians, Chinese, Assyrians, and others, modern chiropractic traces its roots to Davenport, Iowa. In that small town, a man named David Daniel Palmer first practiced manual manipulation in an attempt to correct spinal abnormalities, which he surmised were the root of illness. Palmer was not a trained doctor; in fact, he was a grocer, who, because of spiritual beliefs, felt a calling to find a single cause for all disease. According to Palmer, this one cause underlies the entire range of human illness, and by treating the cause, all other disease—from the common cold to heart disease—will be eliminated. Palmer determined this single cause to be abnormalities in the alignment of the spine.

In modern terms, chiropractic can be viewed, at least in part, as an energy therapy. If any of the skeletal parts are displaced or out of perfect alignment, the nerves, which are the energy pathways, become blocked. In addition to back pain caused by injury, poor posture, lack of exercise, or weak back and abdominal muscles, impeded energy flow can cause such complaints as indigestion, headaches, and even seemingly unrelated disorders such as asthma, menstrual cramps, and skin eruptions such as psoriasis.

According to Palmer, misaligned vertebrae were the cause of the blocked energy flow to—and through—the nerves. Therefore, if the vertebrae were realigned, energy flow would be restored and the symptoms would be relieved. Palmer called the misalignment "subluxation," a term that has lasted for the one hundred years of the evolution of chiropractic treatment and philosophy. Like homeopathy and naturopathy, chiropractic concentrates on the cause of the problem, in this case, subluxation, rather than on treating and eliminating symptoms.

Chiropractors, like many other healers, believe that we have an innate "body intelligence" that is always working to keep us well. Symptoms—pain, hypertension, gastrointestinal problems, fatigue, and so forth—are the body's way of telling us that we need to focus attention on the organ or part of the body affected. In a sense, the seat of this intelligence is the spinal column because all body functions are ultimately regulated by the "communication" between the nervous system and all organs and systems.

Palmer's son, Bartlett Joshua, known as B. J., eventually took over his father's work and turned chiropractic into a well-known healing treatment. However, before chiropractic became widespread in the United States, both Palmers were arrested for practicing medicine without a license, and David Palmer served a prison sentence. Ultimately, he abandoned his vision and his theories to the care of his son.

B. J. took over the early promotion of this new philosophy; when he died in 1961, he was a very rich man who had used high-powered promotional techniques to establish chiropractic as a force to contend with. Unfortunately, B. J. Palmer's early promotional practices worked against the philosophy's acceptance by most traditional doctors and by homeopaths and osteopaths. For example, the younger Palmer aggressively advertised for students and boasted about the lack of educational requirements to get into his chiropractic school. Eventually, he became more of a motivational salesman than a healer. He lectured widely on the psychology of business and blatantly trumpeted the profit motive in chiropractic practice and training.

Fortunately for the future of chiropractic, there were early dissenters within the field who realized that practitioners needed to be both better educated and more diverse in their diagnostic and treatment methods. In time, a schism developed and two distinct groups resulted. Those who continued to follow Palmer were known as "straights," and those who expanded chiropractic to include such things as nutritional counseling and physical therapy became known as "mixers." (Mixers are the majority today, a trend likely to continue.)

After B. J.'s death, his son, Daniel David Palmer, worked hard to change the image of chiropractors and establish them within the mainstream of health care—at least in the minds of much of the public. He professionalized the original school (still located in Davenport, Iowa) and continued the fight for insurance reimbursement of chiropractic treatment. Today, Medicare and Medicaid programs cover this treatment, and most comprehensive health insurance plans reimburse for chiropractic treatment. This is not necessarily a sign that the therapy is truly recognized by the medical establishment as effective, but rather is an indication that chiropractors and their patients have become powerful enough to demand and win these benefits. The profession has also produced numerous studies that demonstrate the efficacy of this care. In addition, the general population has voted with their bodies and their dollars, because so many people have found chiropractic to be effective for numerous health complaints. (About fifteen million people seek chiropractic treatment each year, although they may not tell their allopathic physicians about it. Some of the prejudice against this philosophy lingers on.)

Try as they would, organized medicine has been unable to suppress chiropractic. It is currently a licensed treatment in all fifty states and the District of Columbia. In 1963, the Committee on Quackery of the American Medical Association (AMA) labeled chiropractic "quackery" and called for its elimination. Unable to accomplish this, the AMA continued to harass this branch of healing and physicians were strongly admonished not to associate with chiropractors or refer patients to them for care. However, between 1978 and 1980, the AMA revised its code and removed the stigma it had encouraged. It was pressured to do this by a lawsuit filed on behalf of chiropractors. This effectively put an end to the charge that chiropractors are essentially medical heretics. While chiropractic organizations had to carry on this struggle virtually alone, millions of consumers helped this new health care treatment establish itself by continuing to seek chiropractic treatment even though they were discouraged from doing so.

Despite the long-term attacks against chiropractic theory and therapy, it has thrived because so many people report improvement in certain conditions, particularly lower back and other skeletal-related pain. Most of Western Europe, Canada, Australia, and the United States now accept that chiropractic treatment helps people with a variety of conditions. (Acceptance in these other countries generally came much earlier than in the United States.)

Although results of chiropractic treatment have been difficult to measure by such methods as double-blind studies, it has been established that many conditions are successfully (and economically) treated using chiropractic methods. Some of this research has been conducted in other countries.

A Canadian study, funded by the Ontario Ministry of Health, concluded that chiropractic is significantly more effective than what they term "medical management" for treating lower back pain. Similar to studies carried out in the United States and elsewhere, it also established that workers' disability time is significantly cut when chiropractic care is sought for back injury. The increasing trend in many other countries is to use chiropractic treatment as the primary therapy for most lower back pain. Medical management is recommended only when chiropractic treatment fails.

Because chiropractors are enjoying more respect and recognition, some have affiliated with hospitals and discussions of national health care programs have included continuing coverage for chiropractic treatment. The expanding role of alternative therapies, combined with the extensive training chiropractors currently receive, ensure that chiropractic will maintain its important position in health care.

How Are Chiropractors Trained?

All states require that chiropractors pass a licensing exam, which may be taken after graduating from an accredited chiropractic college. Much of their training is similar to that included in naturopathic and orthodox medical schools. No one can practice chiropractic medicine without passing a licensing exam.

Chiropractors have active professional associations that promote research and continue to work for wider respect for their techniques and therapies. Today, many chiropractors will eventually expand their skills to include Chinese medicine, homeopathy, and naturopathy. Other chiropractors study massage and physical therapy.

Are There Specialties Within Chiropractic?

There are both formal and informal specialties within chiropractic medicine. For example, some chiropractors will specialize in dealing with sports injuries and rehabilitation.

There are a few alterations in basic technique philosophy that represent a specialty as well. For example, a method of treatment known as Network Chiropractic is considered a more gentle form of chiropractic adjustment. Rather than the abrupt, forceful motions associated with typical adjustments, this therapy uses light touching and tapping motions that promote relaxation, increase energy, and is said to have psychotherapeutic benefits as well. For example, some people say that the body work triggered memories they had repressed for years, and when they relived painful events and were able to understand them, they experienced great relief and healing.

Another specialty has come to be known as NUCCA, from the acronym for the name of the professional association established by its practitioners, the National Upper Cervical Chiropractic Association. This specialty within chiropractic maintains that the most important part of the nervous system is the brain stem, in that the two main nerve centers in the brain stem control the muscles down the spine. Those chiropractors who specialize in NUCCA use adjustments to correct misalignment of the atlas, the first cervical vertebra. When not properly aligned, all the muscles down the back will tend to be abnormally contracted, which in turn can cause misalignment in the rest of the spine and pain in the muscles of the lower back.

Readjustment of the atlas will then have a cascading effect on all the back muscles, as well as clearing interference in the network of nerve pathways. With the nerve pathways clear and the back muscles relaxed, long-term musculoskeletal problems will be relieved and all organs and systems benefit.

What Conditions Are Commonly Treated with Chiropractic?

A typical chiropractic patient is a person who has experienced back, shoulder, or neck pain for a period of months or years, and bed rest or muscle relaxants, prescribed by medical doctors, have not provided relief. Many chiropractors, like other health care providers, urge people to seek evaluation before they are in pain, because, like family physicians, they prefer to do preventive care and would rather concentrate on helping patients stay well. Chiropractors are generally skilled in teaching people techniques to improve posture and avoid future injury. They also teach exercises to stretch the back muscles and improve mobility of the spine.

Spinal manipulation, also called chiropractic adjustment, is traditionally used for lower back pain, sciatica, neck and shoulder pain, stress (tension) headaches, chronic pain in the legs and feet and the arms and hands, pain caused by TMJ (temporomandibular joint syndrome), pinched nerves, and tingling or numbness in the extremities.

We can safely generalize and say that most people see chiropractors for the first time because they are in pain. They may have experienced pain on and off for long periods of time or they may have recently sustained an injury and are in acute pain. Chiropractic adjustments attempt to correct any distortions in posture, restore mobility to the spine and joints, and correct irritation to the nerves caused by misalignment.

People often return to chiropractors for adjustments to maintain the benefits of treatment or to have other conditions worked on. For example, the concept that a block in energy flow can cause a variety of conditions and disorders often leads people to continue to use chiropractors for primary or adjunctive care. For example, many women get chiropractic adjustments to help relieve menstrual cramps or other menstrual irregularities, and chiropractic care is often used to treat premenstrual syndrome (PMS). These patients may continue to see a gynecologist, but simply use chiropractic in addition to medical treatment. Some people may seek treatment for migraine headaches, even though this type of headache is considered vascular, as opposed to muscular. They may want to discontinue medications prescribed to treat or prevent migraines and consider chiropractic safer in the long term. (Many people seek chiropractic care in order to avoid taking medications that merely mask the pain rather than treat the underlying problem.)

Those chiropractors who believe that subluxation is the cause of all illness may use adjustments to treat just about anything—from allergies to heart disease. However, most chiropractors will use adjustments to improve circulation and energy flow to particular areas of the body and organs, and while they expect a wide variety of conditions to improve, they don't discourage patients from seeking traditional medical care or other forms of alternative health care.

In other words, few chiropractors today will claim that their primary treatment philosophy will heal anything and everything. However, chiropractors who are trained in additional healing techniques, such as nutritional therapy, biofeedback, acupuncture, Chinese or American herbalism, homeopathy, and so forth, may use therapies from all these philosophies to treat such things as ulcers, asthma, allergies, infertility, hypertension, anemia, and respiratory problems. In many cases, the chiropractor will have other alternative health care practitioners on staff to treat patients.

It is important to note that a "condition" in and of itself is not treated directly. There is extensive anecdotal evidence that individuals who receive adjustment for one problem notice that other, seemingly unrelated conditions improve. For example, there are reports of vision and hearing problems that have been reversed, sometimes dramatically, when adjustments restore the proper function of the nervous system. Spinal adjustments may also affect such conditions as hypertension, ulcers, or heart disease. These secondary benefits come about by correcting subluxation, not because the circulatory or digestive system was directly treated.

What Conditions Do Not Respond Well to Chiropractic Treatment?

Some people believe that chiropractors should not treat any condition that isn't related to spinal alignment. They do not believe that improved circulation and restoration of the flow of energy through the spine and nerves will improve overall health. Many physicians and scientists simply don't believe in the "energy" theories inherent in chiropractic, homeopathy, and Chinese medicine. Therefore, they say, any condition not related to joint and back pain cannot be effectively treated with chiropractic and it is a waste of time and money to expect relief.

Even those people who do believe that chiropractic therapy has wide application would not recommend seeking treatment for acute infections or life-threatening trauma (broken bones or internal injury, for example). Chiropractors are not licensed to prescribe drugs, perform surgery, or set broken bones. Chiropractic care should not be relied on as the primary or initial treatment for conditions such as previously diagnosed cancer or heart disease. (However, the treatment might be part of a holistic approach; certain serious conditions may improve because the spinal abnormalities are corrected.) If you use a chiropractor as a primary care physician, you should seek referrals to other providers for treatment of these illnesses. Your chiropractor may continue to monitor your progress and work with other health care practitioners. (This may be problematic in certain situations, usually because some conventional physicians are not willing to work as part of a team that includes alternative providers.)

Are There Any Risks Associated with Chiropractic Care?

There are a couple of oft-repeated warnings about chiropractic care that we wish to list here, not necessarily because they are valid, but because you may still hear them in other practitioners' offices. The first is that getting chiropractic treatment may delay seeking help from more "appropriate" sources. This was one of the arguments the medical establishment used in their attempts to discredit chiropractic; it doesn't hold up under scrutiny. Most patients seek chiropractic care when they have not received relief from conditions under treatment with traditional doctors. In addition, today's well-trained chiropractors are not likely to continue treatment when it clearly isn't working. These professionals will refer patients on to others who can diagnose and treat conditions that have not improved with their care.

There have been reports that chiropractic treatment can result in serious injury, even permanent paralysis and stroke. However, it must be pointed out that these incidents are extremely rare, and in general chiropractic is viewed as very safe. Even those who don't believe it is effective will agree that it rarely harms patients.

The x-ray has been a standard tool of chiropractic, mainly as a way to visually demonstrate to patients the nature of their problems, and some people believe that the profession has become "x-ray happy." Most chiropractors have their own x-ray equipment and part of a standard evaluation has included an x-ray of the spine, often with follow-up films performed to demonstrate improvement. This practice developed when x-rays were overused by just about every practitioner who was licensed to use them, which included most physicians and dentists (and even the unlicensed—remember the shoe stores of the 1950s!). Most chiropractors have adjusted their diagnostic work to include fewer x-ray tests and, like their physician colleagues, have invested in modern, low-radiation equipment.

Some criticism has also been directed to chiropractors because of the tendency for lengthy treatment recommendations, which some say fosters a dependency and ends up being quite costly. No doubt, there have been unscrupulous chiropractors who have used a smoke-and-mirrors approach to treatment, resulting in unnecessary tests and procedures. The chiropractic organizations have professional ethics committees to investigate claims of impropriety or pocketbook gouging. Competition operates in the chiropractic world as it does in all other health care settings, thereby offering a way to compare chiropractors' fees. If you have questions about the treatment plan a chiropractor recommends, it is wise to seek a second opinion and compare diagnoses, treatment recommendations, and fees. Of course, not all chiropractors treat the same conditions, or even necessarily treat musculoskeletal problems, in the same way.

What Happens During a Visit to a Chiropractor?

The first visit to a chiropractic clinic will probably take at least an hour or so. A chiropractor will always take an extensive history prior to a physical examination. This history is part of an initial visit, even if the presenting problem is acute back pain. Like other holistic healers, symptoms affecting one part of the body are viewed as affecting the whole body—or the whole person.

In some cases, x-rays are performed during the first visit and blood and urine studies are performed. Neurological studies are usually included in order to assess the state of the reflexes and to evaluate any reported numbness or tingling in the extremities. Part of the physical examination includes testing the mobility and agility of the spine and joints in the legs, neck, shoulders, and arms. These physical examinations take place on a treatment table, which is often adjustable and contoured to accommodate the spinal adjustments. Some chiropractors will use a heated pad to warm the muscles before they begin the manipulation.

One reason that some people have been reluctant to seek chiropractic care is that the adjustments can appear—and especially sound—odd and even frightening. The cracking, crunching, or popping in one's neck and back can be startling to a person who has never experienced it. There is a hands-on quality to these treatments that is unlike any other therapy and the practitioner uses the strength in his or her own body to manipulate the spine. This often feels like a jerking or abrupt pulling motion. The chiropractor should explain each step of these adjustments before they are performed, insuring that the patient knows what sensations and sounds to expect.

Many people report feeling immediate relief following the adjustment, although more than one treatment is almost always needed to correct spinal misalignment. In some cases, the pain will return in a short time and may even be worse than before. However, this is considered part of the "healing" pain and depending on the severity of the condition, relief should last longer as treatments continue. Eventually, pain and discomfort should be alleviated and a maintenance program (including self-help measures) will be recommended.

A treatment session could also include application of heat or cold packs, depending on the nature of the injury or condition being treated. Some chiropractors will also use mechanical devices such as TENS (Transcutaneous Electro-Neural Stimulation). This involves applying electrodes to a tender area in order to suppress the pain. This technique does not actually affect the cause of the pain, but acts to block the message of pain to the brain. It may also stimulate natural endorphins, which in turn relieve the sensation of pain.

Nowadays, a chiropractor will usually demonstrate exercises to do at home as part of the treatment that will prevent further deterioration of the alignment of the spine. If obesity, for example, is contributing to long-term back pain, the person will be counseled and advised about various weight loss programs.

In some cases, a nutritionist will be on staff. Patients may be given advice about posture, general exercise, the choice of mattress and pillows, and occupational hazards. (Chiropractors are often called upon to treat spinal problems caused by occupational injury. They also treat repetitive stress injuries affecting many different kinds of workers today.) Stress management programs may also be recommended.

Because of the holistic nature of modern chiropractic, many practitioners are familiar with self-help techniques. For example, a chiropractor might tell you that he or she can alleviate the specific symptoms that are causing discomfort right now, but for long-term prevention and maintenance, you will need to start yoga or T'ai chi, practice relaxation techniques, change your eating habits, and so forth. (One reason some people tend to avoid chiropractors is that they intuitively know that they will not be given a magic pill that cures them, leaving them free to continue living in the same old way.) The best chiropractors are effective lifestyle counselors, so you must be prepared to be advised about what you can do to help yourself.

Depending on training, a chiropractor may suggest—or perform—homeopathic treatments, acupuncture, massage, and in some cases, sensory therapies such as sound and light therapy or aromatherapy. These may or may not be available in chiropractic clinics in your area; there is wide variation in the services that individual chiropractors offer, a trend that is likely to continue as alternative therapies gain wider acceptance.

How Can You Find a Competent Chiropractor?

Chiropractors are available in virtually every corner of the country, and word of mouth referrals are the most common way to find chiropractic care. The national organizations can provide phone numbers for state and regional associations that may provide referrals. Chiropractors are well organized as a profession and there are many continuing education programs that serve the ongoing evolution of both the philosophy and practice.

The following is a list of relevant chiropractic organizations:

American Chiropractic Association
1701 Clarendon Boulevard
Arlington, VA 22209
703/276–8800

This organization provides extensive continuing education to chiropractors and is one of their primary professional associations in this country.

International Chiropractors Association
1110 North Glebe Road
Suite 1000
Arlington, VA 22201
703/528–5000

Among other things, this organization is concerned with health care policy issues and offers continuing education.

Association for Network Chiropractic Spinal Analysis
P.O. Box 7682
Longmont, CO 80501
303/678–8086

This organization offers training in network chiropractic and referrals to those using these techniques.

Osteopathy

Modern osteopathic training is barely distinguishable from allopathic training. However, this wasn't always the case. While often considered a close cousin of chiropractic, the manipulation techniques used in osteopathy also has much in common with other body work techniques and with the "energy" therapies. Osteopathy survives in this country today because its training and licensing practices put it on a par with conventional medicine. Some argue that it is a dying school of medicine precisely because its practitioners do everything a conventional physician does, and many have abandoned its original philosophy. However, the advent of holistic medicine and the increased interest in alternative therapies have resulted in a reexamination of this healing philosophy.

What Is the Philosophy of Osteopathic Medicine?

Unlike chiropractic, osteopathy was developed by an allopathic physician, Andrew Taylor Still, who became disenchanted with the methods he had been instructed to use. In particular, drugs of any kind became a kind of enemy to Still, and he declared them all toxic and refused to use them for any condition.

Like some others who developed unorthodox treatments, Still was a dynamic, colorful man with an intense desire to find a drug-free treatment that would cure all disease, or rather, allow the body's innate healing ability to work. Still was deeply religious and believed that the body's capacity to heal itself was a gift from God. His study and techniques revolved around finding the secret to restoring the body to its natural state of health and then keeping it healthy.

As a small town physician in the Midwest, Still experimented with manipulating the bones of his patients and claimed to have cured many common, but often fatal, diseases (pneumonia, typhoid, flux, etc.) without drugs. Where chiropractic talks about the nerves and the nervous system as the key to restoring the flow of energy, osteopathy emphasizes the circulatory system. Osteopathic manipulation of bones and joints is intended to restore the proper flow of blood to all organs and systems of the body.

Still's greatest motivation was ridding health care of drugs—even homeopathic remedies, still popular in the last half of the nineteenth century, did not escape his disdain. (He referred to homeopathic remedies as "sugar-coated pills.") Still successfully treated many patients and as word of his treatments spread, he soon established a large practice. In the 1870s, he attempted to present his ideas and methods at a university in Kansas. He was refused permission and out of anger and frustration, he moved to Kirksville, Missouri, where he opened a practice and eventually founded the American School of Osteopathy. Unlike conventional medical schools of the day, Still opened his doors to women and African-Americans. (Still had been a passionate abolitionist and had served in the Union Army during the Civil War.)

After Still's death in 1917, some osteopaths began to use standard diagnostic tests, surgery, and drugs in their treatment approach, which ultimately led to a trend that made them practically identical to their allopathic colleagues. Their training became almost identical too, and an osteopathic license has become the legal equivalent of an allopath's license.

Most osteopaths gradually stopped using manipulation in their practices for reasons entirely unrelated to the potential effectiveness of the treatment. The last years of the nineteenth century and the early part of the twentieth century were characterized by political struggles for power within the health care community. Many osteopaths stopped using bone manipulation techniques in order to disassociate themselves with the much-maligned chiropractors and other practitioners (naturopaths and homeopaths, for example) who were labeled heretics and quacks. However, osteopathy retained its reputation as a more holistic approach to health and healing, one reason it is enjoying renewed respect today.

The revival of interest in structural and energy therapies has led to a second look at manipulation treatments, which osteopaths are taught in medical school (whether or not they use them later). In today's health care climate, osteopaths are considered versatile primary care practitioners precisely because they have an additional skill. Osteopathic physicians have hospital affiliations, can perform standard diagnostic tests, and some perform surgery. Yet, they have long been associated with preventive medicine and holistic health care and may encourage patients to use complementary therapies.

What Conditions Do Osteopaths Treat?

Because of their nearly identical medical training, osteopaths treat any condition that allopaths would normally treat. Some will also perform bone manipulation to treat common back injuries and chronic pain, headaches, arthritis, and other conditions affecting the joints and connective tissue. The joints of the shoulders, knees, ankles, and those in the hands and feet may also be worked on with bone manipulation. An osteopath might also use manipulation techniques on soft tissue, similar to those used by massage therapists.

Andrew Still believed, as do chiropractors, that the health of the spinal column is crucial to the health of all organs and tissue. He originally used the term "lesion" to describe the systemic imbalances occurring when the spinal vertebrae are out of position. The lesions can result in muscle spasms or in the over-sensitivity of the nerves radiating from the affected area of the spinal column. (The term lesion does not refer to an actual physical injury that is visible on an x-ray, but rather to a subtle displacement of vertebrae.) In turn, these lesions or, as they are referred to today, segmental dysfunctions, can result in everything from headaches to digestive problems to respiratory or reproductive complaints. These conditions develop because spinal misalignment compromises the flow of blood (with all its nutrients) to all the organs, making them vulnerable to disease.

Today's osteopaths will generally have a wide network of conventional medical specialists to whom they refer patients, in a manner similar to that of medical family physicians. Those who retain their more holistic roots may also refer patients to alternative practitioners.

It is difficult to predict if osteopathy will continue its absorption into conventional medicine, largely leaving manipulation techniques to the chiropractors and others, or if it will reclaim its original roots and reestablish bone manipulation as a primary treatment.

What Happens During a Visit to an Osteopathic Physician?

In most cases, visiting an osteopath is much like visiting a conventional medical doctor. He or she takes a history and recommends appropriate treatment for your problem, and if necessary, will prescribe medication. However, if the particular osteopath you visit uses bone manipulation, then your spine and joints will be evaluated as well. The osteopath will take each joint through its range of motion, and then gradually and gently he or she will increase the motion until full movement of the joint is restored. This can be subtle bone manipulation, and you may not be in pain or experience stiffness in the joint that is worked on. Your walking, standing, and sitting posture will be observed to note asymmetry, which adds stress to your musculoskeletal system.

Osteopathic physicians use a number of manipulation techniques, including those that apply pressure on various parts of the body in order to correct misalignment and restore proper circulation to connective tissue and surrounding organs. As in chiropractic, manipulation is generally painless (though it might feel awkward and produce clicking or popping sounds), and while some of the techniques are abrupt and use a thrusting motion, many involve gentle movement of the joints and muscles. Cranial osteopathy uses gentle manipulations of the head and neck.

It is important to remember that many people have used the services of an osteopath without ever having bone manipulation. Some present-day osteopaths simply do not use these techniques, and some may not believe strongly in their efficacy.

Are There Any Conditions that Should Not Be Treated with Osteopathic Techniques?

The nature of osteopathic training means that, in general, osteopaths treat the same conditions that any medical doctor can treat. In fact, the comprehensive nature of the training removes the argument that having bone manipulation may delay more appropriate treatment for serious illnesses. Osteopaths diagnose cancer, heart disease, infectious illness, and so forth using the same methods as their allopathic colleagues. They also refer their patients to medical specialists.

For our purposes, osteopathic physicians are included in the alternative health world because (1) they have always had a "whole person" approach to treatment, or (2) many are returning to their bone manipulation roots, so to speak.

How Do I Find an Osteopath?

The professional schools and associations listed below can supply information about modern osteopathy. In addition, state associations can refer patients to osteopaths practicing in their region. However, the best way to determine if the osteopath uses bone manipulation is to call his or her office and ask. There is so much variation among practitioners that you should not make any assumptions.

You may also find that osteopathic care is available in some holistic health centers, which may be staffed by both allopathic and osteopathic doctors and other types of practitioners. They may use therapies such as orthomolecular nutrition (see Chapter 8) and chelation therapy (see Chapter 15), and have joined together to provide a variety of services under one roof.

The following are two associations that can provide information and referrals:

American Academy of Osteopathy
3500 DePauw Boulevard, Suite 1080
Indianapolis, IN 46268
317/879–1881

Affiliated with the American Osteopathic Association, this group of providers uses osteopathic manipulation in their practices.

American Osteopathic Association
142 East Ontario Street
Chicago, IL 60611
312/280–5800

This is the national organization that represents all osteopaths, through which you can find the referral service for your state.

Chapter Three

Reemerging Homeopathy

I n 1900, there were fifteen thousand homeopathic physicians in the United States and twenty-two homeopathic medical colleges; by the 1940s, the last homeopathic training institute was forced to close its doors. However, homeopathy has reemerged and is now a major component of the alternative health care world. Currently, there are numerous professional organizations that conduct research or offer training and certification in homeopathy.

While homeopathy is practiced in many European countries, often in conjunction with allopathic treatment, most Americans know almost nothing about this way of looking at health and healing. Yet they may find themselves referred to a homeopath by another alternative health practitioner, as this philosophy and treatment approach has much to offer. In addition, nutritionists, naturopaths, chiropractors, and others may suggest homeopathic remedies as treatment for some illnesses and conditions. Traditionally trained physicians who are interested in offering safe and noninvasive treatment may also expand their treatment options and include some homeopathic remedies. This is still not the norm, however, and many conventional doctors are skeptical of homeopathic treatment.

What Is the Philosophy of Homeopathy?

Homeopathy is one of few health care systems whose beginnings can be almost entirely credited to one person. The atmosphere in which this system developed is also important, as is the way it was initially received by the medical world and the manner in which it was subsequently repressed.

Samuel Hahnemann was a highly respected physician and chemist practicing in Germany in the late 1700s. Trained in the medical treatments of the time, which included bloodletting, blistering, and administering strong purgatives, he eventually became discouraged by the fact that patients often became worse instead of better. This historical period has been called the age of "heroic medicine," because of the drastic nature of many of the treatments. Troubled by what he saw, he began a series of experiments, using himself as the laboratory animal. The important theories he developed remain the core of homeopathic treatment.

The most widely known of Hahnemann's experiments was among his earliest, and involved taking doses of quinine, a substance derived from cinchona bark. In Europe, using quinine to treat malaria was new and still not a universally accepted treatment. Hahnemann did not have the illness, but when he took the quinine, he began to manifest symptoms of malaria.

From this and other experiments, Hahnemann developed his theory, technically known as the Law of Similars, and commonly referred to as the principle of "like cures like." In other words, Hahnemann had discovered that a substance that produces a set of symptoms in a healthy person can be used to treat an ill person who is experiencing those same symptoms. Quinine worked to treat malaria because it could produce in a healthy person the symptoms associated with the illness.

Hahnemann's experiments led him to develop others theories about the nature of health and illness. For example, Hahnemann viewed the body as a whole, not as a collection of separate parts; his was a new attitude in Europe at that time.

When a person is healthy, a state of balance exists and the body's innate intelligence, what Hahnemann called the vital force, is working to maintain its harmony. When this balance is disturbed, the symptoms produced are the body's way of working to restore balance. Nowadays, this does not sound so odd; for example, conventional physicians now understand that a fever is the body's way of fighting infection. Therefore, your family doctor may not automatically attempt to reduce low-grade fevers.

Homeopaths do not believe in treating an illness by suppressing the symptoms, and in fact, they believe that doing so prolongs an illness. Instead of treating the symptoms, they prescribe a remedy that, in a healthy person, will produce the very symptoms the ill person is manifesting. It is important to grasp that in the homeopathic system, symptoms are not viewed as either the illness itself or the cause of it; the symptoms are part of the curative process. It is believed that a remedy based on "like cures like" will help stimulate the body's own healing mechanisms.

After Hahnemann published his early findings in 1810, homeopathic principles were embraced by large numbers of his medical colleagues. Not only were they found to be effective in many cases, they were also relatively safe compared to the other treatments available. From the beginning, homeopathic remedies were used to treat common disorders such as colds, bronchitis, influenza, digestive disturbances, and arthritis, as well as widespread outbreaks of epidemic diseases such as cholera.

Hans Gram, an immigrant from Denmark, introduced homeopathic medicine in the United States in 1820. In 1844, the first Homeopathic Institute was established. For many years, homeopathy was a respected system of health care that coexisted with a variety of other schools of thought and with the myriad "folk" medicines of the time.

Although Hahnemann's Law of Similars remains controversial, it is not without precedent. Two thousand years before

Hahnemann, Ayurvedic medicine based its restorative remedies on a similar principle, and Edward Jenner, a contemporary of Hahnemann's, discovered that a small amount of cowpox introduced to a human being could produce an immune response to the smallpox virus. Indeed, the principle of vaccination could be called "like prevents like."

It is both the nature and preparation of homeopathic remedies that continue to cause controversy. Along with the Law of Similars, Hahnemann's experiments also led to his Law of Potentization (also called the Law of Infinitesimals). In short, this law applies to the strength of the dose of the remedy and the way in which the substance is diluted. Western-trained scientists often point out that in the highest dilutions, there is often barely a trace of the substance left. They use this as proof that homeopathic remedies, while not inherently dangerous, are little more than a placebo. Yet in homeopathic studies, the more diluted remedy often produces better results than those that are stronger. The arguments on both sides continue, and probably will for a long time.

The remedies homeopaths use are extracted from biological sources, and no attempt is made to synthetically reproduce them. Given what we know about the healing properties found in many plants, minerals, and animal tissue, it is not surprising that over the nearly two centuries of experimentation such substances as bee venom, deadly nightshade, phosphate of iron, sulphur, and comfrey have become the bases of many homeopathic remedies. Because of the principle of like cures like, some of the remedies include substances that cause the presented symptoms. Dilutions of poison oak may be given to relieve skin eruptions, for example. Homeopathic remedies for various illnesses are listed in numerous books and research materials and form a homeopathic *Materia Medica*, from which these physicians work.

Nowadays, there are books and journals about homeopathy written for the purpose of training other types of health care practitioners, such as naturopaths and acupuncturists. Lay people interested in prevention and self-healing can also use these publications. In addition, there are numerous homeopathic remedies sold in health food stores and through mail-order catalogs. However, most people find this array of products confusing and are better off seeking the services of health care practitioners who have studied homeopathy.

Today's homeopathic practitioners may also use nutritional supplements, herbal preparations that are not traditional homeopathic remedies, and other substances. Some homeopathic physicians are initially trained as allopaths and hold a medical degree and license. They then receive additional training in homeopathy and consider it their primary philosophy. These homeopaths often have hospital privileges, can order all medical tests, and prescribe nonhomeopathic medications if they consider them necessary. Some people prefer this situation because, in a sense, they have the best of both worlds available to them. (There are a few conventional physicians who use homeopathic remedies from time to time, but they still consider themselves conventional doctors.)

Homeopathy is used widely in Europe, often in conjunction with conventional medicine. While there have always been attempts to suppress it as a valid health care philosophy (some of them successful in Europe for periods of time), it enjoys more public acceptance in other countries than in the United States. For example, there are more homeopaths in India than anywhere else in the world.

Although there is a statue of Hahnemann in Washington, D.C., few medical students know that he was once considered a hero of medicine, and homeopathy part of mainstream health care. Unfortunately, homeopathy was suppressed by orthodox medical practitioners in the United States. These orthodox physicians had fallen from favor during a period in the nineteenth century and were forced to struggle to regain prestige and control within health care. In the mid-nineteenth century, there was wide experimentation in health care and a Popular

Health Movement called for many treatments that were later discarded and labeled as frauds and quackery. However, this movement also included a women's health care component with its emphasis on hygiene, herbal remedies, and prevention. These ideas were either suppressed or gradually adopted by the medical establishment.

In addition to regaining control over medical licensing, in the late nineteenth century the American Medical Association demanded that homeopaths be removed from state medical societies. It is interesting to note that these efforts to discredit homeopathy would most certainly have failed had not orthodox medicine already abandoned such practices as bloodletting. In addition, homeopaths experienced a period of internal dissension and some, rather than losing the ability to practice, allied themselves with the American Medical Association and gradually changed the way they practiced medicine.

There are some indications that the renewed interest in homeopathy is a logical outgrowth of our new "Popular Health Movement" and is a reaction to our current age of technological medicine with its emphasis on invasive procedures and prescription drugs. Although interest in homeopathy took a drastic dive early in this century, it never completely disappeared from the health care arena. There have been a few recently reported cases in which state medical societies have attempted to prevent licensed physicians from using homeopathic remedies.

What Training Is Required?

In this country, homeopathic medicine is practiced by professionals trained and licensed in another type of health care. Some organizations, such as the International Foundation for Homeopathy, hold training conferences for those who are licensed as medical doctors, chiropractors, acupuncturists, registered nurses, naturopaths, dentists, osteopaths, and physicians' assistants. Other organizations have similar training programs that serve as a basis for assessing qualifications. There are also practitioners who do not hold a recognized license in another health care field and are sometimes referred to as homeopathic educators. These individuals may discuss homeopathic remedies with clients, but are not trained to diagnose or prescribe. (This restriction is in place because state and federal law is quite vague about homeopathic practice and most states do not have clear licensing requirements. However, because homeopathy is recognized as a medical treatment, the legal right to practice it is generally linked to the license issued in another field. This varies from state to state as well, and in coming years, it is likely that licensing laws will be challenged and tested.) A homeopathic educator may help you understand what the over-the-counter remedies can and cannot do for you. In other words, this person may be a resource if you are interested in self-care.

Naturopathic schools include homeopathy as part of a four-year training program, and some other alternative health care practitioners using homeopathy have attended lengthy seminars for which they receive certificates of completion. You may find in your community that a few medical doctors studied both conventional and homeopathic medicine in Europe, where practicing both philosophies is quite common. Remember, it's up to you to ask questions about the practitioner's training and alleviate any concerns you may have about the person's qualifications. Some of the organizations listed at the end of this chapter provide referral sources and guidelines, as well as information about training in homeopathy.

What Conditions Can Homeopathy Treat Effectively?

This is a very broad question, in that trained homeopaths often serve as primary care practitioners. Therefore, they treat the whole array of common health complaints from allergies to depression to heart disease to reproductive problems. While homeopathy was not traditionally used as a "second choice" method, in practice, many people in this country visit homeopaths when orthodox medicine does not offer either symptomatic relief or a cure for the illness. In some cases, the treatment offered by the conventional physician is viewed as too dangerous or too drastic and a person seeks other alternatives. The rapid growth of modern homeopathic practices can often be attributed to the decision to search for better answers to common problems, those that conventional doctors are not adequately able to explain or cure.

For example, treatment for migraine headaches usually involves powerful drugs, and after years of taking these medications, a migraine sufferer might decide to seek the advice of a homeopath, who may offer a variety of treatments, including traditional homeopathic remedies. Some of the treatments may address problems that underlie the tendency to develop migraines. That person might then return to the homeopath for treatment of other conditions as they arise. Similarly, a person might seek the advice of a homeopath before agreeing to surgery for a heart condition or for reproductive problems. While homeopathic treatments may not be successful in every case, many people consider it worthwhile to try noninvasive treatments before resorting to surgery.

It is probably unwise for a lay person to try to choose among the many over-the-counter homeopathic remedies in an attempt to self-treat chronic health problems that have been resistant to treatment. This type of treatment is by nature complex and sometimes treatment is subtle. Therefore, if you want to use homeopathic remedies, it is best to consult with a trained practitioner.

Sometimes a patient will appear to become worse before he or she gets better. Homeopaths call this a "healing crisis" and it is considered a positive sign that the person is responding to the treatment and the body is now being stimulated to heal itself. An example of a common healing crisis that people often induce in themselves is the headache that can occur during a fast when the body is ridding itself of toxins. There is even a headache known as the "caffeine withdrawal headache."

It can safely be said that well-educated homeopaths can treat the entire array of common conditions from digestive problems to allergies to arthritis to heart disease. There are also homeopathic remedies for colds and influenza and remedies that help people withdraw from nicotine addiction and those that help recovering drug addicts and alcoholics. However, remember that homeopaths do not treat diseases or conditions; they treat individuals, each of whom is constitutionally unique. The same remedy given to one person with a cold may not be given to another person with similar symptoms. To a homeopath, the symptoms might actually appear to be quite different. A treatment plan for one patient with severe allergies may look entirely different from the plan designed for another patient with the same basic complaint.

What Are the Risks Involved in Homeopathy?

There are few risks associated with homeopathic remedies themselves. Dangerous side effects are few and, in general, the worst that can happen is that the treatment isn't effective in your particular case. However, in some usually obvious cases it could be unwise to delay conventional treatment and use homeopathic remedies in the hope that they will eventually result in a cure. For example, if you have a virulent infection for which immediate treatment with an antibiotic is usually recommended, delaying treatment could make your condition worse. For this reason, most people in this country do not see a homeopath for the first time when they have a serious acute condition or illness. Homeopathic treatment is more frequently sought for prevention or for treatment of chronic conditions. They may then continue to see the homeopath for all subsequent illnesses and health complaints.

If you are seeing a nutritionist or herbalist who recommends homeopathic remedies, be aware that this person is not necessarily a homeopathic physician. You may get good results, but other treatments could be required if your condition persists. However, practitioners who are both acupuncturists or chiropractors and homeopaths, for example, might have the range of skills you need. This remains a confusing area and our best advice is to ask plenty of questions about the homeopathic remedy that is offered to you. Always ask what the treatment is intended for, how it works in your body, and why this treatment is recommended at this time.

Those who are interested in incorporating homeopathic treatment into their lives should set up a consultation when they are relatively well or have questions about some chronic condition that is not debilitating or life-threatening. The homeopathic practitioner can then become familiar with your unique health history and treat you more effectively when a serious problem arises. The same infection that might require antibiotics when viewed through conventional eyes could be treated without them when the practitioner knows your history. He or she might also recommend additional treatment with other types of health care practitioners.

What Other Health Care Methods Are Compatible with Homeopathy?

In many cases, orthodox medicine can be compatible with homeopathic remedies. For example, you may need a conventional physician to put your broken bone in a cast, but you can also use homeopathic remedies to promote healing and reduce stress on the body. Your mild hypertension can be treated by conventional drugs and homeopathic remedies can be used to restore balance in the body. In some cases, the dosage of the conventional medication can then be reduced.

Most homeopaths are willing to work with their patients to make choices about combination methods. However, in certain cases, they will recommend that you use one homeopathic remedy at a time and exclude other treatments, at least for a while, to see if the homeopathic treatment is effective. For example, it is of little use to take over-the-counter cold medications and then add a homeopathic remedy that is not intended to suppress symptoms.

Today, it is common for people to seek a treatment, such as acupuncture, and consult with a homeopath at the same time. Because both treatments affect the basic energy that regulates the whole person—"vital force" in homeopathy and Chi or Qi in Chinese medicine—you may be advised to stop acupuncture treatments in order to give the homeopathic treatment a chance to work. On the other hand, chiropractic treatments, massage, nutritional counseling, biofeedback, and some other treatments may work quite well in conjunction with homeopathic treatments. The best situation, of course, is to find health care practitioners who will consult with each other and work out a joint treatment plan. Truly mutual treatment decisions will come about only as more and more patients demand them.

If you are suffering from a very serious condition, such as cancer, your homeopath may be able to work with your oncologist and suggest remedies to improve your general health and stimulate your immune system. (Your oncologist may or may not approve of these other treatments; many patients make these decisions independent of their conventional doctor's advice. This is an unfortunate situation, but it is still a reality that must be dealt with.) If you are consulting a homeopath after other treatments have been performed, he or she may suggest remedies that will improve your overall health in an attempt to prevent recurrence of the cancer.

As with all other practitioners, a homeopath who claims that he or she can absolutely cure you and discourages any other treatments is engaging in the same behavior that we complain about with conventional practitioners. If you find yourself in this situation, then you probably won't be receptive to the treatments that are offered to you. Trust is an important component in any relationship with a health care provider.

What Happens During a Visit with a Homeopath?

Like other practitioners, a homeopath takes a history, but you will probably be surprised by the kinds of questions you are asked. A homeopath is interested in you as a total individual and even your cold or flu symptoms are considered unique. Your overall constitution is considered crucial to a homeopath.

Like Chinese and Ayurvedic medicine, homeopathy is truly a holistic system and no one fact about you is considered apart from others or is viewed as irrelevant. Therefore, your preference for spicy foods over bland, your cold hands and feet, your sleep patterns, or the seasonal allergies you experience are all considered important. How you feel on cloudy or sunny days is even a significant piece of information to a homeopath who is trying to form a picture of you.

You will be asked about the stresses in your life and the activities you engage in on a regular basis. In addition, you will be asked for a detailed health history. To a homeopath, your childhood illnesses, the appendectomy you had when you were seventeen, and the pneumonia you had three years ago may be connected with each other. Your treatment history may also be important because a homeopath might suggest remedies that, in a sense, undo damage that other treatments have done. For example, antibiotics are used for a variety of conditions, often beginning in childhood. A homeopath might concentrate on restoring the body's natural balance, which has become compromised by years of overuse of antibiotic drugs.

We've heard of initial visits to a homeopathic physician lasting as long as two hours. Most of that time is spent taking the detailed history and assessing the person's current condition. However, homeopaths are individuals with different treatment styles. In addition, homeopaths who are also medical doctors may order tests and perform a more conventional physical examination. Other alternative practitioners who use homeopathic remedies may approach the health history in a different manner. Again, this is changing rapidly because of the way in which homeopathic methods have entered the consciousness of a wide variety of healers.

How Can You Find a Homeopathic Physician?

Probably the best way to find a homeopath is by word-of-mouth referral. If you believe you would like to try this form of health maintenance and treatment, begin asking others about their experiences. You may be surprised to find that there are a variety of practitioners who use homeopathic principles in their practices. Ask friends and relatives about their experiences, including the types of conditions they were treated for. What were the long-term outcomes of treatment and what kinds of recommendations were made? Learn what you can about the person's training and ask questions about the range of diseases treated. (For example, many practitioners will not claim to treat or cure a serious illness, such as cancer. They will recommend that you use their treatments as support and in conjunction with traditional therapy.)

You may find referral sources from the following organizations:

International Foundation for Homeopathy
    2366 Eastlake Avenue, East
    Suite 301
    Seattle, WA 98102
    206/324–8230

This organization has a directory of those who have completed the courses they sponsor. They will send you a complete listing for five dollars. They will also send you a pamphlet with listings of books and journals about homeopathy.

National Center for Homeopathy
801 North Fairfax Street
Suite 306
Alexandria, VA 22314
703/548–7790

This center maintains a directory of homeopaths with a wide range of education and training. They also offer courses on homeopathic treatments.

Homeopathic Academy of Naturopathic Physicians
14653 South Graves Road
Mulino, OR 97042
503/829–7326

You may be able to find a practitioner in your area who has completed the rigorous homeopathic training program from this academy and is currently practicing in your area.

Chapter Four

Acupuncture, Qi, and the Healing Life Force

Traditional Chinese Medicine (TCM) and Qi

Acupuncture is part of an ancient medical system that traces its origins back many thousands of years. Acupuncture began in China, mostly in rural areas, and over the millennia gradually grew to become the standard medical practice of the Chinese people. It is an Eastern way of looking at the world and nature, and represents a philosophy that has evolved over centuries into a many-layered system of examination and diagnosis. Acupuncture is the primary care method for hundreds of millions of people in Asia. It has had a presence in Europe for over three hundred years and has grown exponentially over the last twenty years in the United States.

This therapy works by stimulating points on the surface of the body that affect the physiological functioning of the whole body or, in some cases, specific systems. Points can be stimulated (1) by inserting very fine needles into the skin,(2) by applying heat produced by burning the herb mugwort, usually in a tiny bundle at the top end of the acupuncture needle, or (3) by applying pressure, such as massage, in the form of acupressure, which we will explore in Chapter 6.

Acupuncture is part of the widely used traditional Chinese medicine, or TCM. There are, however, many other Eastern and Western methods that work with acupuncture to enhance health, including herbal medicine, osteopathic manipulation, and what is termed therapeutic exercise, often in the form of T'ai Chi.

This traditional Chinese medicine also makes use of hundreds of herbs. A number of them, anywhere from two or three to a dozen, are combined into a prescription tea to treat particular ailments. We will explore the herbal side of Chinese medicine in detail in Chapter 9. A Chinese doctor or Western-trained acupuncturist may also tell a patient to either avoid or eat certain foods. In addition, exercise plays a key role in how the body's life force, Qi (pronounced "chee"), is built up or depleted.

Qi circulates through bodily channels or meridians called Jingluo. These form a circuit of the body, through which the internal organs are connected to one another. There are a dozen main channels traversing the trunk of the body as well as the arms, legs, and head. These have names like the Spleen channel, Small Intestine channel, and so on, but are not in exactly the same location as the corresponding organ in Western medicine. These channels and the secondary channels that connect with them throughout the body, form the circuit through which Qi is circulated.

The internal organs, or Zangfu, which generate and store Qi, also play a major role in acupuncture. There are five major Zang, or viscera organs, in the body, including the Heart, Kidney, Liver, Lungs, and Spleen. There are also six Fu, or "hollow organs," through which food passes. It is said in traditional medicine that these are very active or "Yang" type of organs.

Traditional Chinese medicine has many similarities with other Oriental medical systems such as Indian Ayurvedic medicine. These ancient medical schools predate Western, "scientific" methods by thousands of years. They also involve principles of body energy and how that energy relates to health. These energy-based systems share a holistic approach to health, meaning that they view the entire person from both a spiritual and physical perspective as a complete or integrated being. Food, massage, herbs, and acupuncture are therapies that can be applied to help people balance their energies and hence remain in good health, or regain lost or diminished health.

It should be remembered that Chinese medicine is, in some ways, a preventative medicine. Many Asian people, and increasing numbers in North America and Europe, will see an acupuncturist or Chinese herbalist on a regular basis, simply to maintain optimum health.

T'ai Chi

Another TCM method for maintaining health is the practice of T'ai Chi. The principle of T'ai Chi is to cultivate and strengthen, through movement and focused thought, the life force energy of Qi. Focus, greater coordination, and increased vitality are some of the effects of a regular T'ai Chi program. The movements of the hands, legs, and whole body are a kind of slow and elegant dance. A T'ai Chi master will stand in front of a group of people and direct movements by example.

These slow and graceful movements, sometimes called postures, are in effect a kind of meditation. They are intended to build energy and increase Qi. The original number of postures was only thirteen, but these have now grown to over a hundred, depending on the master.

As part of an exercise program following an acupuncture treatment or TCM session, T'ai Chi may be recommended. Many YMCAs, church basements and people's homes now function as T'ai Chi centers. Dr. Dean Ornish, one of our cutting-edge, maverick doctors has included T'ai Chi as part of his program of stress reduction for heart patients. T'ai Chi has also recently been shown to benefit people who suffer from multiple sclerosis (MS). T'ai Chi sessions have reportedly helped restore, at least temporarily, some degree of balance and raise energy levels in MS patients.

Types of Acupuncture

Acupuncture has its own highly developed body of knowledge. To be properly used it must be based on the most complete information available. The three types of acupuncture used today include the following.

Traditional acupuncture, which is a preventative technique used for maintaining optimal health, is usually practiced in conjunction with a wide range of traditional medical approaches, such as herbalism. This kind of practitioner will have acquired years of study and practice regarding the history and practices of Chinese medicine.

Acupuncture for anesthesia has and continues to gain wide acceptance in the United States and around the world because of its amazing feats. Not only can localized pain be treated, but major operations have been successfully performed using acupuncture as an anesthesia. You may have seen documentaries about these miracles on your local Public Broadcasting station within the last couple of years.

Treating symptoms with acupuncture is used to immediately relieve pain without a long and involved diagnosis. While more invasive than first aid, it does concentrate on symptoms and relief of pain and stress. A variant of this has been used successfully in a number of American cities to help narcotics addicts who are going through withdrawal. In some cases this is accomplished by inserting acupuncture needles into the soft tissue of patients' ears or hands, or even the nose, in points corresponding to major organ systems.

The Development of Acupuncture and TCM

The earliest origins of acupuncture are shrouded in time and go back at least two thousand years. A Chinese story relates a tale that wounded warriors sometimes recovered from chronic diseases after being shot with arrows in combat. These early anecdotes provide clues to acupuncture and its healing potential for the Chinese. There are sixth century B.C. Chinese medical texts still in existence that describe acupuncture. Sometime between 400 and 200 B.C., *The Yellow Emperor's Canon of Internal Medicine* was compiled and became the first book on acupuncture. Later, a second major book, the *Classic of Acupuncture and Moxibustion,* was written in the third century A.D.

Acupuncture and Chinese medical traditions spread through Asia in the sixth century. During the travels of discovery by Europeans in the seventeenth century, Jesuit missionaries from France came into contact with acupuncture and carried the first glimmerings of this knowledge to Western Europe. The Jesuits christened it with the name acupuncture, from the Latin "acus," for needle, and "punctura" for puncture. Acupuncture, after enjoying a brief period of popularity in the nineteenth century, remained obscure in Europe, only to reappear in 1939 when M. Soulie de Morant, a French diplomat, published a treatise on acupuncture and its healing effect on the human body.

Though Western medicine had gained a foothold in China in the early decades of this century, traditional Chinese medicine remained the primary care system for the Chinese and many Asian people. Both before and during the second world war, traditional Chinese medicine was the main type of medicine available to the nationalists, and later the communists under Mao Tse-tung. When Mao's revolution triumphed in 1949, he sent his so-called "barefoot doctors" into the country side of China armed mostly with a simple form of acupuncture. Currently, traditional as well as Western medicine are both practiced in China.

In the United States, throughout the 1960s and 1970s, acupuncture remained the butt of jokes by the American medical establishment, particularly when quack medicine was discussed. Then in 1971 the unexpected happened. While on a visit to mainland China, an American journalist was operated on for appendicitis. That journalist turned out to be *New York Times* columnist, James Reston. Reston was given only local anesthetic during the appendectomy and was conscious throughout his operation. Not only was acupuncture used in conjunction with the local anesthetic, but his post-operative pain was also treated with acupuncture. When the story of his successful operation was circulated in the world media, acupuncture began its rapid move into the realms of Western medicine.

What Is Qi?

There is no easy translation of the concept of Qi. It is generally translated as "energy" or "vital force," but perhaps "essence" is the best word. This essential life force within us can be harmed by the way we live our lives through diseases and environmental stresses, along with excesses in lifestyle. It can also be built up by proper nutrition and exercise and leading a balanced lifestyle. Qi helps the body function at an optimum level by keeping the blood and bodily fluids circulating properly. When Qi becomes blocked through a deficiency or excess, as we outline below, then illness can occur.

In the Chinese system, the patient and practitioner believe that Qi is an energy that each of us has from birth. The Qi flows from one meridian into the other, completing a cycle once a day.

This Qi gives vigor to and drives all the life forces within us, on both the physical and spiritual planes of our lives. The amount and quality of this life force is determined, to some extent, by individual heredity, but it is also shaped by how we choose to live our lives. We enhance Qi by eating the foods that have a balance of Yin and Yang, taking proper exercise, and using herbal medications. Likewise, our Qi is depleted by inappropriate living habits: excesses in alcohol, stress, drugs, and the like. The fundamental theory behind traditional Chinese medicine states that certain life factors can lead to pathogenesis and illness. These include:

- The seven emotions (*Qi Qing*): fear, anger, joy, obsession, anxiety, sorrow, and horror
- The six environmental excesses (*Liu-Yin*): fire, damp, dry, cold, heat, and wind
- Insufficient or excessive sexual activity
- Insufficient or excessive exertion, as in exercise or work
- Bodily excesses in eating and drinking

As you can see with the lists of possible causes of illness, balance is the key factor. Any of these excesses or deficiencies can block or slow the flow of Qi to different parts of the body or within the meridians. *Illness manifests itself when there is an excess or deficiency in the energies of the body.* If Qi becomes blocked, pain is sometimes the result. If the body is not performing properly, then a deficiency is usually the problem.

Acupuncture therapy stimulates points on the energy meridians to release and balance blocked or deficient energy. If the energy is flowing too fast, acupuncture will slow it down. Placing the needles in the energy points corrects the unbalanced energy flow that has been negatively affecting our internal organs or spiritual essence. The result is dramatically improved health.

Westerners have become fascinated by acupuncture and there have been some attempts to know exactly why it works. Our culture seems to always want "proofs," and to be able to break down and often dissect something before we accept it as real. There have been many Western theories advanced to explain how and why acupuncture works, especially as an anesthetic.

One theory is that acupuncture is a painkiller. In the mid-1970s, researchers on several continents confirmed the existence of endorphins, which are natural painkillers produced by the body. These biochemical pain inhibitors produced in the brain, can also relieve allergies, speed healing, and produce states where exceptional physical endurance is possible. Acupuncture has been found to increase the production of endorphins, thus promoting a beneficial effect on the bodily organ or system being treated.

In order to explain the success of acupuncture in treating a wide range of ailments, as well as the anesthetic properties that it produces, numerous Western-grounded medical theories have been proposed. We mention them here simply as a way to round out the Western picture of acupuncture. Whether one wishes to believe an Eastern or Western explanation is purely an individual decision. Some of these Western explanations include:

1. *Electricity within the human body.* Human beings generate a bioelectricity that flows through the nervous system and brain. Thoughts, decisions, and memories are examples of this process at work. The meridians we spoke of earlier make this electricity accessible to the practitioner at acupuncture points that relate to bodily organ systems. The insertion of acupuncture needles redirects this electrical flow to induce healing or maintain health.

2. *Self-hypnosis.* Sometimes called the "power of suggestion," these concepts are associated with relaxation techniques and positive suggestions inducing the body to heal itself. Many people have used hypnosis to stop smoking or cure compulsive behaviors. Some Western researchers, who tend to be skeptical of the belief system of acupuncture, suggest that its healing power comes as a result of self-induced hypnosis, which, in turn, produces a beneficial effect on the body.

3. *Gate or polarity theory.* This theory sees the life force that sustains the body as a field of electromagnetic energy with specific switches within the brain and body. When the channels

are blocked or not balanced, illness occurs. Acupuncture "needling" opens a pathway within the body so that energy can flow and healing can take place. It has been proposed that anesthetic acupuncture, for instance, closes off certain of these gates, blocking pain messages to the brain.

Yin and Yang and the Five Phases

The Qi life force of which we have been speaking flows through all things according to both ancient and modern Chinese thought. But what makes Qi move about in us? The continuous movement of energy between the two poles of Yin and Yang provide a dynamic tension that give the life force its power. Simultaneously, this theory proposes that everything in nature is governed by the complementary and opposite forces of Yin and Yang. In Chinese medicine living beings are either predominantly Yin or Yang.

The Yin-Yang symbol of dovetailing halves is a reminder of this opposite wholeness. Everything contains the essence or seed of its opposite. Yin, embodying the feminine, is nurturing and receptive; Yang is active, or masculine. These two work as interactive opposites. This wholeness is dynamic and moving with one essence flowing into the other continuously.

Individual human beings have a singular combination of Yin and Yang. When this basic harmony is unsettled or unbalanced, disease and illness result. The traditional view in Chinese medicine is that too much Yang energy causes a fever, for instance, and that too much Yin causes a chill.

The acupuncturist will describe each meridian of the body by both an element and an energy. The heart, for instance, is said to be Yin and fire, while the small intestines are Yang and fire.

The Five Phases is a fascinating circular model that beautifully represents the world of traditional Chinese medicine and plays an important part in diagnosing illness for the TCM and acupuncture practitioner. The Five Phases, sometimes called the five elements, represented by earth, fire, water, wood, and metal, are used to observe natural processes that occur and change with the seasons of the year.

Each phase is representative of the natural world during a given season. Spring, for instance, is represented by wood, the birth process, and the color green. The summer season is fire and creative growth; the color red; sharp, sometimes bitter tastes; but also joyousness. Fall, by contrast, is metal, dryness, the color white, pungent tastes, and pensive moods.

Each phase demonstrates the cyclical nature of all life and the strong influences that these forces have on our health. These characteristics described above are used to diagnose and describe the condition of the patient.

What Happens in an Acupuncturist's Office?

During an initial interview an acupuncturist will ask numerous questions and make a case history. Patients will be asked the history of their problem and the symptoms involved. Questions such as how a person is feeling both physically and mentally, and how he or she is getting along with family and friends are usually asked and are not meant to be intrusive. Questions about environment, both physical and social, as well as other lifestyle factors are often explored. The patient will also be asked about his or her reactions to changes in climate, how food tastes, and whether there have been any changes in sleeping habits. Preferences or dislikes in food and drink are other areas the acupuncturist will likely probe. Family medical history will be noted, as well as appetite and bodily secretions, including such things as sweating and regularity.

The Examination

The practitioner will begin the examination itself by taking your pulse, which is a primary method for assessing the status of your body's energy flow. This is different from the simple pulse taking that an allopathic doctor would perform. Several different pulses are taken on the wrist at different depths of flow. Believe it or not, ancient acupuncture texts list twenty-seven different pulse qualities.

Of equal importance is the appearance of the tongue. The acupuncturist will look at the color and shape of your tongue, as well as the condition of your eyes, fingernails, skin, hair, and face overall. The thickness, moisture, and the location of any swelling or coating of the tongue are all extremely important to an accurate diagnosis. The practitioner will also listen to the quality of your voice, its volume and force, and to the sound of your breathing.

With the information gained from your interview, pulse readings, and overall examination, the acupuncturist will determine your imbalance and the point or points where acupuncture will be used. This should be explained to the patient prior to treatment. The number and frequency of treatments should be discussed along with any diet, exercise, or lifestyle changes that are indicated. Acupuncturists generally break down diseases according to pathological categories. There maybe *Jingluo* or *Zangfu* disorders, or possibly Yin-Yang imbalances. The practitioner should give you at least a brief explanation of how the treatment is related to a system or a specific imbalance. (Remember: One treatment may be considered enough for a given problem, but four to seven treatments is about average.)

Finally, you will come to the insertion of the acupuncture needles. We recommend that you ask for disposable needles if the acupuncturist does not offer them. About seventy percent of all practitioners now use the disposable type. A charge to your bill of about two dollars per twenty needles is well worth the price. As a patient, you should know that the needles used are very thin. You may feel a slight prick when the needle goes in or a slight tingling when it reaches an energy flow. Once the needles are in, however, it is easy to forget where they are placed. Moving around during treatment is not advised.

Most acupuncture is performed on the hands, feet, legs, and forearms. There are conditions, however, where other parts of the body are involved. After the needles are inserted, the practitioner may, occasionally, briefly twirl or wiggle the needles as they rest in the points. This stimulates the flow of Qi and is painless. The patient may then be asked to relax with the needles in place for twenty to thirty minutes.

The acupuncturist will probably be recommending more than just acupuncture therapy. Herbal therapy, as we mentioned, usually involving the taking of certain herb teas or herbs in capsule form, is sometimes indicated. Moxibustion may also be recommended: that is, heat produced by burning an herb called mugwort. This treatment is frequently used in connection with acupuncture.

The mugwort, in the form of dried leaves, will either be attached to the top of the acupuncture needles in very small bundles and burned, or, in the form of mugwort sticks, burned and held close to the acupuncture point. Either of these sends heat comfortably to the acupuncture point to warm and tone the body's Qi, especially when dampness or coldness are the symptoms. Small paper discs are placed at the base of the needles so that ash does not touch the skin. The goal, as always, is to alleviate your symptoms and build your Qi.

Where Is Acupuncture the Most Effective?

A recent guide, put together by the World Health Organization, highlights the types of illnesses with which acupuncture has had the best track record. Be aware that this is not the full range of the application of acupuncture.

- Eye problems, including myopia (in children), cataracts, and acute conjunctivitis

- Digestive disorders, including hyperacidity, acute and chronic duodenal ulcer, hiccups, constipation, and diarrhea
- Bone and muscle disorders, including frozen shoulder, sciatica, osteoarthritis, and general lower back pain

Additionally, numerous other major disorders have been shown to be highly treatable in many cases with acupuncture. These include insomnia, arthritis, depression, headaches, some pains associated with menstruation, and general anxiety.

Cautions

As we discussed in our description of Qi, acupuncture is a medical practice that alters the flow of energy in the body—it is a life force medicine. By changing the flow and quality of Qi, it seeks to heal and maintain our bodily systems. It is best used to address imbalances of the body and illnesses that involve improper functioning of bodily systems, rather than the acute conditions that require emergency treatment in a hospital or Western type clinic.

Trauma wounds and vaginal discharges are not recommended for treatment with acupuncture. Pregnant women should approach acupuncture carefully.

Acupuncture, while not a panacea for cancer, can work as a complementary therapy with other treatments, including herbal and nutrient therapies. It is also useful in raising energy levels and has positive effects in helping patients cope with the side effects of chemical and radiation therapies associated with cancer treatments. Bacterial infection is an area where acupuncture is not used as a sole line of defense. Infections, in a few cases, could be spread to other parts of the body by increasing blood flow and circulation caused by the needles, so some caution is advised. However, some viral infections do respond well to acupuncture treatments.

Finding the Right Practitioner

Acupuncture and traditional Chinese medicine have spread widely across the American landscape. Many small towns now have acupuncture practitioners, and major cities offer a wide array of treatment options. The American Acupuncture Association in Flushing, New York, is one of the professional organizations to which many acupuncturists belong. The National Commission for the Certification of Acupuncturists (NCCA) in Washington, D.C., is the organization that administers the examination of people practicing acupuncture.

Thirty-eight states now license acupuncturists. The NCCA examination is the basis for licensure of acupuncturists in most of these states. We strongly recommend that you see a practitioner who has graduated from an accredited school of acupuncture and passed the examination given by NCCA. Most programs are three years, and a minimum of two years of study or training is considered essential. There are about two dozen schools of acupuncture in the United States at this time. We have listed four of the most well established at the end of this chapter. There is nothing wrong with asking your practitioner if they have malpractice insurance. We recommend that you do.

The examination that the NCCA provides twice a year to graduates of accredited schools of acupuncture has several parts. Included in the examination is the Practical Examination of Point Location Skills (PEPLS), and the Clean Needle Technique (CNT) course. Both of these must be successfully completed before a person can receive NCCA licensure. Currently there are over 4,500 practitioners in the United States who have passed this stringent examination. Certification from the accrediting institution should be clearly posted.

There are subtle, and not so subtle, variations among acupuncture practitioners. Someone trained in China may have a different approach regarding the herbal-medical side of acupuncture, for instance, than someone trained and practicing in North America. Chinese-trained doctors may have a greater knowledge of herbal treatments and request that you take herbs that may only be available through a traditional Chinese pharmacist.

On the down side, they may also ask what your complaint is, conduct only a cursory examination, insert needles, and then leave for the thirty to forty minutes the treatment takes. There is not much patient-practitioner interaction in some instances. The result can seem very much like an assembly-line type of treatment. This detached view of the patient is, unfortunately, a remnant of the bureaucratic 1950s in China when the government of Mao Tse-tung was, first and foremost, interested in getting patients back to work in the field or factory. It was medicine without a human face.

We advise looking for an acupuncturist who has knowledge of TCM, including herbs, nutrition, and T'ai Chi exercise, as well as acupuncture itself. This practitioner should also have the interactive people skills associated with the interview, pulse taking, and observation that we mentioned earlier. Pulse taking is an important technique and should be part of the examination. Consider too how long the acupuncturist has been in practice.

Locating the acupuncturist that is right for you will involve talking with friends and learning about their experiences with practitioners, along with visiting several practitioners. This is frequently the way patients locate a good acupuncturist. Though it is rare, beware of acupuncturists who make wild promises or who speak mainly of treating symptoms. Each person is unique and a good acupuncturist will always be considering the complete person when treatment is administered, and not simply suppressing a symptom.

Some acupuncturists practice through wellness centers where a number of alternative practitioners, such as chiropractors and homeopaths, may also be located. Others, working in conjunction with chiropractors or chiropractic clinics, will have office space under the same roof, while still others will be sole practitioners. At the end of this chapter several colleges where acupuncture is taught are listed along with professional organizations.

Professional Acupuncture Associations

National Commission for the Certification of
    Acupuncturists
    1424 16th Street, NW
    Suite 501
    Washington, DC 20036
    202/232–1404

This organization administers exams to individual practitioners.

National Accreditation Commission for Schools and
    Colleges of Acupuncture and Oriental Medicine
    1424 16th Street, NW
    Suite 501
    Washington, DC 20036

This organization provides accreditation.

American Acupuncture Association
    4262 Kissena Blvd.
    Flushing, NY 11355

American Association for Acupuncture and Oriental
    Medicine
    4101 Lake Boone Trail
    Suite 201
    Raleigh, NC 27601–6518
    919/787–5181
    919/787–4916 (fax)

Acupuncture Research Institute
313 West Andrix Street
Monterey Park, CA 91754

International Association of Clinical Laser Acupuncturists
10704 Tesshire Drive
St. Louis, MO 63123

National Acupuncture Foundation
1718 M Street
Suite 195
Washington, DC 20036

Colleges of Acupuncture

New England School of Acupuncture
30 Common Street
Watertown, MA 02172
617/926–1788

This school offers a multi-year, master's level training program in acupuncture and Oriental medicine. Also offered is a three-year herbal medicine program that totals over four hundred hours of study and practice.

Traditional Acupuncture Institute
American City Building
Suite 108
Columbia, MD 21044
301/596–3675

The institute offers courses in traditional Chinese medicine, as well as numerous seminars with speakers representing ground-breaking views on acupuncture.

American College of Traditional Chinese Medicine
455 Arkansas Street
San Francisco, CA 94107
415/282–7600

This college offers a Master of Science degree in traditional Chinese medicine. In 1992, the college opened a clinic to provide acupuncture and herbal medicine to HIV-positive people. The Ryan White Resources Emergency Act provides funding for this model program.

Midwest Center for the Study of Oriental Medicine
6226 Bankers Road
Suite 5
Racine, Wisconsin 53403
414/554–2010

The Midwest Center offers a full three-year program in acupuncture. The Center has a foreign internship program with Chinese universities that takes students to China as well as an internship program with approved clinicians in Illinois and Wisconsin. Also offers a single-year Oriental Massage program.

Chapter Five

Naturopathy

Naturopathy, sometimes referred to as the "nature cure," is not a new approach to health and healing. It incorporates principles from many systems, and other noninvasive health care philosophies use similar approaches. It has firm roots in traditions associated with European spas, which developed in the eighteenth and nineteenth centuries and still flourish in many countries today. For example, naturopaths offer recommendations about proper diet, exercise, rest, and the use of water (hydrotherapy) to relieve certain conditions and as a means to build—or rebuild—health.

These principles are, of course, emphasized by many health care systems. When your physician suggests bed rest for your cold and heating pads or ice packs to treat your injury, he or she is operating from ancient and lasting principles of healing. Naturopaths, however, emphasize these noninvasive approaches as a primary means to maintain health and treat illnesses. Today, naturopaths may also use treatment methods shared by others, including homeopathy, Chinese medicine, herbalism, and body work. Some naturopaths may also suggest such techniques as hypnotherapy and biofeedback as part of their treatment plans.

How Did Naturopathic Philosophy Develop?

The first naturopathic college in the United States was established in 1900 by a German medical doctor. Considered a heretic in his time, Benedict Lust had become disgusted with orthodox medicine and increasingly convinced that nature held the key to healing. The health spas of Germany, Austria, and Switzerland, which were considered far more than vacation destinations, inspired him to look at fasting and water cures as part of a program to maintain health. Naturopathy, as much as any other alternative health care philosophy, maintains that healthful living habits serve as the key to prevention of disease. Some of these principles appeared a bit eccentric to those who were beginning to look to science to solve every problem.

One prominent advocate of the "water cure," later named hydrotherapy, was Father Sebastian Kneipp, an Austrian priest who claimed that he had cured his tuberculosis by using cold-water baths. Later, Kneipp refined his healing system to include exercise, fresh air, herbs, and light.

As Benedict Lust was developing his curative techniques, he subscribed to hydrotherapy and it became associated in this country with naturopathy. However, it is a mistake to limit our definition of naturopathy to this one—or any single—healing technique or remedy. The American School of Naturopathy, founded by Lust and located in New York City, also taught its students to use herbal remedies, homeopathy, nutritional therapy, and manipulation techniques similar to those found in chiropractic and osteopathy.

Diet is considered a cornerstone of naturopathic treatment, which is again consistent with ancient thinking. Today, however, we would find naturopaths serving as leading advocates of organic farming and gardening and strict environmental laws, because they believe that physical and mental health cannot be separated from the healthful state of air, water, or soil. To a naturopath it seems ludicrous to think that human beings, or any living organism, can maintain health in a toxic environment.

Naturopaths believe that the body is designed to maintain health, and symptoms of illness are essentially signs that the body is ridding itself of toxins. For the most part, the common acute illnesses, such as throat infections, common colds, and many varieties of influenza, are not considered negative by definition. Rather, cold symptoms are part of restoring balance (homeostasis); rather than suppressing a fever or congestion with medications, naturopaths will likely recommend rest, a healthful diet, and nowadays perhaps some vitamin supplements and homeopathic remedies.

The naturopath would not advise taking over-the-counter cold medications or antibiotics. While the family physician might talk about a cold as an illness, the naturopath would take the view that the body is working to restore its natural balance. To repress symptoms is to interfere with the body's own work.

While not giving it a formal name such as Qi, naturopaths believe that there is a vital life force that provides us with an instinct for self-preservation and healing. Every cell has the ability to maintain its natural health and vigor. Some have compared naturopathic followers to those who believe that poor health is the result of bad "hygiene," defined in its broadest sense. Naturopaths believe that health is the natural order of things, and therefore, given nutritious food and exercise, clean water and air, and, perhaps, health-building vitamins and herbs, the body will stay healthy in most situations.

Naturopaths also believe that we cannot separate the mind from the body. If we're emotionally troubled, we are likely to suffer ill health, and the stress of modern life will take its toll on our physical and mental well-being. If we're living under the weight of emotional stress, our bodies will be adversely affected. Naturopaths believe that chronic diseases are often the result of stresses, both physical and emotional. Perhaps this is the reason that the "health spa cure" has enjoyed a revival in this country.

It's as if we intuitively know that our modern lifestyle leaves us over-stressed, physically depleted, and often emotionally spent as well. A break from our daily routine in order to restore balance to the body is an attempt to overcome these realities of life in the late twentieth century. A stay at a European spa is still part of medical treatment in some countries. Naturopaths could be credited for keeping alive the belief that nature can cure us, and in fact our bodies and minds are designed to respond favorably to this natural approach.

How Are Naturopaths Trained?

Today's naturopaths are trained much the same way medical doctors, homeopaths, osteopaths, and chiropractors are trained, in that basic anatomy and physiology are covered along with the symptomatology associated with various diseases. Naturopaths are trained to do only minor surgery, such as suturing of superficial wounds. They are well trained in body work techniques and spinal manipulation. They are also given extensive training in the herbal and nutritional sciences and homeopathic remedies. Naturopaths are trained to use colonics, enemas, fasting, and hydrotherapy (in many forms).

There is wide variation among naturopaths concerning which treatments they emphasize in their individual practices. For example, some naturopaths might be quite traditional in that they emphasize hydrotherapy, fasting, diet, and a balance of exercise and rest. Others might add an emphasis on meditation and other psychophysical techniques, while others rely on herbal therapies and vitamin and mineral supplements. Many incorporate all these approaches.

In recent years, naturopaths have added elements of Chinese medicine, including acupuncture, acupressure, and Chinese herbal remedies. This is an example of the fluid nature of current alternative health care practices. In addition, recent technology has affected diagnostic techniques used by naturopaths, and it is not unusual for patients to be given hair analysis (a controversial testing procedure used to determine levels of heavy metals in the body and nutritional status using hair samples) and sophisticated blood analysis testing, used, for example, to diagnose food sensitivities.

Because naturopathy did not develop as a scientifically unified system or philosophy, it is not surprising that it has developed to incorporate many techniques. However, the original mainstays of naturopathy are still emphasized in training. While naturopaths might once have been viewed as eccentric because of their insistence on a healthful diet and lifestyle, their recommendations have always been much like those we are beginning to hear from mainstream medicine today. From the beginning, naturopaths have espoused low-fat, high-fiber eating, abstinence from drugs and tobacco products, and moderate use of alcohol. Many naturopaths recommend that their patients use only unprocessed, preferably organically grown food products. Some recommend a vegetarian diet, while others believe that small amounts of animal protein are compatible with a healthful diet. However, they never advocated the high-protein diet rich in meat and dairy products that was once the recommendation of orthodox physicians.

While small in number, there are some medical doctors and osteopaths who are also naturopaths and who therefore have hospital privileges and a network of other specialists to which to refer patients. There are many naturopaths who have taken additional courses in Chinese medicine, herbology, and homeopathy. In addition, there are chiropractors who incorporate naturopathic principles in their practices. However, unless they have completed formal naturopathic training and passed the certification exam, these other practitioners may not call themselves naturopaths.

Naturopaths are licensed through the American Academy of Naturopathic Physicians, a national organization that also provides a referral service. The basic naturopathic course is four years of post-college training, and a license is issued after board certification examinations are completed.

What Conditions Do Naturopaths Treat?

In short, naturopaths can be primary care practitioners who offer a broad range of diagnostic and treatment services. This is especially true in Great Britain and elsewhere in Europe. In this country, most people visit naturopaths for the first time after orthodox treatment has failed to help them with common diseases and conditions, such as chronic sinusitis, menstrual or other reproductive difficulties, arthritis, recurrent respiratory ailments, and allergies. However, it is important to remember that naturopaths believe that chronic conditions usually develop after symptoms have been suppressed by drugs or other treatment. Their emphasis remains on prevention and promotion of a healthful lifestyle. Today, much naturopathic healing involves "undoing" the ill effects of our environment and toxic medical treatment, such as the overuse of antibiotics. (Herbal formulations, hydrotherapy, fasting, and colonics might well be part of their cleansing or "detoxifying" treatment.) Naturopaths will also treat nonemergency injuries and work with patients in rehabilitation programs after serious injuries.

Patients can also turn to naturopaths for adjunctive treatment for illnesses such as cancer and heart disease. While a naturopath cannot treat cancer with chemotherapy, radiation, or surgery, he or she can recommend support treatments (such as diet and nutritional supplements) that will boost the body's ability to fight the cancer and heal itself. Similar advice can be given to patients with high blood pressure and heart disease. A conventional physician might strongly advise patients with heart disease to alter their diet and lifestyle, but naturopathic physicians will offer specific information and more thorough follow-up than is generally found in a typical internist's office. (There are exceptions, of course, and these exceptional physicians appear to be growing in number.)

What Are the Risks Involved in Naturopathic Treatment?

In general, naturopaths recommend seeking drug treatment or surgery as a last resort. Therefore, if you are using naturopathy as a primary treatment, there is some risk in waiting too long for conventional treatment for certain acute or chronic conditions. This is not to say, however, that naturopathic treatments are dangerous in any specific way. Generally speaking, they are quite safe and noninvasive and may be used by most people for most common complaints.

While it is probably true that many illnesses can be healed with a "nature cure," not everyone is willing to take the chance that pneumonia or a diseased gall bladder, for example, will become worse while they fast, use hydrotherapy, rest, and so forth, which may be of great help but work more slowly. Therefore, it is best not to expect naturopathic treatment to work quickly on conditions that are advanced or where treatment has been delayed and a near emergency exists.

Given the current state of diagnostic testing and sophisticated services available through naturopaths, it is possible to get general care and referrals to other practitioners, conventional or alternative, should the need arise. Some naturopaths offer gynecological and obstetrical care (in an out-of-hospital setting) and perform minor surgery that requires only local anesthesia. Naturopaths do not have hospital privileges and aren't licensed in all states, so it is probably necessary for most people to maintain a relationship with a conventional family practitioner.

What Happens During a Visit with a Naturopath?

Naturopathy is a holistic health care system, much like homeopathy. A naturopath is interested in all phases of your life and health history. You will be asked questions about your current health complaint or the condition that led you to seek treatment.

However, the naturopath will also record an extensive history. In addition to the standard questions about childhood and adult illnesses and conditions, you will also be asked about the health history of your parents and grandparents. Genetic tendencies— or weaknesses—are considered important in treatment, and if you have a family history of arthritis, for example, then your recommended diet could be slightly different from that of a person who has no such genetic connection.

Your diet history is also important to a naturopath. Are you now overweight? Is there a history of obesity in your family? What foods comprise your standard daily diet? How are these foods cooked? How many meals do you eat every day? You will also be asked questions about your sleep habits, stresses in your life, what kind of weather affects how you feel, and so forth. Your first visit could take an hour or more because of the extensive history that is necessary to advise you as an individual.

If you are suffering from an injury, you could be given hot and cold compress treatments or manipulation, or both. If you have cold or flu symptoms but no fever, you could be given heat therapy to induce a fever, which then helps mobilize the immune system. You may also be given blood tests and in some naturopathic offices, x-rays. Depending on the reason for your visit and the qualifications and practices of the naturopath, it is possible that you will be given an acupuncture treatment.

Your "prescriptions" might include herbal or nutritional supplements and recommendations about your diet. These recommendations could be quite specific if it is believed that you suffer from food allergies. Your emotional well-being is also considered. For example, naturopaths believe in using natural remedies and recommend using full-spectrum lighting to help relieve depression and Seasonal Affective Disorder (SAD), and to maintain mental well-being. You could also be given advice about exercise, sleep, hydrotherapy techniques to use at home, and so forth.

How Do I Find a Naturopath?

We always recommend word-of-mouth referrals, but since naturopaths are not as widely distributed geographically as other alternative practitioners, you may need to rely on referrals from professional associations. While currently licensed in a few states, naturopaths practice in most states using their credentials from the professional associations listed below.

Many other systems use naturopathic principles, just as naturopaths incorporate many techniques from other philosophies. However, only those practitioners who have completed a four-year course and have passed the certification exam are entitled to call themselves naturopaths.

The following organizations can provide referrals to naturopaths.

> American Association of Naturopathic Physicians
> 2366 Eastlake Avenue
> Suite 322
> Seattle, WA 98102
> 206/323–7610

In addition to providing referrals to naturopaths, this organization publishes a quarterly newsletter and materials to educate the public about naturopathy.

> National College of Naturopathic Medicine
> 11231 Southeast Market Street
> Portland, OR 97216
> 503/255–4860

This college offers a degree in naturopathic medicine and also offers referrals to naturopaths.

Canadian College of Naturopathic Medicine
60 Berl Avenue
Etobicoke, Ont. M8Y 3C7
Canada
416/251–5261

This school offers a degree in naturopathy and can offer information about naturopaths in Canada. Currently, naturopaths are licensed in six Canadian provinces.

Chapter Six

Massage Therapy: Touching to Heal and Invigorate

We all know what the modern world of schedules and deadlines has become. This world of accelerated demands at both work and home has resulted in a numbing of the psyche and the body. As the Reichian therapists are fond of saying, we have "armored" our bodies to survive in the hyperpressured, computer-driven world of the late twentieth century.

As a result, our bodies have all the tell-tale signs of this battle with the electronic age. Our posture looks like a question mark from sitting and staring into the computer screen; our shoulders, neck, and back often feel like pieces of iron at the end of a hectic day of working at a desk, lugging around groceries, or sitting in traffic gridlock. Our frustration and blood pressure rise. It's clear that the human body has suffered in this environment. Various kinds of chronic pain, including sciatica, TMJ, and carpel tunnel syndrome top the hit parade of abuse to the body. Add to this the increased numbers of people suffering with debilitating migraine headaches, twisted torsos, and numbed extremities, and you have a pretty good picture of the average adult person's physical state.

But to the rescue comes the balm of the hands of the massage practitioner. The professional massage therapist is the person who knows everything about the body from anatomy to muscle masses to where the nerves and tendons are and how they all work together. If you have not used massage to ease the stresses and strains of the 1990s "stressed for success" pressure cooker, we strongly recommend that you do.

Massage at the Threshold

The mainstream of America no longer considers massage an exotic practice. The scientific and research communities are now actively involved in assessing and measuring the healing, beneficial effects of human touch on the human body. Studies conducted in 1992 at the University of Miami School of Medicine Touch Research Institute show that premature babies who were massaged had a nearly 50 percent greater weight gain and a six-day shorter hospital stay than babies who were not massaged. Additional research conducted by the institute showed that men infected with the HIV virus who were massaged daily for a month showed increased levels of natural killer cells and the neurotransmitter, serotonin. Serotonin calms the body and is one of the neurochemicals necessary for sleep. Studies also conducted by the medical school in Miami show that teens who were massaged reported less depression and had lower levels of stress hormones in urine and saliva. As an added sign of wider acceptance, the federal government, through its National Institutes of Health Office of Alternative Medicine, awarded several research grants in 1993 to investigate the healing properties of massage.

Clearly therapeutic massage has come into its own in the United States. Indeed, over the last five years the American Massage Therapy Association has experienced rapid growth in the number of people who have graduated from massage schools, passed their exams, and joined the association. From about 7,500 therapists in 1988 to over 18,000 today, the numbers tell the story of the increasing acceptance of massage as a therapeutic alternative for people suffering the gamut of ailments.

Over the last decade, massage has become a widely used method to deal with the abuses heaped on us by the modern world, as a way for the body to repair itself, and as a way for a person to simply let go and enjoy the true pleasure of someone kneading, stroking, and pressing away the fatigue and malaise daily life generates. Perhaps more important, massage is also an avenue to put one in touch with the deeper parts of oneself. Massage can be a centering as well as a sensual experience. Deep insights can be achieved when the conscious defenses are dropped and the body is thoroughly relaxed. There can be a profound connection between the body and mind that returns a sense of spiritual wholeness to a person, which in turn brings new creative insights.

Various terms have been used in connection with massage: body work is one that is commonly used and misused. This term covers a wide range of manipulation therapies, including such procedures as Rolfing and Myotherapy. At the other end of the body work spectrum is the low-impact Alexander Technique. In this chapter, however, we will cover the types of massage that are widely practiced in the United States for relaxation and general body health. These include:

- The earliest massage of China, known as **Amma**, has spread around the world and now has many practitioners. These practitioners have helped move massage into the workplace and made it a part of daily life for thousands of people.
- **Western** or **Swedish** massage, with its standard long strokes, is the massage used in health clubs and spas with which most Americans are familiar.
- The Esalen Institute in Big Sur, California, lent its name to **Esalen** massage, which is a combination of Eastern and

Western techniques, and, as a kind of hybrid massage, offers the best of both worlds.

- **Acupressure** massage uses the same energy points along the meridians as acupuncture (see Chapter 4).

Massage Terminology

There are a number of basic movements that the massage practitioner will use when massaging the body. Depending on the type of massage being offered, some or all of these hand movements may be used.

Kneading. This is simple lifting and squeezing of the flesh, usually in an easy rhythmic fashion, and is always used in Swedish massage. Kneading will be a part of a number of the following movements.

Tapotement. This is light tapping or short, quick blows over the fleshy parts of the body. There are a number of variations of this routine. Hacking is done with the edge of the palm, slapping with the open hand, cupping with the hand cupped inward, or tapping, an especially relaxing method, done with the fingertips. When tapotement-type work is used on a particular muscle for thirty seconds to one minute it will exhaust the muscle. This is especially effective for stopping cramps or muscles spasms, including those associated with multiple sclerosis and spastic and flaccid paralysis.

Effleurage. This is light touching or stroking that is gentle, but firm. These are the long, even strokes that cover large sections of the body. A special kind of effleurage, called spiral effleurage, stimulates the smallest blood vessels, the capillaries, in the skin.

Petrissage. This is the firmer type of stroking. It also involves the squeezing, pressing, and rolling of muscles performed with the hands and thumbs. Petrissage stimulates blood flow to the muscles and removes wastes and toxins, such as lactic acid, from muscles. This can be used on the deep tissues or the tissues closer to the surface of the body.

Vibration. This routine is performed with either the fingers or hands and includes rapid shaking and pulsating of the flesh by the practitioner. The vibration of the skin stimulates blood circulation, the nervous system, and often the digestive organs of the body. In some cases a vibrating device may be used.

Friction. This type of stroke involves a greater degree of pressure being applied to the body than the movements described above to reach deeper muscles or pressure points. Quick circular pressure over an area of the body is applied with palms on the large surfaces or with thumb and forefingers on smaller areas. Friction can be combined with other movements, such as petrissage, to enhance the effect of massage. Friction is especially effective for treating deep tissues and joint problems.

Brushing. This is an optional, light fingertip contact of the skin that is done slowly and rhythmically. When it is included in a massage it is usually done as the final series of touches in a massage session.

Swedish Massage—Getting the Whole Body Relaxed

Swedish massage is the kind of massage we are most familiar with in the United States. Developed by Dr. Peter Ling of Sweden nearly 150 years ago, it uses several basic movements, such as shaking, stroking, friction, and kneading, and applies these movements to the soft tissues of the body. If you have been to a health spa or your favorite sports club the type of massage you have probably received is basically a Swedish massage.

The Swedish method often works the large muscles of the body on both the front and back before work on specific muscles is attempted. Both practitioners and receivers of Swedish massage agree that there is a profoundly positive impact on the physiology that follows. Improved blood circulation is an obvious benefit as well as the deep cleansing of muscle wastes. These wastes build up in the tissues as a result of exercise or daily activity, and their removal is an additional benefit of massage. The lactic acids and other toxins that build up in muscle tissue after exercise or any exertion can clog the muscles, causing a reduction of range of motion in muscles. If the body does not burn these toxins, they will be converted into glucose that the body must use or store.

It is known that massage also releases endorphins, the body's natural painkillers, into the bloodstream. The endorphins and their relatives, the enkelphalins, have a natural tranquilizing effect. Studies have also shown that massaging the back, for instance, can increase nervous system activity. Almost any type of massage, but especially Swedish massage, releases knotted muscles, stops spasms, and allows blood vessels of the body a chance to push out any excess or built-up fluids. The cleansing of the cells is accelerated, and this in turn benefits the immune system.

The typical session will last thirty to sixty minutes and will cost anywhere from twenty-five to eighty-five dollars. Some health clubs include a certain number of massage sessions as part of the membership fee. Although they will probably ask, tell the therapist of any recent pains or injuries to your body. Remember, you will have removed your clothes before the massage and you will always be draped with a sheet or towels. Sections of the covering will be moved and then replaced as needed so the therapist can work on each section of the body in turn. Massage oil or lotion will be applied to each area of the body as it is worked. Remember, too, that diagnosis is not part of what happens during a massage session. Massage therapists will often tell you that they do not diagnose or prescribe treatment.

That said, you should let the expert hands of your massage professional put you into the altered state of consciousness that you have been needing. As the body is relaxed and toned you will experience the healthful effects you have been looking for; you will let go of the cares of the day and the emotional baggage of past problems.

Remember that massage can either stimulate the body or relax it, depending on the kind of strokes that are used and the effect that you intend from the session. If you want to take care of an insomnia problem or a bad back, you will definitely want a relaxation response from the massage. If you are having indigestion or neuromuscular problems you may be looking for a massage that will have a stimulating effect on the system.

Acupressure Massage—Pressing the Energy Points

How Acupressure Works

Acupressure is a term that covers a range of massage practices, emphasizing the energy points on the body that correspond to acupuncture points. These points are pressed and held for specific periods of time in order to correct any imbalance of Qi energy that could be at the root of discomfort or illness. These points, called *Tsubos*, (pronounced "su-boes") are situated along the meridians discussed in Chapter 4. As a component of traditional Chinese medicine, acupressure is part of the healing systems of China, dating back thousands of years. Acupressure is a totally noninvasive technique (since no needles are used) and is, for some people, more readily approachable than acupuncture.

Many theories have been advanced to explain why acupressure, like acupuncture, works. We described in detail a number of these in Chapter 4. Suffice it to say that miracles of pain relief as well as a general feeling of mental clarity and revitalization of the energy centers of the body are real and tangible. Acupressure performed on the hands and back of the head has been especially effective, for instance, in relieving insomnia, back pain, PMS, TMJ, some kinds of arthritis pain, and migraine headaches.

Acupressure by Any Other Name

Within acupressure there are different varieties that reflect the approaches of individual systems.

Shiatsu, literally means "finger pressure." This is a form of acupressure from the Japanese tradition. It uses points along the same meridians as TCM, but involves rhythmic finger pressing or deep, gentle finger pressing that lasts from three to six seconds on each point. The Japanese use the term "Ki," for Qi, in Shiatsu, so energy imbalances are considered Ki imbalances. Shiatsu is probably the most widely practiced form of acupressure in this country.

Jin Shin Jystsu was developed by Jiro Murai, an early-twentieth century Japanese philosopher. This system of pressing acupuncture points eventually made its way to the United States over the ensuing decades and became known as *Jin Shin Do*. Today there are several forms of Jin Shin, each with its own trademark or unique ending to the Jin Shin prefix. Jin Shin is a gentle type of acupressure that involves extended holding of acupressure points. This type of point holding is done for periods of time ranging from one to five minutes. Part of the procedure includes meditating on the part of the patient to maximize the benefit to the body.

Tui Na is an ancient Chinese-based system of massage and acupressure-type movements. This involves vigorous pushing, squeezing, and vibrating, as well as stretching of muscles and skin. Tui Na attempts to address a long list of specific health problems. The technique, and its trademark of fast repetitions of rolling hand movements over problem muscle areas, is taught widely in the United States and China.

Do-In is a form of self-acupressure, brought to the United States by Michio Kushi, an advocate of macrobiotic diet. It emphasizes breathing, stretching, and the massaging of acupressure points, especially on the face and head.

Acu-Yoga is the creation of Michael Reed Gach, founder of the Acupressure Institute in Berkeley, California. This system uses various yoga postures to press acupressure points on the meridians of the body against the floor.

An Acupressure Session

Depending on the type you choose, acupressure may be part of an overall massage therapy session, part of a reflexology session (some practitioners combine the two), part of your traditional Chinese medical routine, or may simply be solely an acupressure session. In any case, the goals will be similar—the reestablishment of the natural flow of your body's Qi. Whether Qi is congested and blocked, or Qi is lacking in certain meridians, the acupressure therapist will be pressing and holding points along the meridians in order to restore the normal flow of this vital force, balance your Yin and Yang energies, and enhance the body's ability to heal itself.

Most, if not all, acupressure therapists will take an assessment. As in acupuncture, a medical history will likely be recorded, followed by the pulse taking described in Chapter 4. This is conducted to ascertain any imbalances or acute conditions you may have. Examination of the tongue and face is also generally part of the examination. Remember to report any current or chronic conditions.

Acupressure can be given while you are lying down or sitting in a chair. As the practitioner begins to press on the energy points you will notice that your body will relax deeply, and your breathing will become deeper and slower. The first part of the session will be devoted to rebalancing your energy. Then, any meridians that are blocked or that are causing Qi to be congested will be worked. If your acupressure therapist is conducting the session as part of a larger program, herbal remedies or T'ai Chi may be discussed.

There are some variations of and embellishments to this general technique. In Shiatsu, for instance, the stretching of the muscles of an area that is about to be worked is important. This stretching or massaging will be away from the heart. It is considered standard to bend the legs toward the torso before an acupressure session on your back begins. Jin Shin practitioners will take pulse readings and decide to work on a particular energy channel to reestablish energy balance to the body. After that, specific patient problems can be addressed. As we noted earlier, the positive meditative state of both the practitioner and the patient is considered a necessity. The acupressure session will last anywhere from thirty to ninety minutes. An hour-long session can cost from thirty to sixty dollars.

Ailments that May Benefit from Acupressure

Some conditions can be successfully treated with acupressure. Backache and sciatic nerve problems are two complaints that are routinely treated by acupressure, often with positive results. Chronic fatigue, migraine headache, menstrual problems and PMS, TMJ, carpel tunnel syndrome, impotence, allergies, and hay fever problems are just a sample of the illness that acupressure can address. A list of the ailments that should not be treated with any type of massage are listed at the end of this chapter.

Finding the Acupressure Therapist You Need

Word of mouth recommendations are always important when locating a massage therapist of any kind. We recommend seeing an acupressure therapist who has graduated from an accredited school, with at least a basic training certification in acupressure, and preferably a certificate in one of the many specialized areas of acupressure such as pain relief, sports acupressure, or Oriental medicine. The advanced therapy program offered by the Acupressure Institute in Berkeley, California, takes seven to twelve months to complete and is probably the most comprehensive acupressure training program in this country. An acupressure therapist with a strong background in TCM will also be a good indicator of a high level of competency.

The Esalen Experience

The Esalen Institute, located in Big Sur, California, is over thirty years old and has always been on the cutting edge of the human potential movement. All the major proponents of the movement, including Fritz Perls, Ida Rolf, and Abraham Maslow, have shared their knowledge and insights at Esalen as either teachers or lecturers.

Course listings at Esalen cover the gamut of human exploration. Everything from the Language of the Drum, Self-Empowerment for Trauma Survivors, Enhancing Communications Hypnotically, to Singing Gestalt are offered. Esalen also provides an array of self-discovery, dream exploration, arts, biofeedback, and other healing modalities too numerous to name in our limited space.

Overlooking the Pacific Ocean from beautiful cliffs, the Esalen Institute may just be the place you have been looking for to get away from the maelstrom of the megacity. As part of this seaside experience, guests at Esalen can luxuriate in spring-fed hot tubs, and, after attending a seminar, indulge themselves with one of the famous Esalen massage sessions.

Esalen may be known best for its massage techniques. These are a blend of Eastern and Western styles. While there are Swedish and acupressure influences at Esalen, Feldenkrais, Rolfing, and Aston Patterning are other methods that have gone into the mix of massage styles individual practitioners may use. Indeed, a number of the founders of these various schools of body work have taught at Esalen over the years, and the institute's practitioners have absorbed and tried to synthesize the best that each has contributed.

General Characteristics

A hallmark of an Esalen massage is the flowing body strokes that cover the body from top to bottom. The idea is that the entire body should be worked in a session. Depending on which practitioner you choose at Esalen and the type of massage in which that person may be specializing, the experience can vary. Whether you are looking for a deep tissue massage, stretching exercises, Yoga, movement programs such as Feldenkrais, or an acupressure type experience, they all can be found at Esalen.

Prices for the Esalen Experience

If you are interested in attending seminars at Esalen and experiencing the Esalen massage philosophy in action, you should call ahead for reservations. Standard rates per person per week vary from $570 to $1100. Weekends rates vary from $200 to $380. These prices include the fee for workshops.

Locating a Practitioner

Some people claim that anyone who has visited Esalen is capable of performing Esalen massage. However, we recommend someone who has gone through the twenty-eight-day Massage Practitioner Program at Esalen and completed the necessary thirty follow-up massages. When these requirements are finished, a California state approved certificate of completion is issued. Esalen will provide a list of practitioners for a minimum charge.

Amma Massage

Amma is an ancient form of massage, probably the oldest. Amma means "massage" in Chinese. In the first half of this century, Amma was a massage therapy performed mainly by blind people in Asia. Many centuries ago Amma came to Japan and the word "Amma" has since become synonymous with Japanese massage. Amma, unlike acupressure, includes a wide variety of movements over the body, including kneading, stroking, vibration, and circular pressure techniques. The fingers, elbows, and sometimes knees are used in conjunction with the hands.

Amma uses the tsubos or energy points (as in acupressure) located on the meridians of the body to balance and unblock the yin or yang energy that may be impairing health. Amma practitioners believe that this massage routine promotes the self-healing that the body would naturally employ if Yin and Yang energy were flowing properly.

This massage therapy has enjoyed a meteoric growth in America in the last few years. People have become increasingly interested in the origins of massage and how this relates to health today. Likewise, the Amma Institute and its practitioners have helped to move Amma out of the massage therapist's office and into on-site locations where people work and live, to perform their healing magic.

The Amma massage, taught at the Amma Institute in San Francisco, works 140 of the tsubos of the body. As is the case with Acupuncture, Amma practitioners hold that the body is divided into fourteen meridians through which energy flows. Students are taught "Kata," or a sequence of points to massage. This is a ritual sequence of points, one sequence leading into another, so that students can immediately begin practice.

An Amma Massage Session

Unlike Western/Swedish massage, Amma is generally performed with the client fully clothed. Because of this, there are no long sweeping movements as in Western massage. More likely you will experience your skin being shaken, pressed, and kneaded, especially at the tsubo energy points. Amma practitioners often begin their session by working the shoulders and back. Thumbs also play a great part in Amma because they are used to locate and then balance the tsubos. Circular motion may be applied initially over the tsubos sites.

All of the meridian lines of the body will be touched and worked during an Amma session. This is important since the entire energy field of the body should be worked. The practitioner will also be focusing his or her consciousness into the tsubos as they massage. This is believed to bring about a better result in that the practitioner connects with your tsubos. Keep in mind that since either clothes or a towel will always be covering your body, there will be no lotions or massage oils applied to your body. The massage can last anywhere from thirty minutes to one hour.

Amma Certification

Amma practitioners are fond of saying that they teach people how to touch comfortably. Students are taught four routines of massage during their course of study at the Amma Institute of Skilled Touch: the five-minute chair massage, the fifteen-minute chair massage, the thirty-minute table massage, and the one-hour table massage. As noted earlier, massaging a client in a chair enables practitioners to take their massage into arenas where they otherwise could not practice. This has become one of the trademarks of Amma massage in the United States.

Certification as an Amma Massage Practitioner required fourteen hours a week of course work over a six-month period, in an apprenticeship-style program until 1995, when the Institute went to a workshop format. There are now over five hundred licensed Amma practitioners in the United States. We recommend a practitioner who is a graduate of the Amma Institute or its workshops. The address and number at the end of the chapter can put you in touch with a practitioner in your area.

A Note on the State Licensing of All Massage Therapists

Eighteen states have licensing requirements of massage therapists. There is, however, no uniformity to these regulations. In California, for instance, the state has left each municipality to regulate the number of hours of postsecondary massage training a practitioner must have completed to practice. Hence, many more hours are required for Los Angeles than for San Francisco. In the state of Oregon, 350 hours are required. If you are in the city of Seattle, Washington, that number goes up to 500 hours of postsecondary massage training. In general, a licensed massage therapist should complete at least 500 hours of training.

A certificate from an approved school of massage will usually qualify a practitioner's services for medical reimbursement if the client was referred by a primary care giver: a medical doctor, osteopath, etc. We strongly recommend that you consider a massage therapist who meets all state and local regulations, is accredited by one of the massage schools listed at the end of this chapter, and is a member of the American Massage Therapy Association (AMTA).

Massage Oils—Using Herbal Alchemy to Make a Good Massage Great

Whenever you receive a massage, other than perhaps an Amma massage, oils of some kind will usually be applied to your skin. Many therapists will use an oil you have brought along for your massage. If you are being massaged by a friend or loved one, scented oils add a dimension of relaxation to the experience.

A wide range of oils can be used for a massage session. It is even fun to vary the oils from one part of the body to another. Sunflower or safflower oil are used as the basis of many massage oils. These have little or no flavor by themselves, are readily used for blending with herbs or essential oils, and make excellent lubricants. But sesame, avocado, peanut, coconut, olive, and any number of other oils can also be used. We recommend avoiding ones that contain mineral oil, as this simply clogs the pores. Though it will make your skin supple and hold in moisture, it is not especially healthful for skin in the long run.

Remember that a few drops of your favorite herb or extract can turn your hour of massage into an aromatherapy experience as well. Here a number of scents can work. Perhaps your favorite flavor is cinnamon, or a strawberry/kiwi combination. Want to feel like a big twist of licorice? Try a little licorice extract in your massage oil.

Scenting for Specific Conditions—Bringing Aromatherapy to Your Massage

Aromatherapy requires infusing herbs in your massage oil. Scenting can be achieved by placing herbs in a four-ounce, eight-ounce, or sixteen-ounce bottle of oil and then letting the bottle steep on the window sill, in the sun, for several days. You should shake the bottle periodically. When your concoction is aromatically correct, strain off any remaining herbs, or, if you wish, leave the herbal remains in the oil as an additional scenting factor.

Specific herbs and scents do, for many people, seem to have specific impacts on health. Remember that the essences and herbs that you mix with oils will be absorbed by the skin and eventually, in small quantities, into the bloodstream.

- When massaging someone who has an insomnia problem, we recommend crushed chamomile infused in the oil. Other potential calmers of the spirit include lavender, catnip, and rosemary leaf.
- If you are looking for relief from bronchial or cold-related congestion, peppermint, rosehip, or ginger can provide some relief. The vapors rising off the body reach the air passages and make breathing easier.

- To increase circulation, citrus oils and oil of thyme often have a beneficial effect. Ginger, as always, acts as a good general tonic, even when inhaled.
- Muscular pain often responds well to ginger, clove, or juniper. To produce heat on the skin, try a little oil of wintergreen.
- Fennel can act as a laxative or diuretic.

General Precautions

While massage has incredible benefits for the body and spirit, there are some circumstances where massage is contraindicated. People with active tuberculosis or cancer should not be vigorously massaged. People with insulin-dependent diabetes, varicose veins, or other blood vessel problems, especially in the arms and legs, may want to avoid therapy or have a consultation with your primary care provider before having a massage. Edema or swelling also disqualifies a person from a massage session until the underlying problem has been remedied. This is true with fevers, as well. People with peptic or gastric ulcers should avoid any deep massage of the abdomen. Those with serious and infectious skin problems should have their illnesses looked after by a primary care giver.

Osteoporosis is another condition, depending on one's age and severity of the condition, where massage should be approached cautiously. Massage may be too painful for people with severe arthritis. In other milder cases of arthritis, some forms of massage can provide pain relief. Bone fractures that have not completely healed are another situation where it is better to wait until healing is complete. Remember that sports injuries, or any injury to soft or hard tissues, such as tendons, ligaments, or the muscles themselves, sometimes require long healing times. Make sure that the torn ligament or sprained muscle you have been nursing along is capable of withstanding the vigorous strokes of some massage therapies.

Massage Schools and Associations

The Amma Institute of Skilled Touch
1881 Post Street
San Francisco, CA 94115
415/564–1103

Esalen Institute
Big Sur, CA 93920
404/667–3000

Acupressure Institute
1533 Shattuck Avenue
Berkeley CA 94709
510/845–1059

American Massage Therapy Association (Swedish and other)
820 Davis Street
Suite 100
Evanston, IL 60201
708/864–0123
708/864–1178 (fax)

AMTA has over eighteen thousand members and is the largest and oldest organization of massage therapists. All of its members subscribe to a code of ethics. Members must pass a certification exam or be a graduate from a massage therapy program approved or accredited by an AMTA commission on massage training. There are fifty-eight AMTA-affiliated schools around the country that offer at least five hundred hours of classroom instruction.

Chapter Seven

Structural Body Work and Energy Therapies

In this chapter, we are going to explore a range of therapies that attempt to integrate or reintegrate the often disconnected states of body, mind, and spirit. For the sake of clarity, we will start with techniques that involve no discomfort, and in which there is little physical contact between patient and practitioner. These include such therapies as the Alexander Technique and the Feldenkrais Method. We will then proceed to the areas of Applied Kinesiology and Reiki that include the laying on of hands. And finally we will describe the more active forms of body manipulation, such as Rolfing, which involve the deep movement of tissues. The energy therapies should not be seen as primary medical care, but more in terms of complementary health care.

Alexander Technique

This technique was developed by an Australian actor, Frederick Matthias Alexander, around the turn of the century. As an actor, Alexander was constantly faced with the loss of his voice from overuse. He began to study his own posture and balance as a way of diagnosing his voice problems.

His self-study, along with the observations of others, convinced him that the sloping shoulders, humped backs, and crooked necks that many people carry around were caused by a lack of awareness of how the body moves and how it reacts to stress. Vastly restricted and inhibited body movement was the result, according to Alexander, of not knowing one's innate self. In everything from the startled reflexes that people go through in fight or flight situations, to the simple ways we walk along the street, Alexander saw that people were not allowing the head, neck, and back—the whole body—to move freely and automatically.

According to Alexander, we are being forced by the stresses of our environment to lose our innate posture. He further believed that the body's balance was being adversely affected. To remedy this situation, Alexander taught students how to "use" the body. This new consciousness about the head, neck, and entire body is the basis of his technique.

By 1932, Alexander had published *Use of Self*, a book that brought him notoriety and some degree of acceptance. Alexander's idea was that a teacher, usually using his or her hands, would guide pupils to relearn their natural body posture as well as learning free and automatic movement and balance. By using the technique, students can learn to loosen compacted shoulders and squashed or shortened necks that are locked in defensive positions. The technique can also restore some muscular and neuromuscular coordination that may have been lost through years of habitual abuse of posture and improper breathing.

In Alexander technique classes pupils are taught kinesthetic or movement skills. These include awareness of body position as well as fluid, conscious movement skills. The head and neck are of primary importance in Alexander Technique training. The proper way to carry the head and neck in relationship to the rest of the body and the relearning of balance have a dramatic effect on the entire body. Students relearn how to walk and carry themselves all over again through a new consciousness of the body and its motion through space.

An Alexander Technique Session

A session will often begin by the teacher instructing students to sit or stand. The teacher then observes how they are holding themselves. People, whether they are conscious or not, are fighting the force of gravity at all times. A student will then be placed on a massage table and the instructor will gently exercise the body as a way of lengthening the muscles. Following from this, the student will begin movement exercises using an ordinary chair. The instructor will repeatedly have the student get in and out of the chair. An instructor may put a hand at the base of the spine to guide movement or gently tilt the head up at the chin, in order to correct the posture and suggest a new way of standing or moving.

There will likely be much repetition, as old ways die hard, but almost immediately people recognize a change not only in body posture—to a more fluid and comfortable way of standing and moving—but also a new clarity of thinking after using the technique. Images and verbal suggestion are often used to help meld the new movements into subconscious action free from the direction of the conscious mind. The session will generally last forty-five minutes. Costs range from thirty to seventy dollars, depending on your teacher.

Precautions

The Alexander Technique is readily accessible to everyone. The technique does not prescribe and there are no manipulation-type procedures whatsoever, simply rapport with your teacher. The number of teachers in the United States has grown to several hundred. We recommend a teacher who has completed the three-year course of study and has been certified by the North American Society of Teachers of the Alexander Technique. The address and phone number at the end of the chapter can put you in touch with the nearest Alexander Technique teacher.

Feldenkrais Method

The Feldenkrais Method is a system of learning that stresses the way the body functions and its relationship to behavior and the learning process. It was founded by Moshe Feldenkrais, a Russian-born Israeli physicist who spent a good part of his life studying the martial arts, especially judo. Feldenkrais also read and studied everything from psychology and anatomy to linguistics, prenatal development, and neurology to determine how these each affect the body. Feldenkrais briefly studied with Frederick Alexander and in some ways his system reflects Alexander's influence.

Much of the Feldenkrais Method is explained in detail in his book *Body and Mature Behavior: A Study of Anxiety, Sex, Gravitation, and Learning.* The method is taught either in private lessons, called "Functional Integration," or in group sessions called "Awareness through Movement." The basic concept is that, with the proper instruction, the skeletal and muscular structure of the body can be taught more natural and healthful ways of holding and moving itself. This, in turn, creates a new sense in a person as a physical being, better able to sense and deal with the stresses and strains of everyday life. As in the Alexander Technique there can be a cascading effect; as bodily coordination improves, you may notice other generalized enhancements in your health.

The cornerstone of Feldenkrais is movement and learning how the body is being used and misused in daily life. Every activity that human beings engage in involves movement, even the act of thinking. Our joys, our sorrows, our hopes, and our fears all imprint on us and involve movement as an exploration of the self. According to the method, there are four states of being: these include asleep, awake, consciousness, and awareness. Awareness, according to Feldenkrais, is the combination of consciousness with knowledge.

The goal of Feldenkrais is to increase the range of motion and improve flexibility and coordination, and through this, gain a new knowledge of the body. The teaching of Feldenkrais is designed to create situations where the pupil, through simple exercises, learns how to develop a better and more direct relationship with interior as well as exterior worlds. Consciousness becomes richer when this process occurs. The method contends that many of our routine physical movements are the result of negative behavior patterns from childhood or from distorted movements learned in adulthood that restrict our free movement, cause imbalance and pain, and may even be responsible for distorted bones and skeletal muscle problems.

By relearning and reprogramming our basic movements, Feldenkrais aims to create new knowledge and new instructions for the brain that become subconscious and allow a person to walk, speak, and act in more comfortable and productive ways. People who have multiple sclerosis, cerebral palsy, and even Parkinson's disease have sought out Feldenkrais. People who have been in accidents, those with disc problems and a range of musculoskeletal pain, have also used the method. While not expecting any miracle cures, many people report an easing of symptoms and greater range of movement after sessions. We recommend the book *Relaxercise* as a simple introduction to the Feldenkrais Method. It is available from the Feldenkrais Guild at the address at the end of the chapter.

A Feldenkrais Session

Lessons often start with various kinds of stretching, such as extending and flexing the knees, hands, or feet. Exercises are usually performed on the floor. The method puts a strong emphasis on teaching exercises and movement tasks, including rising from the sitting position. Gentle touch and easy movement exercises are used to reorganize posture, improve the movement of the body, and, the Feldenkrais practitioners say, improve one's self-image.

Teachers will generally ask that the student focus on what is going on internally as well as externally, to notice which muscles are being used and how this is registering in consciousness. This sense of observing the self, like in the Alexander Technique, is one of the primary benefits of this therapy and has benefited not only performance artists but people who must cope with chronic pain or chronic loss of movement or balance.

Precautions

As with the Alexander Technique, Feldenkrais can help people with lower back problems, spinal disc and bone spur problems, sclerosis, chronic pain, and certain kinds of trauma injuries, and in some cases may even mitigate paralysis. Infections, cancer, heart disease, and immune disorders are not considered responsive to this therapy. Since this technique is one that does not prescribe or involve any serious manipulation of the body, it is self-regulated. Sessions can be private or in groups, with the private sessions costing forty to eighty-five dollars and lasting thirty minutes to an hour. We recommend a practitioner who has been accredited by the Feldenkrais Guild.

Applied Kinesiology and Touch for Health

Applied Kinesiology

Kinesiology was founded by Dr. Charles Goodheart, a chiropractor, who introduced his techniques in the 1960s. It is a kind of meshing of energy and meridian-based therapies, such as acupressure, with chiropractic. Goodheart understood from his chiropractic experience that there was a connection between muscle reaction in the body and other, seemingly unrelated, complaints. Applied Kinesiology, for instance, says that the muscle under the shoulder blades, the latissimus dorsi, is related to the pancreas gland and that when insulin is not flowing properly, this muscle will be weak. Allergies and an intolerance for sugar are other types of disorders "reflexed" by muscle weakness in this area.

Kinesiologists believe there is a triad of health. The first leg of the triad is nutrition. This includes the biochemical side of the body, how food nourishes the body, and what foods are contraindicated in certain situations. Also included in this area are the ingestion of both prescription and nonprescription drugs, and the effect that these drugs have on health. The second leg is the body's structure, which concerns all the body's skeletal, muscle, and organ systems, and how they function together. Third is the psychological side of the patient, which covers emotions and mental attitudes. Each of these systems affects the other two systems of the body.

While kinesiology is a therapy usually associated with the chiropractic profession, osteopaths, podiatrists and even some traditional medical doctors are certified applied kinesiologists. To be a certified kinesiologist a health care professional must possess a license to diagnose in their own specialty and then have participated in training through the International College of Applied Kinesiology. We recommend someone who fits these criteria when looking for a practitioner, whether that person is calling himself or herself a kinesiologist or a touch for health practitioner.

Touch for Health

Dr. John Thie met and studied with Goodheart in the mid-1960s and took Goodheart's methods a step further. He could see that the pushing and rubbing of reflex points that Goodheart had discovered could be done by anyone on his own body. He called this self-help system Touch for Health, and wrote a book about it, also called *Touch for Health*. This self-help guide makes these concepts and treatment available to all. In the book, muscle testing, along with techniques for energy balancing and strengthening of muscles, is described in detail. His concept, and that of kinesiology in general, is that when the body's energy flow can be balanced, the body can heal itself.

Kinesiology Session

If you are looking for a kinesiologist, your chiropractor is a good place to start. Remember that your chiropractor, or other health care practitioner, should be the person who performs kinesiology. Kinesiology, as a diagnostic procedure, will usually begin with muscle testing. Classic testing involves the patient raising an arm to one side of the body and then having the kinesiologist press down on the arm as resistance is offered. Your legs will be lifted or pushed (not painfully) at different angles. Sugar crystals put on your tongue or held in your hand are also a method of muscle testing.

The exam may go on for fifteen to thirty minutes. From your complaint, a history that is taken, and from the muscle testing, the kinesiologist may recommend avoiding certain foods, taking certain vitamins, and perhaps spinal adjustments—if he or she is a chiropractor—or reflex treatments that involve holding certain points on the head and body. To get to the root of problems, nutrition adjustments are often needed.

Precautions

As a way of relieving tension, relieving some pains, and addressing nutrition imbalances, kinesiology can be a simple, low-impact way to go. It uses no special devices or exercises, but changes in diet and nutrition are commonly recommended.

Good results are reported with migraine headaches, allergy relief, as well as alleviation of back pain. Since the practitioner should always be a chiropractor, osteopath, M.D., or other health care provider, and because applied kinesiology is primarily a muscle testing procedure, the cost is generally folded into the total cost of treatment the practitioner provides. The address at the end of the chapter can help you locate further information about touch for health and kinesiology.

Polarity Therapy

This therapy made its debut on the American alternative medical arena many decades ago, but only really took off in popularity in the 1970s. Its basic tenet is that the human body emanates and is part of an electromagnetic energetic pattern, which precedes human structure and function. Within this energy flow there are cycles of expansion and contraction, as well as attraction and repulsion. This field will be unbalanced when disease is present. The purpose of the practitioner is to rebalance the body's electrical field by placing hands on the body at various points. In polarity therapy, the top of the head is considered a positive place while the feet are negative. Similarly, the left hand is negative, while the right hand is positive. A practitioner will place his positive right hand on the feet of the receiver and then touch a positive point on the receiver's body with his or her left hand. The placing on of hands by the practitioner enables energy flow to be balanced and strengthened.

While polarity therapy draws on a number of Eastern medical ideas including those of Indian Ayurvedic medicine, it was an Austrian-born American doctor named Randolph Stone, a chiropractor and osteopath, who pioneered the therapy. Stone lived for a number of years in India and it was there that he synthesized his concepts of bioelectrical fields with those of Eastern medicine. Stone published the findings of his studies in five books in the late 1940s. He found that the human energy field, as he called it, is affected by touch, diet, movement and sound, attitudes, relationships, and environmental factors.

Polarity therapy practitioners say that the integration of the negative, positive, and neutral points between the patient and the practitioner relate to the five chakras of the body in Hindu cosmology and to the five elements of Ayurvedic medicine. Polarity therapy uses the five elements described in Ayurvedic medicine to classify all foods. Food and exercise are part of the total approach of people who practice polarity therapy. Exercise in the form of a polarity yoga, also pioneered by Stone, can round out this therapy.

A Polarity Therapy Session

Therapy usually takes place on a table. As with the above therapies, stretching is involved when the practitioner begins. This is simply a loosening of the muscles to facilitate the transference and balancing of energy that will happen later. Your head will be cradled or the practitioner's hands will be placed on your shoulders to loosen muscles as the procedure commences. A simple relaxing and centering procedure is for the practitioner to put one of his or her hands at the base of your head and the other at the top of your head to balance energy throughout the head.

The crux of the therapy is the premise that touch affects the human energy field. Placing the hands of the practitioner on the body of the receiver affects energy flow. One placement can stimulate, while another may have a sedating effect. The goal will be to allow energy to flow smoothly by unblocking the energy field. It should be emphasized that polarity therapy generally involves light contact, although an increasing number of therapists will use a heavier or deeper touch, digging in hard to the body to find pain centers.

The practitioner often feels a tingling sensation in the hands. The receiver may also get the sense of a gentle warmth or tingling in the area where the practitioner's hands are located. As in acupuncture the view is that when the flow of energy is blocked, illness occurs. Unblocking this energy is the function of the therapist. The goal of the session with a therapist (and there may be either several sessions in a row or an occasional trip to the therapist) is to unblock energy, calm nerves, and reinvigorate the body and spirit.

Precautions

Polarity therapy is a nondiagnostic holistic health system. With the energy balancing and the calming effects of polarity therapy, there is little reason for concern about side effects. By itself the therapy is enjoyable and relaxing. The therapy is often used in conjunction with other healing regimens as a complementary health care technique. As is always the case with energy therapies, this should not be used for acute or emergency conditions.

In some cases polarity therapists will suggest fasting or even high colonics as a system purifier when rebalancing the body. Remember that some of these digestion cleansing procedures cause stress on the body, especially for people unfamiliar with the procedures. If you are going to take these steps, consult a primary care giver and study the proposed program of fasting and colonics before you begin. The American Polarity Therapy Association in Boulder, Colorado, certifies teachers of polarity therapy both at associate polarity practitioner level and the registered practitioner level. We recommend a practitioner who has at least reached associate status.

Therapeutic Touch (TT)

Humans have always used their hands to communicate. In a sense, therapeutic touch is the healing side of this age-old use of the hands. This technique has proven effective in raising hemoglobin levels in hospital patients and speeding healing in some instances. We should be clear about the phrase "laying on of hands" that is sometimes applied to therapeutic touch. In reality, the hands of the practitioner will usually move or hover just above the patient's body (an inch or two), and may, in some instances, be held on the body if your "field" feels deficient or cold.

This technique, somewhat like polarity therapy, sees the body as a field of energy called bioenergy. It is a life energy that extends beyond the physical body. Practitioners believe they can aid the body to heal itself, in many situations, including cases of migraine headaches, back problems, psychological distress, or healing of wounds, by rebalancing this vital life energy. The pioneer in the field of TT is Dr. Dolores Krieger. As a professor of nursing in upstate New York, Krieger began to study the effectiveness of so-called psychic healers. Krieger learned the rudiments of that healing procedure and then refined the technique and began teaching others. She began using the technique in hospital settings with people who were recovering from surgery or were under other forms of physical stress. A number of people in the health care professions studied under Krieger, including nurses who dealt with the chronically or terminally ill.

After learning the technique from Krieger, medical students and practitioners returned with stories of how this therapy had sped the healing of wounds and alleviated pain. In 1979, Krieger wrote the book *The Therapeutic Touch: How to Use Your Hands to Help and Heal*. Krieger and her followers have since spread her ideas and practices to a number of countries and count thousands of health care professionals as students. To this day, many TT practitioners are hospital nurses.

A Therapeutic Touch Session

A session will begin with you sitting in a chair, or if you are in a hospital, lying in bed. The practitioner will move his or her open palm over your body trying to synchronize his or her energy field to yours. From the sensations received, the practitioner makes an assessment, usually within a minute or two, about where your field has problems.

What is termed loose or tight congestion of this field indicates a blockage of energy marked by a feeling of coldness or nonmovement. A deficit in the field is akin to a hollowed out area that is pulling in energy, a kind of black hole. Blocked areas of energy will generally be above deficit areas. Finally, imbalance is like the rapids, or in some cases the backwash, of a river. Here the energy field is moving too slowly or too fast, or in contradictory ways.

By placing the hands over the body and moving in sweeping motions, the TT practitioner will unruffle the bioenergetic field of the body. Therapeutic touch, it is clear, induces a state of profound physical and often mental relaxation in the patient. A spreading feeling of warmth or sometimes pleasant vibration is how people report the experience of therapeutic touch.

Some believe that the Hindu concept of Prana is at work as the hands of the TT practitioner pass over the body of the ill person. Other TT therapists such as Janet Quinn, who was a student of Kreiger, highlight the role of unconditional love in the healing of people. In either case, the effectiveness of TT, whether it is a placebo effect or the power of suggestion or prana, is impressive.

Precautions

The Therapeutic Touch procedure of passing hands over the body is a positive and often healing experience for the recovering person. We can see no side effects from this therapy, other then possibly placing too great a belief in its ability to cure a serious or terminal disease. Here again positive thinking and letting the energy flow from the giver can only have a beneficial effect. For pain, especially after an operation, or as a boost to the immune system, results have shown a positive and healthful effect. Remember that the state of mind of the giver is important.

A relaxed, meditative state is considered the most efficacious. For such conditions as cancer, where increased blood flow may not be indicated, we would recommend caution.

Reiki

Reiki is a nonreligious practice started by a Japanese Christian, Dr. Mikao Usui, in Kyoto, Japan, in the late 1800s. Usui sought through his studies—especially of Buddhism—to investigate the healing power of history's great spiritual leaders. The name "Reiki" is itself a fusion of two Japanese words: *rei*, meaning universal, and *ki*, which is the life force. Reiki is based on the belief in what Reiki practitioners call the universal life energy. They believe that this life force is in all of us and that this energy is a healing power that properly instructed practitioners can tap into.

Reiki was first brought to the United States in the 1940s by Hawayo Takata, a Japanese-American woman who studied under an associate of Usui's in Tokyo. At the time of her death in the early 1980s, the Reiki movement divided and then subdivided. There are now half a dozen different versions of Reiki, including a semisecretive type that is practiced in Japan. However, the successor organization that claims linkage to Takata is the Reiki Alliance, headed by Phyllis Furumoto, a granddaughter of Takata. (The Radiance Technique Association International, headed by Barbara Ray, though it has some roots with Reiki, does not currently wish to be associated with the concept of Reiki).

Reiki is another energy-based healing system that is hard to pinpoint as to its exact effects. The way it works is something of a mystery. A Reiki master will often "attune" a student to the universal life energy. These attunements, or empowerments, the Reiki master believes, calm and heal the body. Many recipients report a relaxation response, including warm feelings in the body during sessions. It should be stressed that Reiki does not advocate any particular spiritual or religious belief. Its belief system is secular in nature.

A Reiki Session

You will be fully clothed in a Reiki session. The hands of the Reiki master will be held in twelve basic positions, for a few minutes each, in a session that will generally last an hour. This is a hands-on healing system that is performed by simply placing the hands of the practitioner on areas of the head, abdomen, arms, and legs. There is no massage or manipulation involved. In the session, universal life energy will be transferred from the practitioner or master to the client.

The Reiki Alliance holds to three levels of initiation, including hands-on healing, distant treatment, and finally teaching—the highest level. Becoming a Reiki master involves the commitment of time and a substantial amount of money. The alliance also has a code of ethics and a one-year apprenticeship that prospective teachers must go through. While there are no specific, scientific studies of Reiki treatment, anecdotal reports indicate some alleviation of pain and faster healing of wounds.

Precautions

Reiki is a therapy that involves only light touch. Our recommendation, as always with undiagnosed pain, cancer, heart problems, broken bones, or bleeding, is to seek treatment immediately from your primary care giver. Use Reiki and other energy therapies as complementary health care and as a positive support position that can expedite healing and improve health.

Reflexology

A number of eastern medical philosophies, such as traditional Chinese medicine and Ayurvedic, have long taught the importance of foot and hand massage. Early Egyptian art shows a kind of reflexology being used almost four thousand years ago. Reflexology represents the North American way of using this ancient system. Dr. William Fitzgerald, a turn-of-the-century physician, introduced the concepts of reflexology and originally called it zone therapy. His theories maintained that the various zones of the body, such as the back and head, carry electrical energy through the body and to certain reflex points on the hands and feet.

These ideas were further developed by Eunice Inghram, an American follower of Fitzgerald in the 1940s, who emphasized the importance of the feet. She stressed that when points on the feet were massaged, they reflexed back to the internal organs of the body as well as the nerve and muscle system. This reflex action, in turn, alleviated illness. Today many practitioners will advertise that they are Inghram-certified, meaning that they have completed course work and have been certified in the practice of foot reflexology. This involves attending a number of seminars and a period of practice of one year.

Much of the work of reflexologists, including that of the English practitioner Robert St. John, has concluded that the pressing of points on the hands and feet correspond, or reflex back, to certain points on the spinal column and hence influence the nervous system. This, in turn, allows the body deeper levels of relaxation, deeper and easier breathing, and a balancing and energizing of all bodily systems. It has been admitted by medical doctors and others that foot reflexology speeds circulation. Results in certain kinds of pain control have also been witnessed. It should be emphasized that there are different kinds of reflexology, including hand and ear reflexology. In each case, points on the hand, feet, or ear reflex back to internal organs, systems, or nerve and muscle centers.

Indeed, reflexology can be performed so easily on oneself that it is frequently recommended by practitioners as a self-help therapy. But why not enjoy the luxury of having a practitioner perform this ancient and increasingly popular therapy on you when you are totally at ease? A professional massage therapist will sometimes perform reflexology as part of a larger massage routine. If you are looking only for a reflexology treatment, there are practitioners who specialize solely in this technique.

A Reflexology Session

In a session with your practitioner, you will probably be seated in a chair and asked to lift your foot up onto a short stool or across the practitioner's knee. Some therapists prefer for the client to be lying on the floor. Using the thumbs, forefingers, and middle fingers, the therapist presses and strokes the entire foot to start and then will zero in on certain tender areas.

Patient response is key to a good reflexology session. The practitioner will ask how the massaging and point touching is going. Do not be afraid to respond and say "too much" or "ouch" if a particularly tender area is pressed too hard. When a tender area is found you will notice that within a second or two, as the practitioner continues to press, the pain recedes. Similarly, communicating when pleasant places on the feet or hands have been located lets the therapist know where to proceed. In some cases a therapist may want to use knuckles or even an elbow. A trademark of an Inghram Certified Reflexologist is what is called "thumb walking," meaning that the thumb is pressed in repeated short moves in a line over areas of the foot, literally walking the practitioner's thumb across the bottom or side of your foot.

Reflexologists are generally people who are certified in one or more of the other alternative medical practices, such as massage therapy, chiropractic, or homeopathy, and use reflexology as complementary health care.

Precautions

Certain complaints, like sinus trouble, headaches and acute stress, back and leg problems, and imbalances of the endocrine glands, have been known to respond quite well to reflexology.

As we noted, reflexology is often used in conjunction with other massage techniques as a complementary therapy to tone the body, relax the muscles, center the body, and raise energy levels. There really are no risks to the therapy with the possible exception being that a preexisting condition such as infection could worsen with increased circulation.

Thousands of people have taken the seminars sponsored by the Reflexology Institute and have been certified. A number of practitioners can be found in almost every locality. Some will work exclusively on hands, feet, or ears, or a combination of all three. We do recommend someone who is Inghram-certified. This requires not only a range of seminars, but a full year of practice for certification. Prices for a session range from twenty to forty-five dollars, and sessions last from thirty to sixty minutes. The American Reflexology Board will only accredit people who have a minimum of one hundred hours of study and practice.

Bioenergetics

This form of body-mind therapy is an outgrowth of the psychoanalytic movement. The roots of psychoenergetics can be traced to the work of Wilhelm Reich, an early disciple of Freud, who wished to liberate the sexual energies of people as a way of curing neurosis. Among his theories was that the sexual drive was a life energy, which he called "Orgone." As part of his treatments, he put people in enclosed boxes called Orgone boxes so their life energy could be retained.

Reich believed that the body "armors" itself against various painful or humiliating experiences, especially in youth, and that these patterns of body armoring maintain themselves throughout adult life. Muscle tensions and spasms, and locked shoulders and necks represent the body trying to defend itself from childhood traumas. Anger is blocked and locked into the body, along with an inability to respond sexually in some cases by this process. The free expression of emotions is prevented. The result is physical and emotional illness. Reich and his successors hoped that the freeing of the body through exercise, massage, and analysis would lead to greater mental health for the sufferer.

Reich himself suffered much persecution in his day for his revolutionary theories and moved around Europe, often vilified and misunderstood. When Reich died in 1957 various followers began their own evolution of his theories and practices. Among them was Dr. Alexander Lowen, who termed the life energy of Reich *bioenergy*. Along with others, he established the International Institute for Bioenergetic Analysis.

Lowen emphasized that the mind and body are one unit; in essence, they are fundamentally the same. His view was that the basic functions of life—respiration, metabolism, and so on—produce energy and this energy is dammed up when the body has been put into the unhealthy state of "armoring."

In addition, over the ensuing years, other therapists, led by Ron Kurtz, established Hakomi Therapy as a less confrontational version of the Reichian method. This particular trend merged certain Eastern ideas, such as meditation and body-mind wholeness with Reich's body armoring and muscle unknotting therapy system. Whichever variant of bioenergetics is used, it is based on certain Reichian assumptions about the human body and memory.

A Bioenergetics Session

In a session, the therapist will have the patient lie down, sit, or possibly stand. Various exercises are used to focus the patient's mental and physical attention. The "grounding" experience is key here. This means being intensely aware of the body's own experience, including one's sexuality. These exercises usually involve stretching, deep breathing, and pushing down on the chest, which a therapist will sometimes do.

There will be some initial discussion of problems. The talking starts a process in which the patient begins to examine his or her bodily feelings. If emotions do not surface the therapist may then begin to massage and press on muscle areas where he or she thinks that resistances are residing. This can be physically and emotionally painful.

As a patient opens up, the emotional release creates a climate in which patients can pound, kick, shake their limbs, and generally give the body free reign to vent feelings that may have been repressed for years. Alternately, certain parts of the body may undergo exercises so the patient understands how closed up the muscle structure of his or her body really has become. Following sessions patients report a great feeling of being centered, and of having increased self-esteem, and a greater sense of power because of the liberation of body and emotion.

Bioenergetic therapists are usually psychiatrists, psychologists, or other professional practitioners who have specialized in Reichian therapy. We recommend someone who has the proper experience and clinical background, as well as some years of practice behind them. Treating the symptoms a person brings to a bioenergetic-Reichian session may take weeks, months, or even longer. Therapy can be once a week or less. Costs vary widely, depending on where a practitioner is located, and fifty to one hundred dollars per session is not unusual.

Precautions

People with sexual dysfunctions and psychologically based muscle-skeletal problems may benefit from bioenergetics. When a person experiences deeply repressed emotion, there can be many unpleasant moments as these feelings are relived and insights achieved. Some people who have migraines or nervous ticks, and pain unresponsive to conventional drugs or therapy that is associated with emotional trauma, can be helped by bioenergetic or Reichian-type therapies.

People with some chronic pain can be helped, but commonsense caution is advised. It is paramount that any therapist working in this arena have the well-being of the patient in mind and have established a great deal of trust with a patient. When a flood of painful incidents or repressed memory starts coming back to an individual, the therapist has to know how to support and bolster the person reliving the painful experience. This kind of therapy is serious stuff, with strong emotions and sometimes body reactions resulting. While deep self-awareness can be a liberating and healing experience, there can be a down side. People not used to experiencing strong emotions, particularly in the presence of others, would be advised to approach bioenergetics cautiously. People with manic depression and schizophrenia are not advised to seek this kind of treatment.

Myotherapy

Myotherapy was created by fitness expert Bonnie Prudden. Prudden was the person who alerted the nation to the unfit and flabby condition of our children in the 1950s and 1960s. After working for years with patients in chronic pain referred to her by Dr. Desmond Tivy, and helping with exercise to reeducate the muscles damaged by trauma and emotional stress, Prudden, in the mid-1970's, developed her system of trigger points. These points on the body are the foundation of her therapy. In 1980, she published her seminal book *Pain Erasure*, which was followed in 1984 by *Myotherapy*.

What is Myotherapy?

Myotherapy literally means "muscle therapy." Myotherapy sees the problems of muscles including spasms, pain, and knotting as related to trigger points. These trigger points, where the muscles contract and knot, are the focus of myotherapy. Prudden recognized that the tender trigger points that have contracted into painful knots sometimes refer pain to other areas of the body, creating satellite pain centers. Various muscle relaxation and massage therapies can provide relief, but Prudden's view is that these usually offer only a temporary respite. Prudden reasoned that the entire system of painful points must be eliminated. Once the points are eliminated and the muscles reeducated, pain relief can be permanent.

According to Prudden, there are two types of trigger points, matrix and satellite. The matrix is where pain often starts and the satellites are where pain may manifest itself as the muscles of the body continually "fire," setting off chain reactions around the body that spasm and tighten other muscles and complicate the problem.

A Myotherapy Session

It should be stressed that a Bonnie Prudden Certified Myotherapist takes only patients who have been referred by a medical doctor. The idea is to make sure that other complicating diseases are not present. We consider this a positive point about myotherapy that highlights the serious manner in which the practice views its patients. Following initial referral, a full medical history is taken as well as background about work and personal habits.

A practitioner will actually begin a session by massaging or pushing into points of pain, looking for trigger points. When a trigger point has been found the therapist applies pressure directly above the point, usually for seven seconds. This will be done with fingers and knuckles on the head and extremities. If the main trunk areas of the body are involved, including the back of the thighs, pressure can be exerted using the elbows of the practitioner. There will be moments of pain, perhaps intense pain, but they are usually followed by the sounds of relief, as pain melts away. Certain areas or zones of the body may be worked on exclusively for a period of time. This is often followed with stretching exercises of the areas that have just been worked.

In a myotherapy session, you will most likely be lying down on a table, such as a massage table or one similar to it. Once a trigger point has been located and worked, surrounding secondary areas may be worked in order to loosen muscles groups. The practitioner will continue to work away from the primary trigger point. Kneading of the area loosened may follow. Practitioners often recommend continued stretching exercises at home after the session.

It would behoove anyone considering myotherapy to read Bonnie Prudden's books. These books describe the exercise and trigger points and the system of reeducating that a person who is dealing with serious pain should understand before approaching the therapy. Headaches, TMJ syndrome, and sports injuries are just a few of the types of pain that Prudden and her practitioners have treated with very positive results. Unlike some trigger point therapies, where procaine or other painkillers are injected into the muscles, there are no injections involved with myotherapy.

Precautions

Because myotherapy often deals with chronic pain and the relief or erasure thereof, sessions can be draining, but also liberating. There is real pain involved in working through and relieving years of knotted muscles and distorted negative body habits. People suffering pain from broken bones and those with disk problems are not always the best candidates for this therapy. Check with your primary care giver. Some arthritis sufferers can benefit, but again, check with your primary care giver. Remember, there will be real discomfort associated with a complete course of myotherapy.

When we contacted the Bonnie Prudden school for Physical Fitness and Myotherapy we were told that Prudden, now in her eightieth year, is still very active in running the school. She interviews every applicant in person or by phone to ensure that they are serious students and will make good practitioners. The myotherapy course of study for those who wish to become an instructor is a 9-month, 1300-hour program. The school has graduated about 100 instructors. To locate an instructor in your area, call the number listed at the end of the chapter.

Rolfing

The founder of this body therapy was Ida P. Rolf, who earned a doctorate in biochemistry in the 1920s. She studied under osteopaths and refined her system over many years. Originally Rolf used yoga and other modalities to work on patients with chronic pain. She eventually found yoga inadequate to the task of strengthening the body and reaching deep down to pain centers.

Rolfing works by massaging with hands, elbows, and thumbs on the connective tissue of the body and then reaching down to the collagen that cements cells together in order to move the supportive tissue of the body's frame to a looser and more fluid state. Rolf termed her procedures *"Structural Integration,"* and to this day, the terms "Rolfing" and "Structural Integration" are used interchangeably. The opportunity to work on the "godfather" of the Gestalt movement, Fritz Perls, at the Esalen Institute in the 1960s, proved to be the beginning of recognition for Rolf. Perls's health improved after the session and very soon others were coming to Rolf for body work.

In 1977, Rolf published her book *Rolfing: The Integration of Human Structures*. Two years later, Rolf died, but a number of students have expanded the frontier of Rolfing to include their own variants of the therapy. One of them was Judith Aston who started her Aston Patterning as a kinder, gentler way of manipulating the body. Joseph Heller, another Rolf devotee, created Hellerwork as a less forceful way of dealing with the body's muscle structure. This therapy also emphasizes greater verbal communication between patient and practitioner as a way of working through memories released by the sometimes intense massage and manipulation that Rolfing and its offshoots involve.

Rolfing puts a great emphasis on the body's struggle with gravity and how the body tries to compensate and overcompensate with poor posture and movement habits. By the mind and body sending painful memories and poorly learned physical habits into the muscles, a state is created where muscle and bone problems can originate. Rolfing works with soft tissues at both the surface and deep levels where negative body patterns have their effect. Chronic stress of various types all serve to put different bones, such as the pelvis, legs, and head, out of alignment.

The Rolfing Session

The normal Rolfing program is a series of ten sessions, each an hour long. Initially, a history will be taken and an evaluation performed. Along with this, as in many alternative therapies, there will be a lot of questions about your past, especially any insults to the body. At the beginning, learning to breath will be an important part of the session. Eventually, depending on your condition, the Rolfer will begin massaging or pushing on the outer layers of skin, called the myofascia. A number of stretching procedures designed to free up the muscles in the limbs may also be involved.

Then the deeper procedures begin. This includes deep pushing and massaging, often on knotted connective tissue and muscle tissue. Pain may be intense for a few seconds as tender areas are worked, but this pain will usually quickly lessen. As these places are pushed on with hands, elbows, and perhaps knuckles, they can also produce relief. The goal is not to just find these sensitive areas, but to reach down into the muscle structure where buried pains caused by past physical illness and emotional hurts lie. Releasing these points and "rebalancing" the body, a favorite Rolfing term, often has intense and positive psychological results, sometimes almost immediately.

Precautions

Obviously Rolfing is not for the faint of heart. It is vitally important to have trust and rapport with your Rolfer. Remember,

Rolfing will not be targeted at specific symptoms. It is designed as a method of realigning and rebalancing the body. While some people in psychotherapy have been known to use Rolfing to help release body memories, this is not the only purpose of Rolfing. Its practitioners have some relationship in their methods and goals to removing the body armoring that we spoke of earlier when describing bioenergetics. Remember, Rolfing is not for everyone. Those with any kind of serious bone problems including osteoporosis, arthritis, and spinal disk problems would be advised to approach this therapy with caution. Serious immunological diseases and cancer will not benefit from Rolfing.

Reaching a Rolfer

Rolfers take up to twenty-five weeks of courses to prepare themselves for practice. Part of this training is a study of anatomy, followed by an eighteen-week program in Rolfing itself, including the study of body movement. There are approximately six hundred Rolfers in the United States at this time. The medical establishment, unfortunately, still sees Rolfers as massage practitioners, which is true in only the most general sense. Because of this situation, some Rolfers become certified in their state of practice through a state massage board. To receive a free catalog listing certified Rolfers and Rolfing movement teachers near you, write to the address of the International Rolfing Institute or use the number listed at the end of the chapter.

Organizations and Associations

North American Society of Teachers of the Alexander
    Technique
    P.O. Box 517
    Urbana, IL 61801
    800/473–0620

The Feldenkrais Guild
706 Ellsworth Street
P.O. Box 489
Albany, OR 97321
800/775–2118
503/926–0981
503/926–0572 (fax)

Touch for Health Foundation
1174 North Lake Avenue
Pasadena, CA 91104
818/794–1181

American Polarity Therapy Association
2888 Bluff Street
Suite 149
Boulder, CO 80301
303/545–2080
303/545–2161 (fax)

Reiki Alliance
P.O. Box 41
Cataldo, ID 83810
208/682–3535
208/682–4848 (fax)

International Institute of Reflexology
P.O. Box 12462
St. Petersburg, FL 33733
813/343–4811

American Reflexology Certification Board
P.O. Box 620607
Littleton, CO 81062
303/933–6921

Nurse Healers and Professional Associates Cooperative
(Therapeutic Touch)
175 Fifth Street
Suite 3399
New York, NY 10010

Bonnie Prudden (Myotherapy) Pain Erasure Clinic
7800 Speedway
Tucson, AZ 85710
800/221–4634
602/529–3979

International Institute for Bioenergetic Analysis
144 East Thirty-sixth Street
New York, NY 10016
212/532–7742
212/532–5331 (fax)

Hakomi Institute
1800 Thirtieth Street
Suite 201
Boulder, CO 80301
303/443–6209

Rolfing Institute of Structural Integration
P.O. Box 1868
Boulder, CO 80306
303/449–5903
800/530–8875

Chapter Eight

Nutrition and Healing

Using the science of nutrition to help prevent and cure disease is not new; various foods, often used with herbal remedies, are probably the oldest medical treatments devised by humans. They were developed thousands of years before nutrition science discovered and explained carbohydrates and protein or vitamins and minerals.

In the United States, nutrition science is not an important part of medical education and far more time is spent training medical students about medications or surgery. One only need look at the advertising in medical journals to see the way in which the pharmaceutical industry has supported this trend. Nutrition, on the other hand, is a relatively unimportant tool, and many physicians recognize only the most severe cases of malnutrition.

In this century, there has been a generalized emphasis on a "balanced" diet, the definition of which changes from time to time. Until the last two decades, the typical North American diet consisted of three meals a day, usually built around meat and dairy products. For many decades the conventional medical establishment denied strong links between diet and heart disease, hypertension, cancer, arthritis, infertility, and a host of other conditions. Most Americans thought that they obtained sufficient nutrients from a "normal" diet. As a result, few physicians counseled their patients about nutrition or asked them about their diets. With the exception of conditions such as diabetes and food allergies, specific diets or food plans were—and unfortunately, still are—rarely recommended. Some physicians provide referrals to trained nutritionists, although this is still not a common practice.

Specific information and recommendations about nutritional supplements are also lacking in most medical practices. Many Western physicians stick to the idea that if we eat three meals a day composed of a variety of foods, then we should have little need for supplements, except perhaps for those providing the recommended daily allowance (RDA) for certain vitamins and minerals. But alternative health care practitioners and some conventionally trained doctors have challenged the view that diet and nutritional supplements are unimportant.

Over the last several decades, many alternative health care practitioners were accused of using unscientific, and even irresponsible, methods. Yet millions of North Americans take nutritional supplements daily; they just don't tell their family physicians for fear of being ridiculed.

Most alternative health care practitioners have always emphasized the role of food, herbs, and nutritional supplements in their practices, and in some cases, their contentions are now becoming part of mainstream thinking. Today's new food pyramid, with its emphasis on a diet low in fat and high in complex carbohydrates, is not novel or new to many alternative practitioners. Because they sought treatment outside conventional facilities, millions of Americans were aware of low-fat eating long before the U.S. government and mainstream advocacy associations (such as the American Heart Association and the American Cancer Society) began to educate the public about this way of eating.

The 1988 Surgeon General's Report on Nutrition and Health added credence to the ancient wisdom that diet has a crucial role in maintaining health and preventing numerous diseases and conditions, from heart disease to stroke to arthritis. Although there is not widespread support among conventionally educated physicians for macrobiotic eating, fasting, organic farming, vegetarianism, and so forth, this is changing as new studies are released.

Is Our Food Supply Adequately Protected?

Only a decade or two ago, "health nuts" were people who shopped in "natural" food stores and ate only organically grown fruit, vegetables, and grains. Today, this has changed as millions of people have become increasingly concerned about the number, amount, and kind of pesticides, preservatives, and dyes used in growing and processing food. In addition, antibiotics, hormones, and other chemicals routinely used in raising animals add to the concern that our food supply is not entirely safe.

Many unorthodox practitioners are concerned about the way these additives are tested. These substances are generally tested one at a time, separately. The Environmental Protection Agency (EPA) does not currently have a method to measure risks involved in multiple chemical exposure, meaning that industrial chemicals are not tested for their collective effects on human beings. But, just as vitamins and minerals act synergistically, that is work together, it appears that pesticides, additives, hormones, and dyes do so as well and should be tested for their effects when appearing in groups in air, water, and soil.

Irradiation, a process that exposes food to radioactive substances to extend its shelf life, is also controversial. There is, of course, skepticism about introducing radiation even if its purpose is to make food free of harmful bacteria and molds. The process of irradiation destroys some valuable nutrients in the food along with the bacteria and molds. There are legitimate questions about the safety of the individuals working in irradiation plants and the long-term risks for the communities in which these plants are located.

The concern about the relationship between toxic chemicals and our food supply extends to seafood, once thought to be the least contaminated food available. Industrial and agricultural pollution affects both vegetable and animal life in fresh and salt water. For example, industrial chemicals such as PCBs (polychlorinated biphenyls) and methyl mercury accumulate in the tissues of some fish. PCBs and methyl mercury pose a specific threat to pregnant women since exposure to these chemicals is linked with some birth defects.

This Calorie Is Empty

Unorthodox nutritionists say that many North Americans eat a diet high in calories but low in nutrients. For example, refined white flour and sugar form the basis of many commercially prepared food products, which offer an abundance of calories but few nutrients. Many nutritionists believe that obesity may result from being undernourished rather than overfed. In other words, while relatively few North Americans are hungry, millions of us suffer from low-grade nutritional deficiencies. These deficiencies are caused by consuming so many nutritionally empty calories.

When a condition is nonspecific and described as "just not feeling well," or as a loss of energy and vitality, physicians will often do a thorough examination and run some tests. When they do not find any obvious condition, they throw the ball back into the patient's court. There are millions of people who find their way to alternative health care providers because, while they aren't exactly sick, they don't feel well either. While it isn't exciting to be told that our poor eating habits might be to blame for our malaise, most of us intuitively know that nutritional solutions often yield the best results. Fortunately, we can get nutritional guidance in a variety of alternative health care settings.

Dietary Solutions

Were you to visit a traditionally trained registered dietitian (RD), you would be advised to alter your diet to conform to the new food pyramid, which emphasizes complex carbohydrates—grains, legumes, beans, and fruits and vegetables. Meat and dairy products and all types of fat should now comprise a lower percentage of your total caloric intake.

A nontraditional nutrition counselor will probably offer similar, but greatly expanded, recommendations. General guidelines include using unprocessed foods, organically grown if possible. Many nutritionists would recommend avoiding red meat and most dairy products. (Milk allergies are very common but are not always detected by traditional dietitians.)

Many nutritionists associated with the alternative health care arena are more likely to consider "hidden" food allergies as a source of many difficulties. By "hidden," we mean those allergies or sensitivities that do not show up on standard allergy tests. You may be asked to keep food diaries, which are analyzed during your consultation. You may be given blood tests, similar to those used by environmental medicine practitioners. (See Chapter 14 for a discussion of these tests.)

If you are consulting a nutrition counselor for a specific health concern, then your diet will be individualized. You may also be given specific vitamin and mineral supplements or herbal preparations. The nutrition counselor you see could be, for example, a naturopath, homeopath, chiropractor, or an acupuncturist, who has taken additional training in nutrition. Some nutritionists are RDs or have master's degrees in nutrition science, and they use their training as a foundation from which they can expand the scope of their work. Many consider themselves nontraditional nutritional counselors. (Associations representing these "alternative" nutritionists are listed at the end of this chapter.) There are also nutritionally oriented medical doctors, who have determined that improved nutrition should be part of any health care treatment plan.

Some alternative practitioners and nutritionists offer more specialized expertise in the following areas:

Fasting

Put simply, fasting involves taking a deliberate break from normal eating for a period as brief as twenty-four hours or as long as two or three weeks. Only water is taken during some fasts; on other fasting regimens juice or herbal tea is consumed in addition to water. (Short fasts are generally done at home, but for fasts lasting longer than three or four days, we recommend seeking supervision from an experienced health care provider.) Some fasts take place at a health center or retreat where the person's well-being can be monitored.

Fasting is an ancient and universal practice, sometimes used for spiritual purposes. In Europe, fasting is part of health spa regimens, and in this country, we associate supervised fasts with naturopathic medicine. If you seek supervision for a fast, you will likely use the services of a naturopath or a nutritionist who has received similar training in this area.

How Does Fasting Benefit the Body?

Our bodies use considerable energy just breaking down the food we eat so it can be used as fuel. Carbohydrates and proteins are converted to glycogen (stored in the liver) and used as energy for the body as it carries out its normal functions. When we fast, we burn the stored glycogen for the first day or two and after that the body uses stored fat for energy.

The break in regular eating allows the body to eliminate toxins while not taking in new ones. When the body isn't dealing with food and its associated toxic elements and possible allergens, the immune system doesn't have to overwork just to keep the body healthy. When energy isn't used in digestion, the body can redirect that energy to the immune system and cell growth. Many people believe that in the long run, a fast will rejuvenate them and increase their energy.

After three or four days, the blood becomes thinner, which increases the amount of oxygen delivered to all the body's tissues. As fat is burned, toxins stored in fat cells (pesticide residues, for example) are released into the blood stream and eliminated over the period of the fast. Toxins are eliminated through the kidneys and the skin, which explains why people sometimes complain that their skin itches or breaks out during the early days of a fast.

What Conditions Will Be Helped by Fasting?

Fasting can be used as a preventive tool and for its curative value. Some practitioners will recommend a two- or three-day fast every few months just to rest the body and cleanse the tissues. There are psychological advantages to fasting, too. Most of us live over-active, stressed lives, and taking two or three days out to stay home and fast can be equivalent to taking a break from the world. Some people will follow a regular fasting schedule just to get this self-enforced rest.

Anecdotal evidence suggests that water fasting can help relieve arthritis, although for long-term relief, more than one fast is usually needed. Hypertension also may improve with water fasting and some practitioners report that patients can dramatically reduce their medication or even eliminate it. (Obviously, with both these conditions, it is important to fast under careful supervision, and we don't recommend altering medications without discussing this step with your primary care provider.)

Fasting also can help identify food allergies because once toxins are cleared from the body, the person's reactions to foods are observed as foods are reintroduced. If you have allergies you might have many symptoms, from sinusitis and headaches to irritability and depression. After a few days of fasting, your symptoms are much better, but when you begin reintroducing foods one at a time, the cause and effect phenomenon is sometimes quite dramatic in that the reaction to the food is immediate and severe.

It is best to start a fasting regimen when you don't have a serious chronic or life-threatening condition. While fasting may help improve symptoms, it is probably best used as a prevention technique.

Are There Conditions for Which Fasting Could Be Harmful?

Any fast that lasts more than four days should be supervised by a health care practitioner, and some people believe that these fasts should be done at a health center or a retreat center where supervision is available. In addition, a fast of any length should not be undertaken by people with diabetes; kidney or bladder disorders; ulcerative colitis; seizure disorders, such as epilepsy; severe bronchial disorders, such as asthma; and while pregnant or breastfeeding. Cancer patients should not fast when already weakened by chemotherapy or radiation treatment. For obvious reasons, it is also not wise to fast if you are already malnourished for any reason. Consult with a health care provider to be certain that you do not have a condition that would contraindicate fasting as a treatment technique.

A Variety of Choices

Some practitioners recommend drinking only distilled or spring water during a relatively brief fast of two to four days. For example, on a weekend fast, you would drink water as your thirst demanded and rest at home without reading newspapers, watching stimulating television programs, or talking on the telephone. You would break the fast with cooked fruit, vegetable broth, or a light vegetable soup. This is a simple, low-risk fast.

Under supervision, a water-only fast can be prolonged for many days, even more than two weeks.

Some practitioners recommend juice fasts, but fasting "purists" will consider them a form of restricted diet. Practitioners who use juice fasts prefer them because the detoxification process is less intense. For example, after a couple of days on water only, some people complain of headaches, severe fatigue, and other symptoms such as hand tremors and dizziness. For most people, these symptoms pass fairly quickly and are only part of detoxification, but they are unpleasant while they last.

Vegetable juices are used in juice fasting because fruit juices contain large concentrations of sugar. For example, it takes four to six apples to produce a small glass of apple juice. Some well-diluted fruit juices can be used if they are not the primary source of liquid. Vegetable juices are also generally diluted as well. Herbal teas also allowed. Because vegetable and fruit juices provide some nutrients, these fasts can generally last longer than water-only fasts.

What to Expect

If you are contemplating a fast, talk with a practitioner about which type is best for you. If you are seeing a naturopath, for example, he or she might decide to run some preliminary blood studies just to be certain that there is no reason for you not to undertake even a brief fast. You also need to find out if you will need colon cleansing before fasting or during a longer fast. Some practitioners recommend nightly enemas for a few days before beginning a fast that will last more than two or three days. Others do not think this is necessary and do not recommend using enemas during a brief, water-only fast. If a juice fast is going to last more than two or three days, then enemas may be required.

While there is no necessity to approach fasting as a spiritual activity, people often report that sitting or walking meditation or their prayer life takes on a different quality while fasting. Mental clarity and an ability to focus and concentrate are often enhanced. This ability to focus may not happen right away, however, because there are physical reactions, some of which may be unpleasant.

You may, for example, develop a headache, perhaps from "caffeine withdrawal." This is sometimes accompanied by slight nausea and dizziness and a slightly irregular heartbeat. (These symptoms sound ominous, but generally they are mild and pass after a day or two. Obviously if any symptom becomes severe, you should contact the health professional who is advising you about your fast. Again, if you have a serious chronic condition or take medications regularly, you may not be a candidate for fasting.) After a day or two, your skin may become dry and itchy and you may have general aches and pains throughout your body. These symptoms, like the headache, are the result of ridding your body of toxins and should be viewed as a positive sign. Women in particular often report dramatic weight loss in the first two days of a fast if water retention has been a problem.

Your practitioner can advise you about ways to relieve unpleasant symptoms and also can tell you how to balance rest and activity during a fast. While a feeling of hunger might persist for several days (on a long fast), it inevitably passes and a hunger-free period can last for several days to up to a week or more. Many people report feeling positive about the fasting experience, and when it is time to break the fast, they feel a great sense of accomplishment.

It is likely that we'll hear more about fasting in the future. Health care practitioners in the Scandinavian countries are conducting research on the potential overall benefits and curative value of fasting. Specifically, they are documenting the effect of fasting on rheumatoid arthritis. In addition, there will no doubt be growing interest in fasting because it obviously is a low-cost treatment, requiring only the services of a professional to supervise the process.

Vegetarian Diets

Most people believe that vegetarians are people who, for a variety of reasons, don't eat meat. But this definition is too narrow. Most vegetarians believe that meatless eating promotes health and is also a choice based on ethical considerations. Ethical vegetarians believe it is wrong to kill animals and use them as a source of food, primarily because it isn't necessary for human survival. (There are people who dispute this contention and maintain that in some parts of the world human beings would not have survived without using animals for food and other products. However, these examples are few and don't affect the basic idea that vegetable sources are nutritionally sufficient for human needs.)

Others are less concerned about using animals than they are about what they believe to be the harmful effects of meat on human health. Vegetarians believe that meatless eating is nutritionally superior and promotes health rather than contributing to disease.

Ecological Eating

In the 1970s, a new reason to turn to vegetarianism appeared. An increasing number of people began to look at the global issue of hunger, specifically the economic and political forces behind the growing number of malnourished people in less developed countries. People argued that they could no longer grow food because their land was increasingly being taken over to grow export crops for rich Western countries. Land that could be used to grow grain for human use was used to grow grain to feed the animals that North Americans consumed. The activists who studied this problem concluded that the only way to stop such practices, which are based on supply and demand, is to cut the demand for meat and make it less profitable for agribusiness to continue to import meat and use valuable grain to feed livestock.

For many people, the issue of global ecology represents a new ethical reason for choosing vegetarian eating.

Protein Becomes an Issue

Those who defend using animal products in our diets say that we can't meet our protein requirements without them. But, vegetarians have proven that with knowledge of food combining, this difficulty can be overcome.

Animal products are complete proteins, meaning that they contain all nine of the essential amino acids necessary to maintain and build many types of tissues and other chemical components of our bodies. Except for soybeans, vegetable products do not contain all these essential amino acids, but foods can be combined in the same meal and thus provide all nine of the needed amino acids. For example, if you eat lentils and corn in the same meal, all the essential amino acids will be present. Those vegetarians who consume some dairy products (lacto-vegetarians) are not concerned about the complete protein issue since milk products contain the essential amino acids.

What Are the Health Benefits of Vegetarianism?

There is an old saying that there's no such thing as an obese vegetarian. By and large, this is a true statement. However, eliminating meat, poultry, and fish from the diet is not a guarantee that the diet will be low in fat. Vegetarians caution that they too must be careful about substituting vegetable fats for animal fats. Nuts and seeds, for example, are somewhat high in fat and vegetarians generally use these foods sparingly. Vegetarians have long been on the forefront of advocating a low-fat diet based on whole foods, with an emphasis on grains and vegetables.

It is believed that vegetarians have low incidence of obesity because they tend to eat high-quality, satisfying foods. They usually avoid packaged and processed foods that provide empty calories and encourage overeating. One reason we don't see many fat vegetarians is that they are relatively free of cravings for the empty foods that can be addictive. Let's face it, we usually don't overeat broccoli and brown rice, but food containing high concentrations of sugar and fat can lead to cravings for more of the same.

Vegetarian diets are recommended for such illnesses and conditions as heart disease, hypertension, allergies, digestive disturbances such as constipation and heart burn, and diabetes and hypoglycemia. This way of eating is also considered a long-term preventive measure for these and other conditions. Many vegetarians believe that if we all ate a vegetarian diet, we would see drastic reductions in the incidence of almost all the major diseases affecting our population, including cancer and heart disease.

Some mainstream health care providers agree that vegetarianism is not just for "eccentrics." The American Dietetic Association has a group of vegetarian practitioners and a hotline to answer questions about this way of eating. Many alternative health care practitioners can offer advice about vegetarian eating and many group practices have a nutritionist on staff who is knowledgeable about vegetarianism.

The Vitamin B-12 Question

One reason mainstream health care providers have questioned the long-term efficacy of a plant-food only vegetarian (vegan) diet is that Vitamin B-12 is available only from animal products. One does not have to eat meat to get this nutrient and dairy products can supply it in sufficient amounts. Many people are lacto-vegetarians primarily because dairy foods provide this vitamin. Because Vitamin B-12 deficiency has serious consequences, including neurological damage and a serious form of anemia, most nutritionists advise vegans to take a supplement of this nutrient. Aside from this important consideration, there are not known health risks (for adults) associated with a vegetarian diet. We recommend discussing the Vitamin B-12 issue with your primary health care provider before eliminating all animal products from your diet.

Macrobiotics

The word "macrobiotic" literally means "great life," and is described as a way of living, not just a way of eating. It has had wide spread exposure in this country because of George Ohsawa, a Japanese man who cured his tuberculosis by using the principles of Chinese medicine, on which macrobiotic philosophy is based. Ohsawa started a center in Japan where he taught his methods and philosophy, and a world-wide tour brought his teachings to Europe, North America, and Africa. The best-known student of Ohsawa's in the United States is Michio Kushi, who has written many books and is largely responsible for the many followers of "the macrobiotic way."

What Is the Macrobiotic Way?

Sometimes macrobiotic living is described in terms of what it is not. For example, it is not a religion, an alternative medicine, or simply a healthful way to eat. Briefly, macrobiotic living is a philosophy, a set of principles, and a way of eating—and living—in harmony with oneself and the world.

Ohsawa believed that most people have lost their intuitive sense of the best way to eat and live, but it is possible to regain this "natural" knowledge of staying healthy through living by macrobiotic principles. It is not enough, however, to labor over food choices and go to the trouble of eating in the macrobiotic way if one's attitude is negative toward the process. In other words, there is a macrobiotic way of living, which for most people involves a spiritual orientation and a belief in a central life force that balances all living things.

Yin and Yang All Over Again

In macrobiotic philosophy, food is central to life. That sounds obvious, but most Westerners do not live as if they believed this to be true. Food is something that we eat to comfort ourselves and feel full, or simply because we enjoy it or know we must periodically refuel our bodies. We rarely think about the actual living nature of the food on our plates as we are consuming it. But a person trained in macrobiotic living knows that food must be chosen with great care because each element in it is important. In other words, food choices make an immediate and long-term difference in how we feel and what diseases we will or will not eventually develop. This is where the principles of Yin and Yang come in, because all foods are classified as primarily Yin or Yang, and therefore are part of the world of complementary opposites. Macrobiotic eating is concerned with the essence of each food that exists on the planet. One should never eat a particular food without understanding the reason for doing so.

The Eastern concepts of Yin and Yang help us visually picture the constant change in the universe, from the cyclic nature of the seasons to the myriad capacities of our minds. Yin, the term used for the expansive quality of the universe, encompasses air and water, for example.

This idea is also applied to those foods that are expansive. Fruit, for example, has Yin qualities; watermelon is on one end of the Yin scale, and cherries are on the other. In general, Yin foods are lighter and may grow in a shorter period of time. Yang is the contracting force. Foods that have Yang qualities are dense and heavy and usually take a long time to grow. Root vegetables are generally more dense than those growing above ground and are Yang foods. Salt is a Yang substance because food contracts when salt is added. The pickling process is an obvious example of the Yang quality of salt.

The Yin and Yang principles are the root of the constant change and balance we experience. For example, most people are more Yang (active) in the morning and more Yin (restful) at night. We go through small cycles throughout the day and no two people have identical rhythms. We also can apply the term "macro" to the large cycles of the earth, including the seasons of growing, harvesting, and resting the land. Our cycles as individuals, which some call our biorhythms, are the micro aspect of the whole.

To a macrobiotic counselor everything about you is important and your unique cycles become part of the basis for suggesting an eating plan. A therapeutic macrobiotic diet might look very different from the diet you will follow if you are maintaining good health. It can take a lifetime to understand macrobiotic ideas, linked as they are with the Chinese philosophy of the universe and of health and illness. In fact, if you waited for complete comprehension of this complex system before beginning a macrobiotic diet, you would probably never start. It is not easy for the average Westerner to comprehend that in this way of viewing the world, every food has an element, organ system, sense, season, direction, color, mental process, and even a sound associated with it. Thus, even the color and texture of food is important in macrobiotic eating; some foods should be eaten only in the winter and others in the summer.

Contrary to popular belief, macrobiotic eating is not completely dairy free, at least for most people, nor is it strictly vegetarian. Some followers eat certain kinds of fish, although red meat and poultry are generally not recommended.

The macrobiotic diet can be described as emphasizing unprocessed grains as the staple food, with certain vegetables such as squash, carrots, cabbage, and onions as regular side dishes. Certain varieties of seaweed, such as dulse and wakame, are regularly used. Some beans, seeds, nuts, and fruits are included, but not necessarily consumed daily or in large amounts. Meat, fish, and poultry are allowed once in a while, as are dairy products and alcohol. This description is very general and people must choose those foods that are right for them as individuals with unique—and changing—needs.

What Are the Benefits of a Macrobiotic Diet?

Macrobiotic eating is generally safe for most people and few would argue with the wholesome nature of the foods it offers. Since macrobiotic philosophy maintains that all illness has an internal source, restoring health is an internal process as well. It involves diet, mental attitude, and balancing of the physical, mental, and spiritual needs.

Although Chinese medicine does not label conditions and diseases in the same way we do in the West, Michio Kushi has written extensively about recovering from serious conditions using this way of eating and living. For example, good long-term results are documented for diabetes and hypoglycemia. Some diabetics have reduced and eventually eliminated their dependence on insulin, giving them an entirely new way to live. Macrobiotic eating is used to treat such conditions as hypertension, heart disease, obesity, infertility, menstrual disorders, all kinds of digestive illnesses, and food allergies, and to rebuild health after traumatic injuries or surgery.

Perhaps more controversial are the claims by some experts within the field that the macrobiotic way can prevent cancer, and in some cases, even arrest or cure it. Macrobiotic thinking concerning cancer, however, does not subscribe to the carcinogen theory behind the disease. Cancer, like all other illnesses, is viewed as the result of long-term imbalances and eating patterns that are destructive to the body. Therefore, the cure involves restoring the balance, instead of removing or destroying cancerous tumors. Cure is also not necessarily a word that applies here, in that some well-known experts in macrobiotic philosophy believe that cancer cells can be prevented from multiplying, rather than eradicated from the body. In other words, people sometimes use the macrobiotic approach after undergoing other cancer treatment to prevent recurrence and arrest the progression of the disease.

There is no question that using macrobiotic principles is an unconventional cancer treatment in this country and a choice made by individual patients who seek information about this approach on their own. We make no recommendations here except to say that an increasing number of people are searching for alternatives to surgery, radiation, and chemotherapy. All macrobiotic counselors would prefer that people think in terms of prevention and not in terms of trying to cure an aggressive disease.

How Does a Person Begin Macrobiotic Eating and Living?

While there are hundreds of books about macrobiotic living, most people find it helpful to consult a practitioner, a person who has studied with other counselors, taken courses sponsored by macrobiotic organizations, and, therefore, has received enough special training to qualify as an adviser. Some people develop a relationship with their macrobiotic counselor, who can function as a teacher and a guide. Followers find that they may eventually seek out others in their communities who are also learning this way of living.

As concern over environmental illness grows, incidence of certain cancers rises, and there is a widening search for alternative health care, macrobiotic living will probably receive more attention. While not an easy program to adopt, those who have successfully improved their health by following the diet and studying the ideas believe that its benefits far outweigh any challenges it presents.

Other Special Diets

There are several detoxification diets or cleansing diets in use today. Some do not have distinguishing names, but could be suggested to you by a variety of alternative practitioners. They include such plans as eating fruits, vegetables, and white fish for up to a week and using colon cleansing methods at home; using protein powder, with fruit juice and cooked vegetables for a week or more, along with colon cleansing; or a rotation diet (described in Chapter 14). There are also special diets used to treat conditions such as infantile epilepsy, attention-deficit disorder, and hyperactivity in children. Many alternative health care providers will be aware of these unconventional diets and can lead you to professionals who are knowledgeable about them.

Nutritional Supplements

Almost 50 percent of adults in the United States take nutritional supplements, commonly known as vitamin pills (although many supplements contain minerals, herbs, amino acids, or enzymes as well). Indeed, as we know, this is a multibillion dollar industry—and growing all the time. For decades, mainstream medical doctors have known little about supplements and have generally not recommended them to their patients. Many people take basic supplements, supplying no more than the RDA, as a kind of "insurance policy," because they know that their diets are not always carefully planned and may be nutritionally inadequate.

Few mainstream health care providers are concerned about their patients taking these small amounts of nutrients. The controversy arises over taking "mega" doses of vitamins, minerals, and herbs. Those who recommend taking supplements maintain that the typical American diet is inadequate and just eating a varied diet will not meet most people's nutritional needs. In addition, nutrients can be used in larger than normal amounts as healing agents.

The reasons for nutritional inadequacy go back to the "empty calorie" idea, meaning that the typical American diet provides many calories but inadequate amounts of basic nutrients. Our nutritional needs are greater than ever before because our food is grown on depleted soils, polluted with chemical fertilizers. Likewise, our bodies must cope with exposure to environmental hazards unknown before this century. The result is a need for additional nutrients to maintain health.

Many practitioners trained in alternative health care methods believe that the recommended daily allowances are minimal dosages, based on amounts of nutrients needed to prevent serious conditions such as rickets and scurvy. The RDAs do not address ways to maintain maximum health through strengthening the immune system and preventing subtle deterioration of our organ systems. In other words, cancer or heart disease or diabetes are gross manifestations of diseases that have been gradually developing long before the most serious symptoms appear. Conventional thinking labels these illnesses as "natural" consequences of aging or genetically programmed, or both.

The symptoms people often consider inevitable parts of life, such as fatigue, chronic indigestion, mental confusion, inability to concentrate, nervousness, menstrual complaints, frequent headaches, and so forth, are, according to many nutritionists, early signs of vitamin deficiencies. Alternative health care practitioners look to nutritional supplements as a way both to prevent and treat these common diseases and disorders.

We're Not All Alike

In the 1930s, Roger Williams, a biochemist who discovered one of the B vitamins (pantothenic acid), maintained that nutrients could be used to fight disease. But it is not simply a question of giving patients large doses of this or that vitamin in a "one-size-fits-all" formula. He believed that we are each unique with individual nutritional needs. This concept is known as biochemical individuality. To many alternative health care practitioners, this is not such a strange idea. Traditional Chinese practitioners, homeopaths, naturopaths, macrobiotic counselors, and so on base their philosophies on the idea that no two individuals have the same nutritional needs—or the same needs for rest, activity, or exercise.

Because we all have special needs, a nutritionist will assess your diet and lifestyle, individual and family health history, and sometimes do sophisticated blood tests to find out which nutritional supplements will meet your needs. Some practitioners use hair analysis, a method that measures the concentration of minerals in the body. These practitioners believe that hair analysis accurately reveals exposure to toxic substances, such as lead and mercury, and can provide information on which to base nutritional supplementation and detoxification programs. (Hair analysis is done by removing a few hairs from the nape of the neck. The hair is sent to special laboratories for analysis.)

The Whole Is Greater than the Sum of Its Parts

Jeffrey Bland, a biochemist and leading nutritional expert, emphasizes the synergistic quality of basic nutrients. Vitamins, minerals, and amino acids occur in groups and therefore must be studied and used in groups. For example, vitamins E, A, and C work as a team to prevent breakdown of body tissues. Minerals such as manganese, zinc, copper, and selenium work together to delay the degenerative conditions of the body. Moreover, the presence of one nutrient acts to help another nutrient do its work. For example, when vitamin C and iron supplements are taken together, more of the iron is absorbed by the body. The presence of vitamin C appears to help the iron do its work.

Free Radicals and the Antioxidant Nutrients

A free radical is a particular kind of atom (or a group of atoms) that can damage cells and impair immunity. There is more than one type of free radical, and our bodies are designed to counteract or prevent the damage they can do. A group of enzymes, collectively referred to as free radical scavengers, have the job of neutralizing free radicals. Certain nutrients, known as antioxidants, are also potent forces working against the harmful free radicals.

Vitamins C and E and the mineral selenium are powerful antioxidant nutrients. Beta-carotene, a substance found in plant foods, is converted to Vitamin A in the liver. It is now believed that beta-carotene, rather than Vitamin A (found in fish oils, for example) is the more powerful antioxidant. Other minerals, enzymes, and amino acids have antioxidant properties too, and it appears that these substances do their best work in groups, providing an excellent example of the synergistic nature of nutrients. Studies involving the antioxidant nutrients have suggested that they play a crucial role in preventing and treating many conditions, including cancer.

Evidence Mounts

There is a growing body of research that supports the contention that taking nutritional supplements may be one way to maintain health and enhance recovery from illnesses. For example, a study conducted by a medical doctor in California established that Vitamin C was effective in treating some infectious diseases, including many childhood diseases, pneumonia, hepatitis, and the common cold. Vitamin C has also been shown to enhance the effect of radiation and chemotherapy on cancerous tissue, while helping to prevent damage to healthy cells.

A Welsh study demonstrated that children who had subclinical nutritional deficiencies (deficiencies not detected on standard medical tests) showed improved academic performance after being given multivitamin supplements. Folic acid deficiencies have been linked to birth defects. These are only a few examples of the type of research that is leading to a greater awareness of the link between subclinical nutritional deficiencies and a variety of diseases and disorders.

Are There Dangers Associated with Taking Supplements?

Vitamin toxicity is quite rare, and most people can safely take most available multivitamin and mineral supplements, even though they contain higher amounts of nutrients than listed in the RDA tables. It is not wise to single out one vitamin or mineral and take large doses of it. Doing so can interrupt the synergistic action of nutrients. But nutritionists might suggest taking a higher dose of one vitamin for a specific period of time because of a condition you're being treated for. For example, Vitamin A can be toxic at high levels because it is not water soluble and it stores in the body. (Beta-carotene, however, is water soluble and is harmless.) An alternative practitioner might suggest a high dosage of Vitamin A to treat a previous deficiency or because you have an infection and this nutrient is being used to treat it. After you are well, then you would stop taking the high doses. You should not take high doses of Vitamin D and Vitamin B^6 because they can be toxic if taken over a long period of time.

Orthomolecular Medicine

Treating certain categories of illness with very large doses of nutrients is a branch of nutrition science, and is sometimes referred to as megavitamin therapy. The late Linus Pauling created the term "orthomolecular" to describe a specific approach to healing using substances that are already present in the body. Some disorders can be treated by correcting nutritional imbalances that occur because of biochemical individuality or because of stressors, such as long-term nutritional deprivation or exposure to environmental toxins.

The principles of orthomolecular medicine became more widely known when two physicians showed positive results using high doses of niacin to treat schizophrenics. While still controversial, the principle of using nutrients therapeutically is now discussed in conventional medical circles. There are orthomolecular practitioners treating depression and other mental disorders with amino acids and other nutrients, but the treatment is still not widely available. Most conventional psychiatrists and other mental health professionals will not even mention nutritional treatment as an option to their patients.

Jonathan Wright, M.D., a conventionally trained physician, has established his reputation as a doctor who uses nutrition to heal. He documented many situations in which specific illnesses and conditions were reversed by using megadoses of nutrients. Treating infertility, hyperthyroidism, skin conditions, allergies, heart disease, and so forth, Wright is another pioneer in orthomolecular nutrition and an internationally recognized expert in nutritional biochemistry. The reward for his efforts was harassment and even a raid of his clinic by Food and Drug Administration (FDA) agents in 1992. His Tahoma Clinic, located in Kent, Washington, was searched for fourteen hours and his treatment and office supplies were confiscated. At this writing, a grand jury investigation is underway; he has yet to be charged with any violation of the law.

Wright's story is important because it shows the divisions that continue to exist in the area of nutritionally oriented treatments. Despite this, some practitioners believe that orthomolecular medicine and its applications to prevention and treatment will eventually become a respected medical specialty. Alternative health care practitioners have been instrumental in the growing awareness of this important science.

The following organizations collectively provide an enormous amount of information about the role of diet and nutritional supplements. Some can provide information about alternative approaches to nutritional healing; some also have referral services.

Sources of Information and Referrals

American College of Advancement in Medicine
P.O. Box 3427
Laguna Hills, CA 92654
714/583–7666

This organization's members are physicians who use diet and nutrition as part of their regular treatment plans. This organization is also known for its advocacy of chelation therapy.

Their directory can lead you to physicians and nutritionists in your area.

The Huxley Institute for Biosocial Research
American Academy of Orthomolecular Medicine
900 North Federal Highway
Boca Raton, FL 33432
800/847–3802

This group can provide referrals to physicians using orthomolecular medicine.

American Association of Nutritional Consultants
1641 East Sunset Road
Las Vegas, NV 89119
702/361–1132

This association provides training and information for its members and may be able to refer you to a nutritional counselor in your area.

International Academy of Nutrition and Preventive Medicine
P.O. Box 18433
Asheville, NC 28814
704/258–3243

An organization devoted to reporting nutritional advances in the treatment of many diseases and disorders, including psychological illness, it can help you find appropriate physicians and nutritionists and referrals to treatment centers.

Nutrition for Optimal Health
P.O. Box 380
Winnetka, IL 60093
708/835–5030

Open to the general public, this organization educates professionals and the lay public about advances in nutritional healing.

The Linus Pauling Institute
440 Page Mill Road
Palo Alto, CA 94306
415/327–4064

This institute is a source of information about nutrition and healing, with an emphasis on Vitamin C.

The American Dietetic Association
216 West Jackson Boulevard
Chicago, IL 60606

While this is considered a mainstream organization, it now has information about vegetarian diets. Many nutritionists using a variety of treatment techniques were first trained as registered dietitians.

The Vegetarian Education Network
P.O. Box 3347
West Chester, PA 19380
215/696–VNET

This group engages in research and education to inform people interested in vegetarian eating. It also produces a newsletter written by and for young people.

North American Vegetarian Society
P.O. Box 72
Dogleville, NY 13329
518/568-7970

Free information about the society and a pamphlet on vegetarianism is available by sending a self-addressed stamped envelope. They also publish a quarterly journal.

Vegetarian Resource Group
P.O. Box 1463
Baltimore, MD 21203
410/366-VEGE

This group provides general information to the public and produces a magazine.

American Association of Naturopathic Physicians
2366 Eastlake Avenue
Suite 322
Seattle, WA 98102
800/206-7610

This organization is one place to start when looking for a practitioner who can supervise a fast. Not all naturopaths will consider themselves qualified for this, but most will know nutritionists or other practitioners who are. These practitioners are also able to provide information about vegetarianism and are likely to know nutritionists who can counsel in this area as well.

Kushi Institute
P.O. Box 7
Beckett, MA 01223
413/623-5741

This is a major macrobiotic educational center in the United States, and certifies practitioners.

The East West Foundation
7 Station Street
P.O. Box 850
Brookline, MA 02147
617/738–0045

This organization is another source of information about macrobiotics.

Chapter Nine

Herbal Medicine

The origins of herbal medicine, sometimes called "phytomedicine," or plant medicine, are as old as humankind itself. Every civilization has used the plants of the earth to treat illnesses and promote healing. The history of these plants, roots, barks, and flowers is many thousands of years old. Whether the herbal tradition is western, Chinese, or Native American, each has a rich storehouse of knowledge passed down from generation to generation. All of these traditions are part of the fabric of human herbal knowledge. According to the World Health Organization, herbal medicine is the primary medical therapy for over three-quarters of the world's people.

Allopathic medicine, with its heroic interventions at the times of health crisis, can be very effective. If there is a broken limb or a heart attack, allopathic medicine is usually the right way to go. The herbalists, however, rather than treating the crisis of the moment by itself, view the human body as part of a greater web of life on the earth. This view of wellness holds that illness occurs when the body is stressed, undergoes nutritional/food imbalances, or has toxins accumulated within bodily systems. These toxins can include fatty foods, tobacco, alcohol, drugs, or environmental pollution from any number of sources. Rather than taking heroic measures that involve antibiotics or invasive procedures, herbalists will try to regenerate health by eliminating toxins and tonifying the body. Plants, whether raw or as extracts, are the herbalist's medicines of choice.

Because of the diverse traditions of herbalism, there are many different kinds of herbal practitioners. Most homeopathic remedies, for instance, are based on plants, animal products, or minerals. Hence many homeopathic physicians do recommend herbal preparations in their practice. Iridoligists, with their study of the eye, will sometimes recommend herbs or foods to promote healing. Naturopathic practitioners will usually include plants, herbs, foods, and essential oils as part of a nature-based health program, often to boost the immune system. Then there are the aromatherapists who use scents from the essential oils of plants and other products to enhance everything from attitude to digestion. Ayurvedic herbalists will also recommend herbs as part of their treatments.

Remember that the approach any herbalist will take is much different from that of allopathic doctors. Herbalists believe in constitutional medicine. Constitutional medicine looks at the body's energy level and how each of the bodily systems, such as the respiratory, digestive, and immune, are working, and assesses the function of glands to understand someone's condition. Deficiency in, say, liver function, or an excess in adrenal function from stress, will tell an herbalist that a certain plant medicine may be appropriate.

An herbalist knows that symptoms are simply manifestations of a deeper, underlying problem. The approach will depend on the particular herbal tradition the person has practiced and studied. Some practitioners may blend parts of the various traditions together. This can be useful, if the practitioner has worked extensively in a number of areas and can grasp the different traditions effectively.

Health-promoting herbs are used as complementary therapy by herbal practitioners. That is, herbs are an additional therapy to be used along with conventional medical care, eating properly, exercising, and having a healthy environment. Herbal practitioners believe that plant medicinals should be used to keep the body well and prevent acute situations from arising in the first place. Many herb preparations are general body toners. That is, the herbal medicine, whether taken as a tea or in capsule form, will be blended to strengthen a certain system of the body, or in some cases, the entire body. Because of the many kinds of practitioners and types of herbal medicine used, we will concentrate in this chapter mainly on the traditional Chinese herbalist and the western herbalist. Native American herbal practice has contributed greatly to current Western herbalism and we will also highlight some of those contributions.

Medicines from the Earth

About 40 percent of all the allopathic medicines conventional medical doctors prescribe were derived originally from plant and earth sources. A number of these are famous. Vincristine, the anticancer drug used to treat leukemia, was derived from the rosy periwinkle. This plant extract medicine over the last two decades has raised the survival rate for certain types of cancer to 80–90 percent, if caught early. The heart medication digitalis was derived many years ago from the foxglove plant. A new drug, taxol, used to treat breast cancer, is taken from the bark of the rare Pacific yew tree. These medicines that pharmaceutical companies have processed from the substances of the earth are every day saving lives around the world. Today, there continues to be a worldwide effort by scientists and others to find and test the thousands of undiscovered plants in the rain forests and jungles of the world.

Western Herbalism

There are, of course, hundreds of plants, herbs, and barks that have been used for centuries with great effectiveness by folk healers around the world. European and Anglo-American traditional herbalism represents an important strand of this world herbal culture. The plants utilized in Western herbology include some of the same plants as those that are utilized in other systems. Many of the herbal and plant sources of Western herbalists are those that are native to the Americas. As these herbalists are fond of saying, "where you live has what you need." Based on the accumulated knowledge from the ancestral European immigrants and what immigrants learned from indigenous people, the plants of North America have become the living apothecary of the continent. Indeed rural and mountain people, as well as Native Americans, have kept themselves healthy for over three hundred years using these medicines.

It would be impossible to trace all of the many contributions to herb lore that are now part of the North American tradition. We do know, however, that the first known herbal record in America goes back to the ancient Aztecs of Mexico. In 1552, only half a century after the arrival of Columbus, Martin de la Cruz, an indigenous physician, produced a manuscript in his native language of Nahuatl. In it plants and flowers are described and cataloged that could cure toothache, alleviate pains of the chest, and aid in digestion. It was translated into Latin and has come to represent the earliest known example of indigenous people's herbal knowledge being passed on to arriving Europeans. This herbal tradition has continued, with much borrowing by Europeans, combining Native American knowledge with the Anglo tradition of healing that has come down to us as the modern Western tradition.

Other people along the way played important roles in this history. One such person was Samuel Thomson, an early Anglo-American doctor, who in the nineteenth century recorded the healing effects of North American earth remedies. Thomson patented some of these preparations and wrote at length about what he had learned. During the nineteenth century, naturopathic and homeopathic doctors used medicines that were based solely on plant and mineral sources first brought to light by Thomson. These doctors fought the trend of the emerging medical establishment and its reliance on synthetic drug substances into the early

1900s. One of the most famous books of herbs and plants, *Back to Eden*, was compiled by the nineteenth-century herbalist Jethro Kloss. Not until the counterculture revolution of the 1960s was this wonderful book rediscovered, and the many healing remedies it contained made widely available to the public.

Even as late as 1894, the *National Dispensatory,* a reference book of medical substances, listed over a thousand plants and plant-related medicines. In the decades that followed this changed. With some of the patent medicine scares and fraudulent cures of that time period, and the entrance of manufactured drugs increasingly promoted by allopathic doctors, many herbal remedies were forced out of the market completely, and prescriptions were left to yellow and fade in drawers and on bookshelves. By the early part of the twentieth century, information on the medicinal properties of plants was being systematically purged from medical compendia, like the *U.S. Pharmacopoeia.*

Slowly, in the late 1960s and early 1970s, the situation began to change again. As people questioned the effectiveness and limits of allopathic medicine, herbal medicine reemerged. As the environmental movement grew, a new respect for the earth, and the herbal storehouse it contained, began to take hold. People saw that the earth could not be pushed beyond certain limits by the human species, and that plant medicines the earth possessed were a great gift that should not be frittered away. In the United States during the last fifteen years, herbal medicine and the wisdom it represents has undergone a much needed renaissance. Like many "alternative" medical practices, herbalism is becoming less alternative every day.

Chinese or Eastern Herbalism

In our chapter on traditional Chinese medicine (TCM) and acupuncture, we describe the eastern medical system of diagnosis. Pulse takings and personal history along with other methods are used to assess the condition of a person's Qi and the general balance, or lack of balance, of Yin and Yang. This is the same diagnostic procedure that an herbal doctor, trained in the oriental method, will use. A practitioner will assess symptoms and then prescribe herbs as a remedy by itself or as a therapy that will compliment acupuncture or other treatments.

In diagnosing a condition, descriptions of a problem may have exotic-sounding names to some American ears. If, for instance, you were to go to a TCM-trained herbal practitioner with a case of strep throat, the practitioner would say that you have toxic heat in the upper burner. This is a traditional description of the imbalance of Qi that is causing your symptoms. Chinese medicine describes disease as a process of the body and Qi, not simply as a listing of body organs that are affected by illness.

In the Chinese system of diagnosis, herbs will have different functions. These functions are related to the five elements of earth, water, fire, wood, and metal (described in Chapter 4), and to what are called the four evils—wind, cold, dampness, and heat. Hence there are "herbs to drain fire," in cases of acute pain and migraine. There are "herbs to cool the blood," when there is a heat problem such as inflammation and swelling. Others "calm and relieve summer heat" or "disperse wind dampness." Symptoms of dampness would include tremors, some fevers, and Parkinson-like disorders. Cold problems are generally demonstrated by a lack of circulation. Infertility is considered a cold problem, while emotional upset is usually a heat or hot problem. Most of the Chinese herbal formulas will perform two functions simultaneously. They will initially have a sedating effect, especially on fire symptoms, as well as a tonifying, or strengthening effect on the body's constitution.

After a consultation and interview, an herbal prescription will be written for you, if the practitioner does not fill the prescription from his or her own store of herbs. How the prescription will be filled can vary, depending on your herbalist. In some cases, the herbalist will recommend, if you are located in a large metropolitan area, that you go to the Chinese pharmacy and fill the prescription from the drawers of the pharmacy with the raw herbs themselves. They will be weighed and you will take your herbs home in an envelope and make a tea with them. Someone trying Chinese herbal medical treatments for the first time should be aware that many of these have a bitter taste that some Westerners have a difficult time swallowing. In Chinese medicine there is a saying that "the more bitter the taste, the better the formula." Over time you can get used to the taste, but in the early stages, a handful of raisins after taking your medicinal tea is not a bad idea.

You may get a prescription for a single formula tea that can be a common herb such as ginseng, used widely around the world as a general tonic. Some "single formula" herbs that have specific effects in Chinese medicine include:

- Ginseng, which is often used to tone or build yang Qi. It is used to raise vital energy.
- Dong Quai is Chinese angelica root and is often used as a blood tonic, but is especially useful for female problems such as dysmenorrhea.
- Ginseng and royal jelly, two products in one (ginseng with the jelly from the queen bee of the hive), is intended to act as a general energy booster.

More than likely you will be given a prescription that includes a number of herbs, not just a single herb. These formulas are called "classical formulas." The herbs that are prescribed and go into these teas, or in some cases capsules, are pharmaceutical grade. This means they were prepared at a Chinese pharmacy or by a Chinese-trained doctor and are up to traditional standards. Other products are not necessarily of a lesser grade, but it is wise to check the origins of any herbal product. They are usually bitter and strong. These formulas are blends of herbs and plant products that can contain anywhere from four to twenty different ingredients or more.

As we have said, diagnostic names can be unusual. The names of classical herbal formulas also can have colorful sounding titles. For instance, if your complaint is bladder-related or a problem with kidney Qi, you could be given Sang Piao Xiao, which translates as preying mantis egg case powder. For a flu or cold, your practitioner may recommend the Soup of Six Gentlemen, which is not a soup, but an herbal preparation for tea, which should help relieve your symptoms. Or for the same complaint, you could receive the much sweeter-sounding formula Yin Quiao San. This is a honeysuckle flower and forsythia powder.

Classical and single formulas can be purchased in a number of ways: The traditional Chinese pharmacy as we described above is where raw herbs are blended to make the formulas to sedate and tonify the body. In the United States and western Europe, there is a rapidly expanding use of freeze-dried Chinese herbs. These have been created by companies from Japan, Taiwan, and China to reach the market of people who have difficulty with the bitterness of classic formula herbs. While the herbs are still medicinally correct, they do have a lighter taste and flavor. In some cases your practitioner will make it clear that it is perfectly acceptable to use these preparations and may even recommend them.

Additionally, there is wide availability in both Chinese and western herbal stores of products called "Chinese Patented Medicines" or "Chinese Prepared Formulas." A number of grocery stores now carry these preparations with prices ranging from a few dollars to eight or ten dollars per preparation. Consult with your herbal practitioner to see if these preparations are useful for your herbal needs.

How Herbal Preparations Work

In order to understand herbs and their effectiveness, it is important to understand what herbs do and how they are made. Herbal medicines can work in several ways to heal the body.

Depending on the dosage and the method the herb is taken, there can be different effects.

Herbal Actions

- Herbs can be used to purge and detoxify the body. This category includes laxatives, blood toners and purifiers, and diuretics. The purpose of the medicine will be to relieve the body of a source of acute illness.
- People in Europe and developing countries often use herbs and plant extracts for their maintenance effects. The idea here is to bolster, support, and rebuild the body's natural defenses. This can include use of immune-boosting remedies or herbs to promote wound healing.
- Certain herbal blends can be used to build up and tone body systems, such as the digestive or reproductive systems. Individual organs in some cases can also be toned with specific herb remedies.

Herbs Can Be Prepared in Many Ways

Herbs can be dried, baked, or simply taken from the earth as they are found. Many times, if an herbalist is making a preparation on site for you to take home, herbs will be ground or crushed and then weighed to get exact proportions. Otherwise a prescription will be written, to be filled at an herbal pharmacy or purchased over the counter. The variety of preparations can include:

- Raw herbs, from the practitioner's office, Chinese pharmacy, or purchased prepackaged over the counter, can be used. These are usually prescribed in capsule or tincture form, or brewed in a tea to be taken over a number of days. Occasionally herbs are eaten raw on the recommendation of your herbalist.

- Lotions, ointments, liniments, and salves that have a carrier such as safflower oil or aloe vera and then have the active herb mixed with the carrier are another form. These are effective for skin problems and are intended for external use only.
- Tinctures are herbs infused in liquid, usually alcohol, in small bottles that are added to drinks a few drops at a time. These are increasingly recommended by herbalists of all kinds because of the ease of use.
- Powders are ground herbs and come in large containers. A person measures the amount of herb according to direction and then stirs the herb into teas, juice, or other drinks.
- Capsules containing either a raw or processed herb can be used in teas or taken by mouth.
- Tablets taken by mouth are herbs combined into a base of rice starch or similar carrier.
- Suppositories, which are intended to purge the body of toxins or to treat such conditions as hemorrhoids or vaginal or rectal infections, are used in a limited way.
- Inhalation of herbs, especially in hot baths, are used for relief of colds, flu, asthma, and bronchial infections.
- Infusion is a method that calls for herbs to be steeped in hot, usually boiling, water. An exception to this is the creation of the Bach Flower remedies, which we cover in Chapter 15, where sunlight alone is used to steep flowers or plants in water and impart their healing properties.

The Effectiveness of Herbal Medicine

There is increasing scientific evidence of the effectiveness of herbal medicinals. We will cite just a few examples here. If you watch the media closely, you can see almost daily new discoveries about the healing and healthful properties of plants and herbs.

In November 1993, the British medical journal *Lancet* reported on the effectiveness of the ginkgo plant. It highlighted two studies, one in Germany and one in Italy, that showed ginkgo extracts were successful in treating cerebral insufficiency in the elderly. The symptoms of insufficiency included dizziness, absentmindedness, confusion, depressive moods and headaches. Ginkgo protects the brain from oxygen deficiency and prevents damage to cell membranes by free radical toxins. Ginkgo also increases blood flow and is used for tinnitus—ringing in the ears—and vertigo. No serious side effects were shown in either trial.

Recent placebo-controlled clinical studies in Germany have also highlighted the usefulness of the purple coneflower plant, echinacea, which is native to North America, in fighting flu and cold symptoms. Some doctors at Cedar Sinai Medical Center are now giving echinacea to children for colds and even ear infections. The evidence from the front line of this cold war is that echinacea acts as an antiviral agent. Doctors note that the severity and duration of colds is cut dramatically using the extract.

Feverfew, a widely dispersed flowering plant, has been shown in placebo-controlled, double-blind studies at the University of Nottingham in England to dramatically reduce the severity of migraine headaches. Feverfew, with its active ingredient parthenolide, has an anti-inflammatory effect that is believed responsible for minimizing migraine headaches. Relief was demonstrated for 70 percent of patients in the study, much higher than the rate for conventional pain medications.

Oil of evening primrose has been used for years as a remedy for PMS. Now the Rhonda Fleming Clinic at the University of California at Los Angeles is recommending evening primrose oil along with Vitamin E as an effective medicine for PMS.

Some herbs and plant products have been used so widely for so long that their safety and efficacy is no longer in question.

Fennel is widely used as a way to ease colic in babies. The carminative (gas relieving) oil in fennel will help the baby deal with the gas that is the cause of colic. Check with your herbalist for the proportions.

Valerian root, as well as chamomile flowers, are common elements of many herb tea preparations. They are both mild sedatives and are highly effective in treating insomnia and improving the quality of sleep.

The bilberry plant has been used in England since World War II. At that time, it was used by British pilots to improve their night vision and is also considered an effective remedy for varicose veins.

The saw palmetto berry was used for centuries by Native American practitioners. New research confirms that saw palmetto reduces the inflammation as well as the pain of an enlarged prostate gland.

A Session with an Herbal Practitioner

When you visit an herbalist the session will vary depending on the kind of herbalist you are seeing. In the Western tradition, as in TCM, you will be asked about your complaint and also a number of background questions regarding your health history. Some professional Western herbalists, such as Rosemary Gladstar, have patients fill out a six- or seven-page form. Personal and family medical history is key. Current illnesses or allergies are always important to note.

The herbalist will likely ask you the kinds and amounts of food you are eating, what your sleep and work habits are like, and how the changes of season affect you where you live. Getting the proper context of a person's life is critical. If there are certain constitutional systems, such as the liver, that are not functioning well, the herbalist will try to access the deeper causes of your ailment.

With Western herbalism, the manner of diagnosis is similar in ways to TCM diagnosis. That is, the Western herbal practitioner will check color of skin, the health of the tongue, and also take the pulse and sometimes blood pressure. Western herbalism, however, does not have the twenty-seven depths of flow and extensive pulse taking the TCM tradition recognizes. It will also not have some of the colorful diagnostic names that TCM uses.

In the Eastern-TCM tradition, pulses at various levels will be taken. The appearance of the face, eyes, and tongue will be noted. The practitioner will ask you about your symptoms and how long you have had them. The Chinese-trained herbal doctor will try to assess your Qi, while the Western herbalist may call this an energy level assessment. The herbalist will determine if energy or Qi is circulating too quickly or too slowly, and if you are excited, depressed, or angry. Any imbalance of Yin and Yang in the Chinese tradition will be assessed, as well as the functioning of Zhang-fu (internal organs) and Jingluo (channels). If you are visiting a Chinese traditional doctor, he or she will very likely also be an acupuncturist or have an acupuncturist at the clinic or office where the examination takes place. Acupuncture may be recommended to facilitate the healing process and help reestablish the balance of Yin and Yang or Qi in the body.

From the interview, observations, pulse taking, and history the practitioner will make a determination of illness. Getting to the deeper causes of the complaint is the goal in herbal medicine. In doing so, the practitioner will determine if the illness falls into an acute category such as cold or flu, or into a chronic category. This can include arthritic problems, allergies, PMS, and immune-related illness. With an acute condition, the remedy recommended will generally be directed to getting you well and up on your feet again in a relatively short period of time.

In chronic conditions as the ones we mentioned here, the program of recovery will be different. To deal with chronic and underlying problems that may have taken years to develop, the idea is to gently and slowly bring the body back to health and reestablish normal body chemistry. Professional herbalists, especially in the Western tradition, say that three months is often the length of time needed to really get that process under way. It took you time to get ill, they say, and it's going to take time to get well. You will likely have a follow-up visit two to four weeks later to check on your progress. The visits may continue for several months with the times between appointments increasing as you recover.

The herbs that the TCM practitioner will recommend have some of the same properties of Western herbs, though the names are different. Some are tonifying herbs. In Chinese parlance, these are herbal combinations to build or tonify Qi, Yang, Yin, or the blood. This will likely be explained to you during the session. Other herbs can transform phlegm in colds and flu situations or stop coughing. Besides the tonifying formulas there are also sedating formulas, opening the orifices formulas, astringent formulas, carminative formulas, warming formulas, and antiparasitic formulas, among others. Western herbalists will often recommend herbs that are organic, wildcrafted, or wild-grown; these are an assurance of quality and potency. Remember that with wildcrafted herbs, the aroma will be clear and strong, and the color should be vivid.

Specific herbs and herbal combination will be recommended for treatment of your complaint. We listed above a number of ways that herbs can be taken. Most likely capsules or tablets, tinctures (which is the herbal extract dissolved in alcohol at a ratio of 1 to 5), or raw herbs for tea will be the recommended form of preparation. Since teas require measuring and brewing and drinking on a schedule over a period of time, increasing numbers of Western herbalists are using capsules and tinctures.

Remember that Western and Chinese practitioners of herbal medicine usually consider herbal medication as an adjunct or complementary therapy. You should let your practitioner know if you are seeing a chiropractor, homeopath, or allopathic doctor. Herbalists recognize this and will frequently recommend other additional therapies to build the constitutional health of the body. Western-style herbalists may recommend yoga classes if someone is really stressed out or has gynecological problems. Massage therapy for back, neck, and headache problems is frequently suggested. Visualization is another area that herbalists sometimes advocate when there are emotional upsets. Chinese herbal doctors, for their part, may recommend T'ai Chi or acupuncture. All herbalists consider the herbal medicinals themselves as only one part of the path to health.

As we mentioned, diet changes are also frequently recommended. Similarly, exercise is another common method of normalizing the vitality of the body, and in cases of insomnia, getting people back in a normal sleep cycle. Finally, in acute and dangerous conditions allopathic doctors will be recommended outright. Patients may be encouraged to use certain herbs as a follow-up, adjunct therapy after the visit to an allopathic physician. The complete session with the herbalist, counting interview and assessment, when it is not part of an acupuncture or TCM session, usually lasts from forty-five minutes to an hour. The charges for a session vary widely across the country. Prices in the thirty-five to seventy-five dollar-per-hour range, at this time, are considered fair.

Choosing an Herbalist

To accurately recommend herbalists from their formal training is difficult. Listed here are some guidelines that we have discovered can be useful. Herbal lore and knowledge is an ancient practice, however. There are many herbalists who have never had formal training and are quite fine. We recommend using the same discretion you would use picking an allopathic doctor, chiropractor, or naturopath when choosing an herbalist. Experience is important and the references of friends are always helpful. In an initial meeting see if your personalities resonate. Ask yourself if the suggestions of the herbalist, after the history taking, interview, and assessment, make sense. Remember to check if the fees being charged are sensible.

If you are considering herbal medicines in the Eastern tradition as a health alternative, we suggest locating a practitioner who has passed the same NCCA exam as an acupuncturist covered in Chapter 4. Remember acupuncture and herbalism are part of the practice of traditional Chinese medicine. As part of getting their certification, TCM-trained practitioners will have to possess at least three hundred hours of herbal training.

For Western herbalists, the California School of Herbalism recommends at least a nine-month series of courses to prepare a person to treat with herbs. These courses include anatomy and physiology, medicine-making, nutrition, plant identification, and herbal actions, among others. Remember almost anyone can hang out a shingle and rent office space claiming to be an herbalist. If you are unfamiliar with the herbalist you are meeting for the first time and do not have a word-of-mouth recommendation, ask about their training and experience. A professional herbalist will not mind in the least.

Precautions

There are some precautions to take when seeing an herbal practitioner. Perhaps most important, ask your herbalist up front if he or she has knowledge of the pharmaceutical interactions that may occur between any allopathic drugs and the herbal medication you may be taking. If you have any strong allergies to particular plants, flowers, or grasses, it is wise to inform your practitioner at the time of the initial interview.

Pregnant women should approach herbal medication carefully. Inform your practitioner if you even suspect that you are pregnant. In this case the earlier the better is the watch word. If you wish to take herbal medications during pregnancy, the practitioner can adjust the prescription. People who are fighting cancer or other immune-related diseases should always pass this knowledge on to their practitioner. Some herbs can be useful in helping the digestive system take in food and allow the body to cope with the nausea of chemotherapy and radiation treatments. By keeping the appetite healthy and helping the body keep weight on, herbs can markedly improve the quality of life for some cancer patients and those with compromised immune systems.

Herbal Associations and Resources

American Herbalists Guild
    3411 Cunnison Lane
    Soquel, CA 95073
    408/438–1700

The Herbalists Guild has several hundred members. It was founded in 1989 as a professional association for North American herbalists and publishes a directory of classes and seminars.

North Eastern Herbal Association
    P.O. Box 146
    Marshfield, VT 05658
    802/456–1402

This association of practicing herbalists, growers of herbs, and students puts out a newsletter and has a directory of herbalists for the northeast.

American Herbal Association
    P.O. Box 1673
    Nevada City, CA 95959

AHA publishes a directory of classes, seminars, and correspondence courses.

Herbal Research Foundation (HRF)
1007 Pearl Street
Suite 200
Boulder, CO 80302
303/449–2265
303/449–7849 (fax)

HRF acts as a clearinghouse for information about herbalism, especially new research on the effectiveness of herbal medicine. The foundation is a membership-based organization.

Books

If you are interested in learning to prepare your own herbal medicines, we recommend the following video and books.

Herbal Preparations and Natural Therapies by Debra Nuzzi. This is an excellent four-hour video with detailed instructions on herbal preparation. Write to Morningstar Publications 997 Dixon Road, Boulder, CO 80302

Herbal Medicinal Preparations by Rosemary Gladstar, P.O. Box 420 East Barre, VT 05649

The Art and Science of Herbology by Rosemary Gladstar. This is a home study course available at the address in East Barre, VT.

Schools of Herbalism

California School of Herbal Studies (CSHS)
P.O. Box 39
Forestville, CA 95436
707/887–7457

Offers a nine-month, two-semester program on foundations and therapeutics of herbalism. CSHS teaches the Western school of herbalism.

American College of Traditional Chinese Medicine
455 Arkansas Street
San Francisco, CA 94107
415/282–7600
415/282–0856 (fax)

This college offers complete course work in pharmacopoeia and herbal prescriptions as part of its Master of Science degree in traditional Chinese medicine.

New England School of Acupuncture
30 Common Street
Watertown MA 02172
617/926–1788

This school offers a three-year herbal medical program. It includes pharmacopoeia, formulas, internal medicine, gynecology, and pediatrics—a total of 465 hours of study and practice.

Chapter Ten

The Mind/Body Connection

B ody/mind health care represents a convergence of many fields, and is the underlying principle of holistic health care. The idea that we are more than a collection of organ systems and cells, separate from our mind and personality, is perhaps this philosophy's most important unifying belief. The rapid growth of the body/mind approach to healing shows that patients have a deeply felt need to be treated as whole persons. Western medicine may have developed into a series of treatments designed to act on and affect "sick" body parts, but this is rapidly changing as the science of physiology converges with psychology and the philosophies of consciousness.

Psychoneuroimmunology (PNI), an emerging science of the body/mind connection, explains that substances (neuropeptides) are produced within our bodies in response to internal and external stimuli. Endorphins, the body's natural pain killing chemicals, are one group of neuropeptides. Initially, it was thought that endorphins and other chemicals are released only in the brain; however, researchers discovered that peptides are present throughout the body and have a profound effect on immunity. Our thoughts and emotions trigger the production of these chemicals, making them a direct link between the mind and the body.

The receptors for these chemicals are the same as those used by viruses to enter a cell. If the cell contains an adequate amount of the peptide, then the virus will have a more difficult time entering the cell. The reverse is also true, and inadequately protected cells may leave us vulnerable to infection. It also appears that the body does not distinguish between a real or imagined stressor. In other words, if you imagine that a tiger is getting ready to attack you, your body will produce a chemical response similar to that produced when your ancestors ran from the real thing. This is an obvious simplification of early, but important work. The field of PNI is scientifically confirming what human beings have observed for centuries: belief systems, attitudes, and thoughts and feelings play an important role in keeping us healthy or leaving us vulnerable to disease. (Genetics, diet, and socioeconomic status also have their parts to play in health and illness.)

What Does the Body/Mind Relationship Mean In Health Care Today?

Millions of people regularly see alternative health care practitioners because, in general, these professionals recognize that healing is something patients do for themselves. These practitioners know that we have an internal and innate capacity to heal, and treatment helps activate this process. Health care professionals (including orthodox medical doctors) who view themselves as holistic practitioners know they are facilitators of healing.

The reality that the mind and body are connected is present in both their treatments and in the way holistic health care practitioners communicate with their patients. The interaction between you and your health care provider can greatly affect both the course of symptoms and your attitude about your illness. If your doctor tells you that your condition is chronic or hopeless, then you are more likely to become discouraged and fearful. On the other hand, if your doctor is reassuring and willing to explore treatment alternatives, you will be more likely to approach your condition with optimism and courage. An effective health care provider can help you cope with the consequences of both the illness and the treatment.

Body/mind health care also puts responsibility on patients. This approach encourages us to ask ourselves if there is a message in the illness. What is the illness trying to say? Is there something we can learn from having this condition or disease? This philosophy encourages us to explore our lifestyle and habits. We have all heard about individuals who were told they had a serious illness and instead of becoming victims, they made major life changes. When people use body/mind techniques to explore the relationship between their illness and their lives, they might quit less-than-satisfying jobs, leave destructive relationships, or nurture healthy ones. Rather than viewing their illness as a disaster, they might view it as an opportunity for a new direction.

A case could be made that all the treatments described in this book are based on a body/mind philosophy, in that they move beyond the mechanical medical model. However, the following techniques are among the most common specific body/mind therapies. Nowadays, they are recommended by many different types of health care practitioners, from homeopaths to massage therapists to cardiologists.

Biofeedback

Biofeedback is a technique taught to patients. We use it to regulate some of those functions normally considered automatic (controlled by the autonomic nervous system) and not under our conscious control. It is a somewhat new technique, often recommended as a stress-management tool. However, biofeedback has many applications, and training patients in the technique may help reduce or eliminate the need for medication. It can even be a substitute for surgery in some situations, usually those involving chronic pain.

The ideas underlying biofeedback are not new. However, the modern theory and techniques were developed at, among other places, the famous Menninger Clinic in Topeka, Kansas. The clinic opened a center devoted to mind/body medicine, of which their biofeedback research is an integral part. Some early researchers studied advanced yogis and learned much about the body's ability to respond to conscious "directions" from the mind. This information then guided their search to discover how this "feedback" system works.

Biofeedback involves gaining information about activity in various systems within the body and then taking conscious steps to alter their function. If you take your temperature when you don't feel well, and then call the doctor or take an aspirin, you are using rudimentary biofeedback. Or when you are working at your computer and your neck and shoulders become stiff and sore, you shrug or roll your shoulders, do some neck rolls, or may massage the stiff, sore areas. You do these things in response to your body's feedback, which alerts you to discomfort. You then act and attempt to loosen your muscles and become more comfortable. It is now evident that it is possible to prevent muscle spasms and induce muscle relaxation in a systematic way, and biofeedback has become a treatment with its own protocols, practitioners, and researchers.

The word biofeedback can be applied to any technique in which individuals learn how to monitor and alter those functions normally considered outside conscious control. For example, in the West, our breathing, heart rate, and blood pressure are considered entirely automatic functions and, therefore, there is nothing we can do to regulate them. But now we know that if we have a way to receive information about these functions, we can learn to influence them. It's a system based on using the information—the feedback—we receive from our bodies to treat and prevent a variety of conditions.

How Does Biofeedback Work?

Biofeedback sparks—or unleashes—the potential that is already present; it uses mechanical techniques to demonstrate and measure what is going on within the body. A biofeedback device can, for example, measure heart rate and produce a signal, such as a beeping tone, or a flashing light, for each beat. A device can also measure the temperature of the skin and its electrical conductivity (the galvanic skin response). An electromyogram can supply information about tension in the muscles; an electroencephalogram (EEG) measures brain wave activity.

When we're comfortably relaxed, our skin is warm and dry; when we're anxious or tense, our skin feels cold, moist, and even sweaty. In a relaxed state, our sweat gland activity is low, which indicates low electrical conductivity. When the galvanic skin response (GSR) increases, this suggests that we are becoming tense. Once a biofeedback device gives us this information, we can learn to alter our stress levels consciously. Our changed bodily responses can then be measured. When a person with a rapid heartbeat (because of anxiety or stress) learns to relax, then the change in the pattern of the beeps or the flashing lights show that the technique is working.

Regaining Control

Some people believe that they are hopeless victims of their bodies; biofeedback provides tangible evidence that they can exert a degree of control over certain bodily functions. Looked at this way, biofeedback is not a cure, but is one technique that can be used to help patients help themselves. In essence, it is a subtle behavioral modification technique that improves with practice. The biofeedback practitioner is there to interpret data and to coach patients in ways they can use the information to alleviate symptoms and change the way their bodies are working. The changes recorded by biofeedback devices monitor progress and are part of the training. Ultimately, patients can learn to get the same results on their own, without benefit of the equipment.

Biofeedback itself does not, for example, lower blood pressure. It simply measures it. Then, using various relaxation techniques, a person can see the blood pressure readings change. Progress is "fed back" to the patient through skin temperature, muscle readings, and, in some cases, brain wave activity.

Biofeedback is a noninvasive procedure and may even be an enjoyable one, especially for people who believe that their symptoms are beyond their control. Currently, most people receive biofeedback training at a clinic that specializes in this treatment. You may also receive the training in a holistic health care center, where a trained and certified biofeedback practitioner is on staff.

The specific device used depends on your condition. The devices are small and not intimidating in any way. Most likely, you will sit at a table, or in a reclining chair. In either case, you can see the monitor that is providing the information about your body. Electrodes are attached to your skin, which is a completely painless procedure. Once you receive instructions about relaxation techniques, you probably will be left alone in a darkened room to practice the techniques and watch your results. To help you relax, the technician may ask you to choose some soothing music to listen to during the session.

Biofeedback is a modern tool that demonstrates what even the most ancient health care practitioners have known all along: the way we breathe has a profound effect on our health. The relaxation techniques generally begin with deep breathing exercises. Watching the body's responses to deep, regular breaths eventually increases the patient's awareness of his or her breathing patterns when not hooked up to the machine.

The goal of biofeedback is to train a patient to relax and pay attention to the body's responses. With practice, the techniques can then be used anytime, anywhere, without the biofeedback machine. For example, a person who suffers with migraine headaches might learn through biofeedback that his or her hands are below normal temperature. Relaxation techniques are used and the patient can see on a meter that the skin temperature rises and pain begins to go away. Outside the clinic setting, this person can relieve a migraine headache by employing a relaxation technique that raises skin temperature. The patient is confident that this will work, because he or she has already had the experience during biofeedback training.

This monitoring system can work well with many stress-related problems, including insomnia, muscle spasms and involuntary twitches in various parts of the body, headaches, fatigue, hypertension (usually along with dietary modification and exercise), and so forth. It also can be used to train asthmatics to monitor and regulate breathing in order to decrease the fear involved in wheezing attacks. An asthmatic will often believe that there is nothing he or she can do once an attack has started. Biofeedback shows that this is not necessarily the case. Additional research suggests that the technique can be effective in relieving the symptoms of gastrointestinal conditions and may play a role in treating eating disorders. Biofeedback is sometimes used with guided imagery and other visualization and meditation techniques.

Biofeedback can be used with other therapies, and in fact, is rarely used alone. A variety of practitioners, including psychologists, psychiatrists, and other mental health professionals, may recommend biofeedback to their patients both to prevent and treat various conditions. Many insurance companies pay for this training because it is an effective complementary treatment. Over the long run, it can lower health care costs.

Once trained, you can continue using the biofeedback techniques at home, using a device recommended by your practitioner. Some people find that this is much like taking a refresher course, allowing them to continue to improve their ability to influence bodily responses on their own.

The associations listed at the end of this chapter can provide information about biofeedback clinics and practitioners in your area. Currently, biofeedback practitioners are certified through the Biofeedback Certification Institute of America (BCIA), which sponsors the national exam.

Guided Imagery and Visualization

We all know that the imagination is powerful. Without it, we would not have art, music, stories, new inventions, or fantasy lives. However, the imagination also can be considered a health care tool. Guided imagery and visualization (terms often used interchangeably) are emerging as important techniques in body/mind medicine.

The imagination can have powerful physiological effects. For example, if you are a parent and your child is out well past the agreed-upon curfew, then you probably will be annoyed at first. Then, as time passes, you begin to worry and you may become angry with your child for causing this worry. As the minutes and hours pass, you might begin to imagine all the terrible things that could have happened. There's been a car accident and you can see your child hurt and trapped in the car. Or your child has been a victim of a terrible crime and you can see images of him or her being held at gunpoint. By the time you are through, you may be sick to your stomach or have a terrible headache or be nervously pacing the floor. In a heightened emotional state, you have created these images with your mind and your body responds accordingly.

Obviously, we also can create positive images. Our fantasy lives and daydreams are often filled with pictures of pleasant scenes and our bodies may feel light and energetic. Sports psychologists often have their athlete clients picture a successful performance in their minds before they execute the play. Skiers often picture the run before they start the race; gymnasts visualize their performance before they take the floor. Basketball players may regularly visualize making free-throws and then follow this exercise with consistent practice sessions. It appears that mental images can help train the body. Imagery also is being used in the business world and even in education to enhance self-confidence and to reduce stress.

How Does Imagery Help Improve Our Health?

This valuable tool can probably be used as a complementary therapy for almost any illness and condition, both chronic and acute. It's certainly an example of a technique that can't hurt a patient and may, at the very least, help alleviate symptoms that are part of a disease process or side effects of treatment. Imagery also can be an important tool in understanding a disease process in the body, and may lead to powerful insights into what the illness means to the individual. There is some indication that imagery may increase the effectiveness of other therapies, reduce the severity of side effects of some treatments, and may promote healing.

Contrary to some popular thinking, guided imagery or visualization is not a substitute for conventional treatment, at least not in most cases. Most patients who seek help from a practitioner trained in imagery are using the therapy to help them cope with an illness and gain insight into it. For some people, learning guided imagery is essentially relaxation therapy, and may be the only such training they ever encounter. Others use it as a psychotherapeutic tool. They work with the images they create in a variety of ways, such as in art or movement therapy, dream analysis, and journaling.

Imagery and Cancer

Dr. O. Carl Simonton, a radiation therapist, is perhaps the best-known pioneer of using imagery as part of cancer treatment. Simonton developed a therapy in which patients would imagine their cancers as entities that could be influenced by their thoughts. Patients were guided to picture their cancerous tissue as material that could be broken apart, neutralized, and destroyed. The immune system could be visualized as an "army," poised to fight the disease.

As the technique developed, it became apparent that individuals have preferences about the types of images that are most effective for them. For example, some people convert the radiation beam into thousands of tiny bombs being dropped on the cancer. Chemotherapy drugs are visualized as tiny soldiers moving through the body on search and destroy missions. Other people prefer the image of radiation as healing, white light, which allows the cancer cells to wither away while preserving the healthy surrounding cells. Drugs are converted into beneficial beings that wash away the cancer.

This technique has been helpful in alleviating some of the fear that the treatments themselves produce. For example, if one imagines chemotherapy as a poison that is making the whole body ill while it destroys the cancer cells, fear is a logical reaction. However, some people report that if they substitute a more benign and healing image of the chemicals moving through their bodies, their side effects are actually reduced.

Dr. Bernie Siegel picked up on Simonton's work, recommended it to his patients, and through his books, gave wide public exposure to guided imagery as a healing tool. However, the work of both Simonton and Siegel, as well as the many other physicians who have recommended the technique, has at times been misinterpreted. No proponent of this therapy has ever claimed that imagery by itself can cure cancer. Some patients who use imagery as one of many treatments recover from their cancers and join the ranks of survivors. Others who use the technique do not recover. Many in the latter group, however, have reported that imagery helped them cope with their illness, gave them a sense of control over their bodies, and offered some pain relief.

Guided Imagery Has Many Applications

It is no exaggeration to say that imagery can be used as a complementary treatment for just about every condition, injury, or illness. It is not a tool reserved for life-threatening diseases. For example, anecdotal evidence suggests that wounds heal more quickly when a patient uses imagery; visualization techniques can help alleviate the inflammation and pain associated with arthritis and other chronic conditions.

Remember that imagery is not the same as "positive thinking." Imagery is intended to produce a positive response in the body, and it uses the power of the mind to that end. However, this technique does not deny the pain or the condition, nor does it encourage the person to simply rise above it, so to speak. It doesn't encourage a patient to affirm that everything's okay, and simply direct all thoughts to something else. Rather, imagery uses the imagination to focus on the problem and work with it directly.

Let's say you have a burn on your hand. First, you would treat the burn medically, and along with that you might create a healing image on which to concentrate. In this case, it could be an image of healing light surrounding your burn. Or you could imagine your body's internal healing resources all rushing to the site of the burn. One therapist taught a child to imagine thousands of healthy cells heading toward the burn to replace those that were damaged. These images help marshal the body's own healing response.

Almost any condition could be treated in a similar way. The same image that promoted healing of a common burn could be used to promote healing following radiation therapy. Imagining that the body's healing resources are rushing to an injury is a technique that could also be used in treating the symptoms of AIDS. In fact, Simonton's techniques have been adapted and used with patients suffering from AIDS, arthritis, and multiple sclerosis.

Using the Dialogue Technique

Some professionals describe imagery as a way of talking to the body. In fact, they claim that our minds are always talking to the body anyway, so we might as well consciously direct the dialogue. For instance, a person suffers from a condition that is causing great distress but seems resistant to treatment. Or, once cured of a disease, an individual is still at a loss to understand why he or she had the illness in the first place. Guided imagery can be used in these cases to establish a dialogue between a patient and the illness.

In its simplest form, there are few among us who have not become extremely annoyed when we come down with the flu or a bad cold. Adherents of imagery would suggest that instead of simply saying, "Why me? I don't need this now," we might enter a relaxed state and ask to have the reason for the illness revealed. Those who have done this have reported some surprising answers to the questions, "Why me, why now?" For example, we could have become sick because we want attention, or we want a break from our routine, or we are angry with someone and getting sick is a pay-back, or because we are avoiding something we are expected to do. We might also have become ill because we won't rest unless we're forced to. While these might seem like easy answers, and perhaps even obvious ones, they don't do us much good if we don't acknowledge them. This dialogue technique is a tool that helps us use the answers we get.

A therapist using imagery may use the dialogue technique to probe more deeply into the cause of a serious, even life-threatening illness. The condition itself can be pictured and named, and then the patient is guided in an exchange of questions and answers. In some cases, the disease image can ask the questions and the patient responds. Therapists employing this technique believe it is one important way to bring information from the unconscious to the conscious mind. Much like the images in dreams, these dialogue images may reveal hidden motivations and fears.

A word of caution here: Imagery is a widely used technique found on relaxation tapes and described in numerous books. For the most part it is a safe technique. However, the dialogue technique can bring up powerful insights, some of which can be frightening, confusing, and even depressing. If you are dealing with a serious illness and the thought of talking with an image of the condition makes you uneasy, then respect that feeling and don't use the technique by yourself. There are numerous trained practitioners who can guide you through such an exercise should you choose to try it. In addition, if you want to use imagery as a complementary treatment for cancer, AIDS, or other serious illnesses, you might consider using it in a support group setting, which may help you feel safe with the process.

Practitioners are usually mental health professionals, alternative health care practitioners, such as naturopaths or homeopaths, and registered nurses and medical doctors, all of whom have taken additional training in order to use these techniques. Professionals trained in guided imagery techniques sometimes work in the cancer and AIDS support groups sponsored by hospitals and associations. These professionals may also work with private clients. If you are looking for someone trained in guided imagery techniques, calling those groups may be a good place to start. The associations with training programs and referral services are listed at the end of this chapter.

Meditation

Since the 1970s, stress has been a catch-all phrase used to describe the way in which our reactions to the world around us and our chosen lifestyles can contribute to a laundry list of illnesses and conditions, from musculoskeletal problems to heart disease. Dozens of medical treatments and psychological therapies are used to treat these conditions, some of which don't sound like treatments at all. Meditation is one of the most commonly suggested stress-management tools, but because of its long history and its place in religious life, calling it a therapy seems inadequate. Nonetheless, meditation is currently being recommended to many patients because it does have therapeutic value. Meditation can be beneficial regardless of prior religious belief. While certain forms of meditation are associated with and taught by followers of Eastern religions, there are many meditation teachers whose methods are generally compatible with and not dependent on a particular spiritual system.

There is no one form of meditation. Even the goals may vary, but there are certain characteristics that all have in common. First, they all work to quiet our mind and to become aware of our breathing. Some practices use a word, known as a mantra, to focus on, while others simply suggest observing thoughts and feelings as they pass through the mind. This is known as mindfulness meditation. Imagery—or visualization—is considered by some to be a form of active meditation in that the person consciously forms and works with images during a meditation session. In all forms of meditation, the past and the future are left behind and the focus is on the present moment.

How Does Meditation Improve Health?

The health benefits derived from regular meditation are numerous, but not necessarily predictable for each individual. For example, there are benefits from regularly entering into a relaxed state. The heart rate slows down, blood pressure lowers, tension in the muscles eases, and there is a decrease in the secretion of hormones associated with stress. There are also measurable changes in the brain wave activity with alpha waves, associated with relaxation, appearing. During deep meditation the mind is said to be in an alpha state.

Meditation is considered a unique kind of rest in that the mind is actually alert as the body becomes increasingly relaxed. Many people report that the benefits of meditation carry over to every aspect of life, which is one of the reasons it is difficult to measure specific health benefits.

Meditation is rarely used as an isolated treatment. Even if it is used without other lifestyle changes, one of the benefits can be a greater awareness and clarity about health related issues. For example, a man may begin to study and practice meditation because he has been told that he is at high risk for heart disease. He may not be ready to quit smoking or change his diet, but he is willing to give meditation a try. As his meditation practice continues, his quality of life might change enough that he becomes motivated to make other lifestyle changes. Likewise, a woman with breast cancer might use meditation as a stress-management tool that helps relieve the anxiety she experiences about both the treatment she is undergoing and the possibility of recurrence. Through meditation practice, she becomes more aware of issues from the past that have troubled her and with her mind more clear, she is able to make decisions about seeking additional therapies or making significant changes in her life.

Much of the information about improved overall health is anecdotal, but results of meditation may be difficult to measure by acceptable scientific means. However, in some ways, the point becomes moot. There are no known dangers of meditation, and except when used alone as a substitute for other treatment, no health care practitioner will tell you that meditation is bad for you.

Meditation Goes Academic

Dr. Herbert Benson, a cardiologist by training, coined the term "the relaxation response" to describe the way the body responds during meditation. He was among the first to measure the physiological reactions to quieting the body and mind. In 1988, after the stress reduction benefits of meditation were scientifically verified, Benson and some like-minded colleagues started the Mind-Body Medical Institute at New England Deaconess Hospital at the Harvard Medical School. Several hundred people are referred to the institute every year to receive stress-management training, including meditation therapy. Individuals come with a wide range of disorders, from asthma to gastrointestinal problems to panic disorder. In addition to stress-management training, patients receive counseling about nutrition and exercise.

Jon Kabat-Zinn, Ph.D., founder of the Stress Reduction Clinic at the University of Massachusetts Medical Center, was also a pioneer in using meditation as a stress-reduction tool. Thousands of people have learned Buddhist meditation techniques at this clinic. Kabat-Zinn's studies with patients with chronic pain problems are worth noting. After 8 weeks of meditation training, over 60 percent of participants had at least a 50 percent reduction in pain. The remaining patients experienced slightly less pain relief, but they also reported a greater sense of well-being.

Critics of using meditation will claim that the results, even those that are measurable, may be the result of the "placebo" effect, meaning that the patients believed the "treatment" would help and therefore it did. However, to those who teach meditation and related techniques, the results demonstrate that we have more control over our bodies than once believed. The physiological changes are brought about by patients themselves during meditation practice and no outside agent (such as a medication) is introduced.

How to Begin

One way to begin meditation is to read books that offer descriptions of the various types of meditation practice. (We've included some on our suggested reading list in the back of this book.) Most also offer instructions and exercises that you can use immediately. If you wish to find a teacher in your area, ask a health care practitioner you trust to suggest someone who either works with individuals or has regular meditation groups. The associations listed at the end of this chapter can also provide information, and some can give you referrals to meditation teachers or health care practitioners who recommend meditation to their patients.

Some books suggest that those of us who are used to rushing around and having our minds on many things at once can begin by sitting quietly in a chair for five or ten minutes at a time. We can pay attention to our breathing or attempt to focus on an object in our minds—a religious symbol, a flower, a peaceful scene in nature, and so forth. This may be more difficult than it sounds, because most of us are used to constant stimulation and we may have forgotten what deep concentration and peace and quiet are. But if you string together a few five-minute sessions, you may gradually notice that the process becomes easier. Others suggest spending a few minutes concentrating on a favorite poem or inspirational phrase, while attempting to clear the mind of superfluous thoughts. The point of this exercise is to understand that meditation is a discipline whose benefits may be subtle and come only with practice. The health benefits we may derive usually come about as a outgrowth of the process, meaning that meditation is usually one method that opens other doors to greater health and well-being.

Hypnotherapy

Hypnotherapy can be used for both physiological and psychological disorders, although there is not necessarily a clear distinction between the two. It is based on the ancient idea of the power of suggestion, with specific, beneficial suggestions given to the unconscious mind during a trance-like state. Our common word "mesmerize" is derived from the name of an eighteenth-century German physician Franz Anton Mesmer, who treated patients by using suggestion. The trance-like state appeared to make patients so suggestible that Mesmer believed he had them under his control, through what he termed "animal magnetism." Mesmer believed that loss of control was part of the treatment and it is said that some of his patients were induced into convulsions. The word "mesmerized" has come to mean the loss of judgment and control that comes about when under the strong influence of another person.

A British physician later renamed the technique hypnosis, which literally means a state of sleep. However, this is actually a misnomer, because the trance state induced by hypnotherapy is not the same as sleep, and is better described as an altered state of awareness. During the earlier years of his work, Sigmund Freud was a proponent of hypnotherapy, but eventually he abandoned it in favor of his analytic approach. His influence was powerful and for many decades, hypnosis was not well accepted as a legitimate tool of psychiatry or psychology. Hypnosis also became associated with entertainment, parlor games, and the occult, and thus had a rocky road to acceptance as a legitimate therapy.

Many people still fear being in an impressionable state, one in which another person can influence them. However, like other therapies described in this book, there are organized training programs and societies whose members promote the ethical use of hypnosis as a treatment for many human ills.

Health care practitioners who use hypnotherapy, or refer their patients to professional practitioners, do so because it has been shown to be effective in treating dozens of conditions, from chronic pain conditions to sleep disorders to chemical dependency. It has been used successfully in dentistry and there are reports of major surgery being performed using hypnosis to anesthetize the patient. Hypnotherapy has also been used to treat certain psychological disorders such as phobias and anxiety.

How Does Hypnotherapy Work?

Like many of the body/mind therapies (and most other treatment techniques as well), hypnosis is effective only if the patient is receptive to it and participates in the process. The hypnotist is there as a guide to facilitate the process, but cannot induce even a light trance state without the patient's cooperation.

The cornerstone of hypnosis is relaxation and there are many ways to promote deep relaxation of both mind and body. The goal is to slow down the concerns and "chatter" of the conscious mind and move the focus away from the person's immediate surroundings. This allows greater access to the unconscious mind, which is then receptive to new concepts and suggestions. While the conscious mind reflects on information and brings in critical thinking and judgment, the unconscious mind receives information without analyzing it. Focusing on an object, idea, or activity, the sound of the hypnotherapist's voice, deep breathing, and so forth are all used to promote the hypnotic state.

Hypnotherapists sometimes speak of a light trance state, one in which a patient generally remembers most of what is said and can be fairly easily distracted and brought out of the state. In a deeper state, referred to as somnambulistic, the patient is more suggestible and the posthypnotic suggestions are more likely to be acted upon. It is currently believed that the vast majority of people are capable of entering the light hypnotic state, but a smaller number, 20 to 30 percent of the population, are able to attain the somnambulistic state. Either state may be used to bring about beneficial change, but those who can reach the deeper state will probably see more direct and faster benefits.

Although hypnotherapy is rarely used as the sole treatment for most conditions, it can be an effective complementary therapy and continues to show progress as a substitute for anesthesia for certain medical and dental procedures. Using it to treat chemical dependency or chronic pain does not preclude the patient from also seeking acupuncture and group support programs.

Critics of hypnosis believe that when it is used as a pain control treatment, for example, it is suppressing symptoms and not reaching the cause of the problem. However, for many patients being treated for chronic pain conditions, the alternative is prescription pain relief medication, which also treats symptoms and not the cause. When used for certain psychological disorders, such as phobia or anxiety, hypnotherapy may be used after the person has already sought many other treatments but found them ineffective. In other words, because many medical professionals don't recommend it, hypnotherapy has sometimes been a treatment of last resort. This will probably change in the future as research continues and the population searches for economical and noninvasive treatments.

What Happens During a Hypnotherapy Session?

The effectiveness of the treatment depends a great deal on the relationship between the practitioner and the patient. For this reason, it is best to get a referral to a practitioner from someone you know and trust. The practitioner should also talk with you about the reason you are seeking help, any other health complaints, other treatments you have had, and your health history. This initial conversation can help you talk about your reservations about the treatment and ask questions about the process. The therapist should not rush you into the hypnotherapy session, and you may use the first appointment to explore what you hope to get from the therapy, followed by a second session that includes hypnosis. Because the first goal is to relax and enter an altered state, many therapists will recommend that you avoid caffeine and other stimulants before hypnosis.

Each practitioner has a unique style of inducing the altered mental state that is necessary before the suggestion phase begins. It almost always starts with deep breathing and drawing attention away from your surroundings and to the sound of the hypnotist's voice. You may be told that although you hear noises around you, they will not disturb you. If you are like most people, you may wonder if you are really "under" because other thoughts may float through your mind. However, in a light trance state, this is normal. It is best to try not to second-guess the process but simply relax into it.

Once relaxed, the suggestions you receive will relate to your condition. You should, however, have an idea about the kind of information you will receive. Hypnotherapists do not want to suggest anything to you that is unacceptable in some way, because the trance-like state will be disrupted. Most people feel a bit mentally fuzzy upon coming out of the hypnotic state, but this lasts for only a minute or two. The predominant sensation is one of relaxation.

Some problems, such as pain control and overcoming some psychological disorders, may take six to twelve sessions, with follow-up sessions always an option. Chemical dependency treatment may require fewer sessions, perhaps only one or two, with a follow-up session scheduled some time later. Sessions generally last about an hour. Tapes of the sessions may also be used at home to reinforce the treatment.

Are There Any Dangers Involved in Hypnotherapy?

As in any field, there are unethical hypnotherapists, some of whom promise too much or in extreme cases, use the hypnotic state to elicit embarrassing information or control patients. There is current controversy over using hypnotherapy to regress patients for the purpose of uncovering memories hidden deeply in the subconscious. In recent years there has been publicity about false memory syndrome, a situation in which people come to believe that events occurred in the past that did not actually happen. This syndrome has received attention in connection with claims of childhood sexual abuse, the memories of which may surface later in life and are sometimes revealed during hypnosis sessions. The controversy arises when the hypnotist, who may or may not be a certified hypnotherapist, has led the patient in some way, possibly even planting the suggestion in the first place. There is much difference of opinion among psychotherapists as to the efficacy of using hypnotherapy for the purpose of probing childhood traumas. We can only recommend that before you use hypnotherapy for that purpose, you explore the process and the possible consequences with a qualified psychotherapist or psychiatrist with whom you have developed a long-term, trusting relationship.

Hypnotherapy is also not recommended for patients with severe psychological disorders, such as long-term clinical depression, psychosis, or disorders that cause antisocial behavior.

Hypnotherapy should never be performed by amateurs, that is, by people who have taken nothing more than a couple of weekend seminars or who have listened to a few tapes. The organizations listed at the end of the chapter have extensive training programs and certify their students after completion of course work and practical application. In most cases, they will refer you to practitioners in your area.

In general, hypnotherapy is a safe and powerful tool for most people, provided it is performed by a qualified practitioner. In recent decades, hypnosis has left the realm of "occultism" and has become one of the respected alternative therapies recommended by many different types of practitioners.

Resources

Following are associations and organizations that can provide information about the therapies described in this chapter. Many have catalogs of books and tapes, and in some cases, they can also provide referrals to practitioners in your area.

Association for Applied Psychophysiology and Biofeedback
10200 West Forty-fourth Avenue
Suite 304
Wheat Ridge, CO 80033
303/422–8436

This organization has an affiliate that trains and certifies biofeedback practitioners. They can lead you to state associations and provide information about local clinics and practitioners.

Center for Applied Psychophysiology
Menninger Clinic
P.O. Box 829
Topeka, KS 66601
913/273–7500

This center has an extensive research program and a psychophysiology clinic. It is an excellent place to find general information and research about using biofeedback and guided imagery for specific conditions.

The Academy of Guided Imagery
P.O. Box 2070
Mill Valley, CA 94942
800/726–2070

This organization has an 150-hour training program for health care professionals, and publishes a directory of trained imagery practitioners.

American Holistic Medical Association
4101 Lake Boone Trail
Suite 201
Raleigh, NC 27607
800/878—3373

This organization's members are allopathic and osteopathic physicians who support mind/body healing techniques. You can get a list of members in your area. These physicians may also be able to help you find meditation centers or teachers in your area.

Simonton Cancer Center
P.O. Box 890
Pacific Palisades, CA 90272
310/459–4434

This center can help you find physicians and other trained professionals who use imagery in cancer treatment.

Institute of Transpersonal Psychology
P.O. Box 4437
Stanford, CA 94305
415/327–2006

This organization is one source of information about research on the benefits of meditation. They may help you choose an appropriate center to learn meditation techniques.

Maharishi International University
1000 North Fourth Street
Fairfield, IA 52556
515/472–5031

This group educates individuals about transcendental meditation (TM). It will lead you to teachers in your area who are skilled in this form of meditation. Because it is tied to a particular philosophy and technique, the information it provides is specific to TM.

Mind-Body Clinic
Deaconess Hospital
Harvard Medical School
Div. of Behavioral Medicine
185 Pilgrim Road
Boston, MA 02215
617/632–9530

Joan Borysenko, Ph.D,. and Herbert Benson, M.D., are the cofounders of this clinic, which conducts research, educational programs, and stress-management training, including meditation.

Stress Reduction Clinic
University of Massachusetts Medical Center
55 Lake Avenue North
Worcester, MA 01655
508/856–2656

This is the clinic that Dr. Kabat-Zinn founded, which teaches meditation techniques to patients. You may be able to get information about a similar center in your area.

The National Guild of Hypnotists
P.O. Box 308
Merrimack, NH 03054
603/429–9438

This organization offers training and certification programs, and an extensive catalog of books and tapes.

The American Institute of Hypnotherapy
16842 Von Karman Avenue
Suite 475
Irvine, CA 92714
800/872-9996

This institute offers a variety of training programs, including a doctoral program in hypnotherapy.

The American Society of Clinical Hypnosis
2200 East Devon Avenue
Suite 291
Des Plaines, IL 60018
708/297–3317

This society's members are medical doctors and dentists who are also trained in hypnosis. They will provide a list of practitioners in your area if you send them a self-addressed, stamped envelope.

Chapter Eleven

Dance and Movement Therapies

Movement and dance therapies are important components of the holistic approach to health care. Movement techniques tone your body, promote relaxation, and help you note and evaluate sensations and feelings in your body. While few people in our country are unaware of the benefits of exercise, movement therapies are far more than exercise programs. The movement therapies we briefly describe in this chapter represent philosophies that have well-established links within body/mind healing.

Movement therapies are different from exercise programs in a few important ways. First, paying attention to various sensations in our bodies may provide information about important physical and psychological issues in our lives. Regular practice quiets the mind and helps us observe the fluid nature of our thoughts and feelings. Second, unlike competitive sports and other exercise programs, movement therapies do not emphasize performance goals or competition. In addition, these therapies emphasize total well-being more than physical fitness and conditioning, although the latter are by-products of regular practice.

Almost everyone can get some benefit from these therapies, regardless of prior physical condition.

Yoga

An ancient philosophy of health and well-being, yoga has had an important influence on mind/body medicine in the Western world. The word "yoga" means union, which implies harmony of mind, body, and spirit. Yoga is one of the ancient religious schools of Hinduism; it has evolved over several centuries and has been adapted for and by Westerners.

While the original roots remain, yoga is often practiced today outside religious or even spiritual settings. Although some students eventually do absorb the spiritual tenets into their lives, it is not necessary to do so to benefit from this psychophysiological discipline.

There are many different types and levels of yoga. In this country, *hatha* yoga is associated with physical movements or postures, known as *asanas*. Students of hatha yoga also learn breathing exercises and meditation techniques. The word "hatha" combines the roots of two Sanskrit words, "ha," which refers to the sun, and "tha," which refers to the moon. In the traditional interpretation of the word, the sun controls the breath through the right nostril and the moon controls the breath through the left. Proper breathing is essential to correctly execute the asanas and develop the mental concentration necessary for meditation practice.

The breath takes on additional importance in yoga philosophy because prana, the life force, is drawn in with each breath and circulates through our bodies. In the most simple terms, prana can be blocked when we are ill, under emotional or physical stress, or when toxins in water, food, and air affect our bodies. Controlling the breath, or learning to breathe correctly, is called "pranayama," which literally means "regulating the life force."

What Are the Health Benefits of Hatha Yoga?

There are over eighty asanas, each of which is part of a group that benefits various systems within the body, although all benefit the entire body and the mind. Each asana is composed of the movement to reach the pose and a phase in which the pose is held; thus, an asana alternates between activity and rest. In addition, the asanas stimulate and help regulate the circulatory, endocrine, and nervous systems.

Several studies have confirmed that yoga has therapeutic value for respiratory ailments, including chronic bronchitis and asthma. Other studies have suggested that patients with hypertension who practice yoga regularly can reduce dosages of medication or eventually eliminate the need for it. Many asanas directly benefit the musculoskeletal system. Yoga is one of the premiere exercise programs for preventing back and joint pain, because the movements involved in the asanas promote flexibility and strengthen every muscle in the body. Some specific asanas are recommended for rehabilitating from muscle, back, and joint injuries. In addition, studies suggest that yoga is an effective treatment for chronic pain conditions and regular practice may both relieve and prevent headaches.

Some postures are used for warm-up and general toning, while others stimulate and benefit specific organ systems. (The line here is a fine one, however, because the asanas work together and each helps tone the entire body.) There are sitting, standing, inverted, or raised asanas; other exercises control breathing and lead to meditative states.

The shoulder stand, an "all-purpose" asana, strengthens the arms, shoulders, neck, back, legs, and the abdominal muscles. The shoulder stand gently stimulates the thyroid gland and is therefore beneficial in weight loss programs. This asana is said to have therapeutic value in the treatment of many disorders involving internal organs, from menstrual problems to gastrointestinal conditions. (Because it can temporarily raise blood pressure, it is not recommended for people with hypertension; however, many other asanas can be safely used.)

An asana called "the half fish" helps to expand lung capacity and is therefore of benefit in treating respiratory disorders. The "half spinal twist" promotes spinal flexibility and helps prevent constipation. The "archer" pose is said to reduce abdominal fat and refresh and revive a tired mind. The "lotus," or Buddha, posture is a classic meditation pose; it increases the flow of blood to the upper body and leads to clear, calm thinking.

These poses may have many additional benefits, and yoga teachers say that they all work best as part of a complete program. In other words, practitioners don't recommend that you randomly practice an asana now and then. Even if this were physically possible—and for most of us it's not—it would defeat the purpose of a unified program that benefits your body and promotes relaxation and meditative states.

Yoga is a complete, non-competitive exercise program for people of all ages, from small children to the elderly. The watchword of yoga is "gentle," meaning that the movements are slow, fluid, and never intended to be forced beyond the point of pain or pressure. You measure your own progress by noting the subtle changes in the way you feel, both physically and mentally.

Because of the many benefits, it is not surprising that a variety of alternative and orthodox practitioners recommend yoga for prevention and treatment of an array of conditions, including but not limited to heart disease, hypertension, reproductive disorders (including sexual dysfunction), gastrointestinal problems, musculoskeletal conditions, chronic pain conditions (including arthritis), headaches, respiratory ailments, chemical dependency, and obesity. It is also recommended as a stress management tool and as a complementary therapy for cancer patients.

There are no specific dangers in practicing a yoga program, although some postures should be avoided in certain situations. For example, if you already have a back injury and are in pain, you probably will be told to avoid certain asanas until you have built strength and flexibility. If you have not engaged in an exercise program for a long time and are not in good physical condition, you should start slowly and never force a movement. In addition, pregnant women should avoid a few of the breathing exercises and asanas. In any case, we recommend that you speak with your primary care practitioner to find out if there is any reason that you should avoid particular movements or postures.

Getting Started

Many yoga teachers recommend doing a series of asanas and breathing exercises every day. There are many videotapes and books available, and yoga teachers can be found in almost every town or city in the country. Some teach privately and others are associated with yoga centers, which are educational and spiritual outreach organizations for particular branches of yoga. Some yoga centers have residential retreat facilities. The centers listed at the end of this chapter can also help you learn more about the various types and levels of yoga.

T'ai Chi

T'ai Chi is sometimes called "moving meditation." Some people believe it more closely resembles a body/mind meditation technique than a movement therapy. (Again, the line is a fine one.) Practiced for at least one thousand years, the discipline of T'ai Chi is related to the martial arts. T'ai Chi comes to us from China, and derives its philosophy from both Taoism and Buddhism. Although it was introduced to the West in the nineteenth century, it was not until the 1970s that T'ai Chi became well known in the United States. Today, there are T'ai Chi teachers and classes in almost every part of the country.

What Is the Goal of T'ai Chi?

Like yoga, T'ai Chi emphasizes strength and flexibility rather than building muscle mass. Each movement has a symbolic meaning and is performed without strain, but rather with circular, fluid motions. Every T'ai Chi movement is important and none is superfluous or wasted; each motion flows from the previous one, which results in one continuous series of movements. If you watch T'ai Chi, you will notice that the movements look effortless and smooth. Indeed, gradual mental detachment and tranquillity are the results of performing the series of movements.

Rather than expending energy, T'ai Chi seeks to contain energy and then gently release it from the body in a systematic way. T'ai Chi is similar to some body/mind therapies, such as biofeedback, in that we learn that we are not helpless observers of our thoughts or our bodies. Through practice, we can gain control over some bodily functions and quiet the mind.

In the West, T'ai Chi is practiced at various levels, but the fundamental Chinese approach remains strong. Learning T'ai Chi also means attempting to understand the underlying principles of Chi (or Qi), the basic energy of the universe, and the concepts of Yin and Yang, the complementary energies. On a metaphysical level, the goal of T'ai Chi is to experience the movements as moving through the body without consciously controlling them. Put another way, the "dance" and the "dancer" become one.

Generally speaking, a T'ai Chi session can consist of a short form, which has thirty-seven movements and takes ten to fifteen minutes to do. The long form has one hundred movements and takes twenty to twenty-five minutes to complete. Although T'ai Chi can be practiced alone, serious students also practice in groups or with a partner. The work with a partner includes a series of movements known as "Push Hands," which helps a person understand another person's energy, or Chi, and the way in which energy flows between people.

In its largest sense, the work with a partner illustrates the ideas of Yin and Yang and provides a way to experience how these complementary energies influence one another. For example, a pushing action is Yang energy and the yielding motion is Yin. Each partner absorbs the other's energy and the actions can then be reversed.

What Are the Health Benefits of T'ai Chi?

Some people begin this movement-meditation program as a stress-management tool, and with regular practice, T'ai Chi may slow your heart rate and bring about a relaxed, tranquil mental state. Because the movements are gentle, it may be an appropriate activity for individuals with conditions that make strenuous exercise inadvisable. While it is a nonaerobic exercise, T'ai Chi will increase your muscle strength, improve your posture, and expand your flexibility. Most practitioners also say that your overall well-being can be dramatically enhanced because your outlook on life fundamentally changes as a result of the inner harmony you experience. These benefits are not immediate, however, and some practitioners say that it takes many years of study and practice to master T'ai Chi.

Getting Started

Most people recommend studying with a T'ai Chi teacher who has been practicing for a minimum of ten years. Fortunately, T'ai Chi has been available in this country for so long that there are probably qualified teachers in your community. In addition, some health clubs and dance studios offer T'ai Chi classes taught by trained practitioners who are also knowledgeable about Chinese philosophy. Nowadays, referrals can come from many sources, including many alternative health care practitioners, particularly those trained in Chinese medicine. Hospital-based stress management programs also may offer information about T'ai Chi training available in your community.

Qigong (or Chi-Kung)

Like T'ai Chi, qigong comes to us from China, where it has been practiced for many centuries. As a self-care technique, it is used for both prevention and treatment, and like yoga and T'ai Chi, qigong uses breathing techniques, specific movements, and meditation. It is a noncompetitive program and once learned, is often practiced alone as a daily self-care ritual. The movements stimulate the flow of Chi, also known as Qi.

The meridians used in acupuncture become important in qigong, because the movements direct energy flow along the meridian pathways. In addition, some qigong exercises are directed to areas of the body (the hands, feet, and ears) that in Chinese medicine are called reflex microsystems. Specifically, stimulating the microsystems helps circulate Chi throughout the body. The hands are also used to massage or rub areas of the body that stimulate organ systems. For example, rubbing your hands over an area of your lower back will move Chi to your kidneys; using your warm hand to touch the skin under your rib cage can stimulate the flow of Chi to your spleen and liver. Other pressure or rubbing motions stimulate specific glands and organ systems in your body.

Breathing exercises combined with movements are also part of qigong practice. The movements consist of gentle twists and bends; some movements end with postures that resemble yoga asanas. Some exercises and postures are done while facing a particular direction (north, west, northwest, and so forth); one exercise involves eight such movements. While this might sound odd to a Westerner, it is consistent with complex Chinese philosophy of energy and the manner in which it moves through the universe, and through our bodies. The breathing patterns that accompany each movement balance and strengthen Chi within the body. When we are ill, these breathing exercises are said to marshal or mobilize healing energies. The meditation practice involves visualizing the healing energy flowing through the body.

We need to point out that qigong is comprised of many different kinds of individual practices and is therefore quite adaptable. A person confined to a wheelchair, for example, may be unable to do the standing movements, but can still benefit from the breathing exercises and the skin massage techniques that stimulate the flow of Chi along the meridians. Exercises involving arm movements, for example, can be used by a bedridden person who is recovering from a serious illness.

What Are the Health Benefits of Qigong?

This question would not be asked in China, where at least two hundred million people practice qigong as a self-care technique. In this country, qigong is less well known than acupuncture, acupressure, or T'ai Chi. But this is changing as Chinese medicine becomes more widely accepted in the West.

Qigong practice can affect the body in ways similar to acupuncture. Therefore, the many conditions that acupuncturists treat may also benefit from qigong exercises. For example, some studies suggest that qigong stimulates the natural painkilling and relaxation response chemicals, thus making it effective for treating chronic pain conditions and stress-related disorders. Qigong also may have a role in preventing a variety of disorders from heart disease to arthritis to respiratory ailments. Some Chinese practitioners recommend qigong for emotional disorders such as depression. There are even studies that suggest that qigong is an effective complementary treatment for many types of cancer.

Are There Any Dangers Associated with Qigong?

There are no known dangers in practicing qigong, although the full range of exercises may not be possible for some people. Qigong is not easy to learn, however, and to get the full benefits you probably will need an instructor to teach you the basic movements. We also do not recommend using qigong as a primary therapy for serious illnesses. It is always wise to check with your primary practitioner before you begin movements with which you aren't familiar.

Getting Started

Practitioners trained in traditional Chinese medicine are probably the best referral sources. In this country, many of the qualified qigong teachers are trained at centers that specialize in Chinese philosophy and health care methods. Because of the current emphasis on preventive medicine, some hospitals and stress-management clinics have begun to offer qigong classes. The organizations listed at the end of this chapter also may be able to refer you to a qualified teacher or to an institution that offers classes.

Dance Therapy

In all its forms, dance is an important part of human cultural and religious rituals and is one of our oldest art forms. But dance as a therapy was formalized in the West only in this century, and the American Dance Therapy Association (ADTA) was founded in 1966. The ADTA offers graduate programs in dance therapy and explores the potential of this form of psychotherapy.

What Is the Goal of Dance Therapy?

Dance is obviously a form of exercise offering many physical benefits. But it is primarily used for psychotherapeutic purposes, generally as a group therapy. A group provides a safe setting in which participants can express their internal fears, anger, and joy through movement. This kind of therapy also may be the only way some psychiatric patients can communicate internal conflicts; for others, it provides an added dimension to therapy and uses dance to recreate feeling states.

Dance therapy is sometimes used to retrain the body as part of a rehabilitation program following a stroke or a brain injury. Movement or dance also is used for conditions in which sensory integration needs improvement. For example, Alzheimer's patients may benefit from dance therapy because it strengthens some patients' ability to perceive themselves in relation to space and time. For this reason, dance and movement may help autistic, emotionally disturbed, and learning disabled children.

Some dance therapists emphasize spontaneous movement, while others use choreographed sequences. Children, for example, may be asked to pretend to be objects or animals through movement. The therapist interacts with each participant and guides both the movements and the discussion of the feelings or ideas that arise. Some people find that movement and dance are powerful vehicles for emotional expression and strong feelings of anger, rage, or sadness may arise. So it's important that the dance therapist is qualified to deal with whatever issues come up.

What Are the Health Benefits of Dance Therapy?

In addition to the conditions discussed above, dance therapy is successfully used in treatment programs for patients with eating disorders and other conditions where body image may be distorted. For example, some cancer patients whose bodies are altered by surgery, radiation, or chemotherapy express their sense of loss and become more accepting of their bodies through movement therapy. For many of the same reasons, the elderly and people who are visually or hearing impaired, or have a physical disability, benefit from movement and dance therapy. Some substance abuse programs and rehabilitation programs for cardiac patients also include dance and movement therapies.

Are There Any Dangers Associated with Dance Therapy?

For the most part, dance therapy is considered safe, and when used under proper conditions, it is generally an enriching experience. Obviously, there is some risk of injury, but this is rare under controlled conditions. A qualified therapist considers your physical limitations and designs appropriate movements for you. If you have any condition (hypertension, heart disease, emphysema, asthma, etc.) where exertion could be dangerous, your primary practitioner should discuss these limitations with the dance therapist before you begin.

Getting Started

Dance therapy usually takes place in hospital settings, particularly in psychiatric programs. Senior centers and special education facilities may also offer dance therapy, and many qualified dance therapists sponsor classes, which usually run from four to twelve weeks. No previous dance training is required, but the therapist may ask if you are currently receiving psychotherapy and what issues you are currently working on. These classes are often held in dance studios, community centers, or health clubs. While generally done in groups, some therapists will hold individual dance therapy sessions. The American Dance Therapy Association is one organization that can provide referrals to practitioners qualified to sponsor private classes.

Sources of Information and Referrals

Sivananda Yoga
5178 South Lawrence Boulevard
Montreal, Quebec H2T 1R8 Canada
514/279–3545

This organization has centers in some U.S. and Canadian cities and retreat centers in Europe, India, Canada, the Bahamas, and the United States.

International Association of Yoga Therapists
109 Hillside Avenue
Mill Valley, CA 94941
415/383–4587

This association promotes research about the benefits of yoga as a therapy.

Himalayan Institute of Yoga, Science, and Philosophy
RRI Box 400
Honesdale, PA 18431
800/822–4747

In addition to sponsoring yoga centers in the United States, this institute has an extensive mail order catalog of books, audio tapes, and videos.

Samata Yoga and Health Institute
4150 Tivoli Avenue
Los Angeles, CA 90066
310/306–8845

This institute specializes in yoga as a therapy for prevention and treatment of back problems.

American Foundation of Traditional Chinese Medicine
505 Beach Street
San Francisco, CA 94133
415/776–0502

Among its services, this foundation offers referrals to T'ai Chi and qigong classes.

The Healing Tao Center
P.O. Box 1194
Huntington, NY 11743
516/367–2701

In addition to offering qigong classes throughout the world, this organization sells videotapes of qigong exercises.

Qigong Institute/East West Academy of the Healing Arts
450 Sutter Street
Suite 2104
San Francisco, CA 94108
415/788–2227

This organization engages in public education and clinical research.

American Dance Therapy Association
    2000 Century Plaza
    Suite 108
    Columbia, MD 21044
    301/997-4040

The ADTA provides referrals to certified dance therapists and offers continuing education for members.

Chapter Twelve

Light and Sound Therapies

Light and sound, like herbal remedies and massage, are among our oldest healing tools. Even our ancient ancestors knew that our bodies have an internal clock that influences when and for how long we sleep, the rise and fall of our energy throughout the day, and even the way our moods fluctuate. We call this internal clock the circadian rhythm (or system), and we now know that light profoundly affects how this rhythm works.

Similarly, it is no accident that sound both relaxes and arouses us and, therefore, has an important role in the religious and cultural rituals of every society. Today, researchers know that different sounds affect specific parts of the brain and influence us in myriad ways.

Light, color, sound, and music are used therapeutically, and current research is identifying the conditions these sensory therapies can prevent and treat. These treatments have many advantages, not the least of which is that they are noninvasive and relatively inexpensive.

Light Therapy

When light enters the eye, it is converted to electrical impulses, which move along the optic nerve to the brain. Once the brain receives these impulses, the hypothalamus gland is triggered to do its work as a first step in regulating many bodily functions. The hypothalamus does this by means of chemical messengers, known as neurotransmitters. Since the hypothalamus is part of the endocrine system, it is responsible for many bodily functions (e.g., the digestive system, blood pressure, sexual functioning, etc.), and it helps coordinate the way these systems work together. This important gland, along with the tiny pineal gland, also governs our circadian system. Therefore, light plays an important role in the way the hypothalamus functions.

John Nash Ott, a photobiologist, is one of the pioneers in light therapy research. He believes that healing or beneficial light must contain the full wavelength spectrum that occurs in natural sunlight. Most of us are not exposed to the complete spectrum for long periods of time because we live so much of our lives in artificial light. This is particularly true in the winter when the daylight hours are fewer and those of us in cold climates spend less time outdoors.

Ott concluded that poor lighting is detrimental to our health and can adversely affect the body's ability to absorb nutrients. There are serious consequences from living in artificial light, without additional regular exposure to full-spectrum light. Many conditions, from mental disorders to dental problems to cancer, may be made worse by inadequate exposure to light.

On the other hand, exposure to full-spectrum light has shown positive results in treating such conditions as insomnia, premenstrual syndrome, migraine headaches, hypertension, and hyperactivity in children. Using light to lower bilirubin levels (that cause jaundice) in newborn infants is a routine use of common light therapy.

Light therapy might also be a preventive tool in certain cases. One study suggested that full-spectrum light therapy could play a role in preventing some forms of cancer. A Russian study correlated full-spectrum lighting in factories with a reduction in the normally expected number of colds and sore throats among workers. Studies done in schools suggest that students in classrooms with full-spectrum lighting had improved academic performance when compared to students in classrooms with fluorescent lighting. Attendance was also consistently better in classrooms with full-spectrum light. These studies found reduced behavioral difficulties and less hyperactivity among students exposed to full-spectrum lighting.

Light and Depression

Perhaps the best-known use of light therapy is among people suffering from a form of depression known as SAD (seasonal affective disorder). Directly related to the circadian system, this is a seasonally related depression, which includes many symptoms such as lethargy, fatigue, cravings for carbohydrates, decreased sex drive, and a need for more sleep than is normal for the affected person. Those who suffer from this cyclical depression also say they feel withdrawn and even hopeless during the darkest months of the year. Some professionals have speculated that the increase of reported depression around the December holidays is attributable to the onset of SAD.

While the cause of SAD is not definitively established, the level of melatonin, a hormone secreted by the pineal gland, is high in people with this disorder. The pineal gland produces melatonin when it is dark, and light inhibits its production. Melatonin is an essential hormone and plays a role in immunity; it also has a sedative effect and helps induce sleep. Overproduction, caused by lack of light, though, can lead to the symptoms described by people with SAD.

SAD is successfully treated with regular exposure to sunlight or by using either full-spectrum light therapy or bright white light exposure. This treatment helps regulate melatonin production and SAD patients report that their symptoms are alleviated or disappear entirely.

Bright white light therapy does not contain all possible wavelengths of light, but it is far more intense than the average home or commercial lighting. "Lux" is the unit of measurement of illumination, and our homes and offices generally have a lux measure of no more than 500 or so, though of course this varies throughout the day as we move from one location to another. Much of our daily exposure is probably much less than 500 lux.

Therapy using bright white light calls for exposure ranging from 2000–5000 lux. This intensity successfully treats SAD, and does not carry the risk of prolonged exposure of ultraviolet (UV) light that is part of full-spectrum therapy. (Long-term UV exposure can damage the eyes.)

Bright white light therapy is also used to treat sleep disturbances and shows promise for treating menstrual irregularity and some eating disorders. In addition, shift workers are perhaps more vulnerable than anyone else to disturbances in the circadian system. Second and third shift workers suffer from some disorders, including sleep disturbances, more than those of us who work during the day and get most our sleep at night. When given bright white light therapy, most shift workers say they feel better and also show general improvement in health.

There are many commercial manufacturers of light therapy devices, usually called light boxes. If you are diagnosed with SAD, it is likely that you will be advised to use a light box and your practitioner may recommend a particular one. This is fine, but we caution you not to diagnose yourself and begin treatment without professional guidance. Light therapy for SAD receives much attention in the popular press and many different alternative health care practitioners probably can guide you to an expert in light therapy. While light boxes are sold over-the-counter, light therapy is not a simple self-help technique.

Ultraviolet Light Therapy

There are three types of ultraviolet light rays: UV-A has the longest wavelength and is responsible for slow tanning; UV-B is the most dangerous to humans and is responsible for damage to the eyes; and UV-C is considered harmful, but little of it penetrates the ozone layer. UV-A is probably the least damaging, although there is disagreement about the potential harm of the three types of UV rays from the sun.

In the late nineteenth century, a Danish physician named Neils Finsen successfully treated tuberculosis with sunlight. Because of his work, he won a Nobel Prize in 1903 and was the first pioneer in photobiology. One hundred years later, an impressive amount of research has accumulated, but UV treatment is still somewhat rare in mainstream medicine. Studies were done with UV-A therapy and lupus erythematosus, an auto-immune disease that damages the kidneys and produces many adverse symptoms, such as joint pain and severe fatigue. UV therapy improved lupus symptoms and patients were able to reduce their medications. UV-A therapy also treats skin conditions such as vitiligo and psoriasis.

Photopheresis

A process known as photopheresis is used to treat many diseases including cancer, and bronchial asthma, infections, and the symptoms of AIDS. Photopheresis is a process that removes blood from the ill person, irradiates it with ultraviolet light, and then returns it to the patient. Photopheresis was pioneered by William Campbell Douglas, a physician in Georgia, but is not yet widely used. (It is important to emphasize that photopheresis is not a cure for AIDS, but only alleviates AIDS-related symptoms.)

Cold Laser Therapy

This therapy uses low-intensity laser light, which stimulates a healing response within the body. It can be used to control pain and promote healing of injuries and is usually used with other treatments. While not yet common, cold laser therapy is a substitute for acupuncture needles in some situations. But the practitioner must have the same skills as an acupuncturist, that is, he or she must be able to determine the points along the meridians that should receive treatment. In other words, this therapy is much like having an acupuncture treatment that uses another type of instrument to stimulate the crucial points. Cold laser treatment may be an alternative for those who are squeamish about needles.

Light and Color

Using color to influence mood and well-being is an ancient practice. However, there are now treatments that combine light and color. A technique using flashing colored lights treats sleep and mood disorders and for pain control, and red light therapy is used for many conditions from diabetes to gastrointestinal conditions to depression. Red light therapy can be both continuous or flashing (pulsating) and also can be used on acupuncture points. Colored light therapies require specialized equipment and are not self-help techniques.

Color is a form of energy, and each color stimulates different psychological and physiological changes. For example, the color red arouses the body, increasing the heart rate and brain wave activity; pink has the opposite effect and soothes the mind and promotes relaxation. Yellow stimulates the memory—if we want to remember something, we should write it down on yellow paper; yellow also has an energizing effect and can lift us out of an afternoon slump. Green, often used in hospitals and nursing homes, is a relaxing but mentally uplifting color. Children are calmer in a room with blue walls. (You can find more information about using color therapeutically in some books listed at the end of this book.)

Art Therapy

Art therapy is a conventional psychiatric treatment, but we included it because it is also a complementary treatment for many illnesses. Patients with cancer, AIDS, multiple sclerosis, chronic pain conditions, and so forth discover that art therapy helps them cope with their conditions. Cancer patients, for example, find that art therapy gives expression to the emotional component of the disease. Art therapy is also an established treatment tool for exploring the unconscious mind. Art therapists work primarily in psychiatric hospitals and with children without language skills that enable them to talk about internal conflicts. It is also useful for people with eating disorders or who are recovering from chemical dependency.

A professional art therapist helps you interpret your art work, and he or she also suggests issues to explore in various art media. You will probably find that you change your attitudes and beliefs about issues as the therapy proceeds, and the therapist will help you integrate your progress into your daily life. As new themes arise in your work, the therapist helps you understand the reasons for these changes. For most people, art therapy is both insightful and enjoyable, but it can bring up painful issues, too. For this reason, it is important to work with a qualified person.

Today, many art therapists work with private clients or with support groups. Qualified art therapists have at least a master's degree from a university with an accredited art therapy program. Some psychotherapists use art in combination with traditional "talk" therapy techniques. Only those with specialized training can legitimately call themselves art therapists.

Sound and Music Therapies

Intuitively, human beings know that sound can have both positive and negative effects, but it is only in the last century that the effects have been scientifically demonstrated and measured. In the 1890s, physicians discovered quite by accident that different parts of the brain are stimulated by different kinds of music. Even ultrasonic sound waves, which are beyond the range of our ears, can affect us.

Sound travels from a sending source to a receiving source in waves, and each sound has a velocity, an intensity, a frequency, a wavelength, and a pitch. We respond to a sound in two ways. The first involves the rhythm of the sound, and our heartbeat can change when external rhythmic sounds are introduced. The technical name for this is "rhythm entrainment." Sound also resonates in our bodies; when we speak of sound vibrating, this is actually our body's response to a sound. A low sound causes vibrations in the lower parts of the body; a high-pitched sound causes vibrations in the upper part of the body.

Sound moves from the ear to the brain along specific cranial nerves. For example, rhythmic sound affects the reptilian brain and can alter our sense of time; the tone of a sound affects the limbic portion of the brain, which is its emotional and instinctual center. There is a growing body of knowledge about the connections between the areas of the brain affected by various sounds and the physiological response in the body. This information is allowing sound to be systematically used to control pain and reduce stress.

Some studies show that music and sound therapy benefit patients in health care settings. Hospital patients report that music helps reduce anxiety, and following surgery, music in recovery rooms may help patients recover from the effects of anesthesia more quickly.

Work with Alzheimer's patients shows that sound therapy enhances communication with caretakers and family members, and helps disoriented patients become focused on their immediate surroundings. These therapies, once considered frivolous, are now used in labor and delivery rooms to help the mother relax. And at the end of life, it appears that music can soothe the dying. Physically and mentally disabled children benefit from sound therapy in that it can be a substitute for speech and help motor and other sensory development.

We mention these benefits because you might find yourself in a situation in which you want to use sound or music therapeutically, and your health care provider scoffs at the idea.

However, you have a right to have your choice of music playing while you are having surgery, for example. This might be very different from the music you take to the dentist's office, where loud music appears to stimulate the release of endorphins.

Toning

Toning has been practiced for many centuries. The well-known "om" sound used in meditation is an example of toning, which uses sound to create vibrations in the body. The vagus nerve, which has a long pathway through the body, is one of the cranial nerves affected by sound. This nerve passes through the larynx and many internal organs, and it appears to be an important part of the mechanism by which sound affects the body. The continuous repetition of a long sound, usually a vowel sound, is thought to be one of the easiest and fastest ways to reduce stress and to stop the "mind chatter" that interferes with mental concentration and focus.

Guided Imagery and Music

Music therapist Helen Bonny, Ph.D. created a technique called guided imagery and music (GIM), which, as the name implies, uses music to elicit images and feelings. Combined with deep breathing and relaxation, GIM is an additional technique in psychotherapy used to explore the unconscious mind. According to Bonny, the material that may arise is comparable to that produced when drugs are used to suppress the conscious mind and probe the unconscious. The technique also reduces pain and anxiety.

Sound, Technology, and the Future

Technological advances allow researchers and clinicians to create devices designed to retrain the auditory system and improve listening skills. Developed by the French physician Alfred Tomatis, the electronic ear is a device used to treat autistic children and those with learning disabilities. A Chinese scientist, Dr. Lu Yan Fang, developed a machine that simulates the secondary sound waves, which, she discovered, come from the hands of qigong masters. The machine was used with over one thousand hospitalized patients and many benefits were reported, including pain relief, muscle relaxation, and increased circulation. This device is now a recognized pain management tool.

Music Therapy

Traditional music therapy is practiced in hospitals, nursing homes, and in special education programs. The therapy varies among its practitioners and some may incorporate specific sounds as well as a wide range of music into their treatment plans. Participatory music therapy is beneficial for children with physical or mental disabilities because it helps improve motor functioning and listening skills. It is also a way to elicit emotional responses in children (and disabled adults) who are unable to use language to communicate.

Some of these sensory therapies have a strong self-help component, but we recommend that you ask a health care practitioner to help you choose those that will benefit you the most. Homeopaths, naturopaths, chiropractors, osteopaths, and Chinese medicine specialists are among the primary practitioners that can help guide you.

Sources of Information and Referrals

Environmental Health and Light Research Institute
16057 Tampa Palms Boulevard
Suite 227
Tampa, FL 33647
800/544–4878

This institute can provide information on full-spectrum lighting. It continues Dr. John Ott's research work.

Society for Light Treatment and Biological Rhythms
  10200 West Forty-fourth Street
  Suite 305
  Wheat Ridge, CO 80033

You can write this society for information about SAD.

American Art Therapy Association
  1202 Allanson Road
  Mundelein, IL 60060
  708/949–6064

This association is a referral source for art therapists.

Sound, Listening, and Learning Center
  2701 East Camelback
  Suite 205
  Phoenix, AZ 85016
  602/381–0086

This organization can provide information about the Tomatis auditory integration programs. Referrals are also available.

Guided Imagery and Music
  Temple University
  Presser Hall 0012–00
  Philadelphia, PA 19122
  215/787–8314

This organization trains practitioners to use GIM and will send information about the method.

The American Association for Music Therapy
P.O. Box 80012
Valley Forge, PA 19484
610/265–4006

This organization can refer you to qualified music therapists. It also accredits music therapy programs.

Chapter Thirteen

Aromatherapy

Using the sense of smell as part of cultural rituals, for cosmetic purposes, and to enhance relaxation are practices as old as human life. Modern aromatherapy is an expansion of the ancient practice of using and studying the effects of certain aromas on the body and mind. Over the last several decades, aromatherapists have compiled formulas and extracts to use in specific ways for selected conditions and ailments. Aromatherapy has been popularized in recent years so that the average person has access to essential oils for home use. If you've used aromatic massage oils, you have engaged in aromatherapy.

The scientific community is currently confirming the importance of the sense of smell (olfaction) in human behavior and in maintaining health. Indeed, losing the ability to smell can have profound consequences, not the least of which may be mild depression that often goes undetected and untreated. A person who has lost the sense of smell will report feeling melancholy and sad, often without understanding why. Too few mental health professionals understand this connection and may not question clients and patients about their ability to smell. However, this is changing, and modern scientific methods are being used to establish the important connection between mental well being and the ability to smell.

The term aromatherapy derives from the French word "aromatherapie," coined in the early 1900s by a French chemist, Rene-Maurice Gattefosse, who considered the use of the essential oils of plants another branch of herbal medicine. A French physician, Jean Valnet, used essential oils to treat wounded soldiers during World War II and became interested in the healing properties of these substances. His work helped establish aromatherapy as a valid treatment approach in France. Aromatherapy is still considered a nonconventional treatment in the United States, but it has gained a wider acceptance in Great Britain and elsewhere in Europe among orthodox practitioners.

While there are aromatherapists who practice this art exclusively, other practitioners, such as massage therapists, chiropractors, herbalists, nutritionists, homeopaths, naturopaths, and so forth, have incorporated these techniques into their practices. In other words, aromatherapy is a complementary or adjunctive treatment, which can be used as one part of a treatment—or prevention—program.

What Is the Philosophy of Aromatherapy?

Until recently, the effects of particular aromas on an individual were known only through anecdotal evidence, that is, information based on experiences reported by those who have used oils for particular ailments or conditions. The Western scientific method had not been applied to the practice of aromatherapy, and thus the anecdotal results had generally been dismissed by the medical and scientific community. However, almost everyone now agrees that aromas do affect human beings, particularly on an emotional level. Until the last decade or two, these effects were largely considered learned responses and while pleasant human experiences, basically insignificant. But as the science of olfaction and the art of aromatherapy converge, the mystery surrounding the way aromatherapy works is rapidly disappearing. The way has been opened to explore wider—and intentional—uses of the sense of smell to improve health and overall quality of life.

Here in the West, the sense of smell is generally thought to be less important than our other senses. Sigmund Freud influenced this easy dismissal of olfaction when he speculated that smell was important when humans were "primitive," but as we become more "civilized" and intellectually sophisticated its significance in our lives decreased. Where the sense of smell once protected humans from eating spoiled food or alerted them to the presence of predator animals, Freud maintained that this ability to detect odors was no longer necessary or important and might gradually disappear through ongoing evolution.

However, research is confirming just how important this sense is, thereby opening the door to further investigation of aromatherapy. We know that olfaction is unique among the senses; it is the only sense whose receptors are in the limbic portion of the brain. The limbic center, known as the primitive brain, is the seat of instinct, drive, and emotion. This explains the universal phenomenon of experiencing powerful emotions when particular odors are detected.

For example, your grandmother has been dead for thirty years, but a particular cooking or cosmetic odor reminds you of her and your mind drifts away from whatever you were doing at that moment. You are suddenly flooded with memories about her. Your recollections touch you deeply and you are moved to tears. This whole episode was first stimulated by the odor molecules that reached the olfactory bulb in the brain. You may not consciously know why you have reacted in this way, but the unconscious does know, and the odor molecules do their work before the intellectual center of the brain can explain your response by applying logic and reason.

Not so pleasant is the fact that post-traumatic stress syndrome (PTSS), which may include episodes of rage or panic, can be initiated by an odor. Some veterans of the Vietnam war, who suffer from PTSS, have reported that episodes of panic and terror were triggered by the odor of burning fuel.

It is also no accident that odors are almost universally used in religious rituals and sexual encounters. Odors help create and extend moods, facts that have been intuitively known for centuries and now can be demonstrated scientifically.

Today, researchers are rapidly confirming the importance of smell in all aspects of human life. While there are some important medical applications for this research, there are also commercial and behavioral components that bear watching. For example, introducing certain smells into an environment has been shown to increase the likelihood of buying particular products.

This recent scientific and commercial study of olfaction and behavior has some goals in common with the field of aromatherapy. However, there are some important distinctions. When a marketing firm introduces a carefully selected smell into a department store, the goal is to coax shoppers into spending more money than they planned to. And it has long been known that used cars are sometimes sprayed with a substance that makes them smell like new cars. These odors are manufactured smells, artificial and mass-produced substances made from a variety of chemicals. The substances used by aromatherapists to aid in healing are derived from plants in a process that makes mass production nearly impossible. An aromatherapist would never use an artificial "look-alike" smell as a substitute for the naturally occurring oils extracted from plants.

Aromatherapy uses essential oils derived directly from a wide variety of plants. These substances occur naturally, but usually in very small amounts, adding to the inability to use the substances in massive commercial ventures. The oils are found in roots, flowers, bark, leaves, the rind of fruit, and in the resin. Formed in various parts of the plant, these oils circulate throughout its structures and may concentrate in different areas throughout the day. For example, the oil may be concentrated in the flowers during the evening and in the leaves during the morning hours. It is the aromatic property of these oils that attracts bees and other pollinating insects, and the oils also serve as pesticides and fungicides for the plant. It's no exaggeration to say that the essential oils have a vital role in keeping the earth's plant life healthy.

In order to use them in concentrated amounts, the essential oils must be extracted from the plant, a process that varies considerably depending on the part of the plant that contains concentrations of the oil. Some oils are distilled, using a process of heat and cooling; others oils are squeezed or scraped either manually or mechanically. Some oils are plentiful and easily extracted, but others can be accumulated in only tiny amounts. Needless to say, the latter are more expensive.

Essential oils may contain several hundred naturally occurring chemicals, some of which can be dangerous when isolated or used improperly. For example, citral, a substance in lemon oil, can be toxic when it is isolated; if it comes in contact with the skin, it can cause severe irritation. It is also unwise to ingest the oils by mouth, unless you are very knowledgeable about the particular properties of the substance. A professional aromatherapist, an herbalist, or a well-trained primary care practitioner will be able to advise you about which oils can be used internally, generally as a mouthwash, a gargle, or more rarely, as a douche.

Oils are classified by volatility, meaning the speed by which they evaporate when exposed to air. Volatility, in turn, is linked with the effects on the body. Oils with high volatility generally have an energizing, stimulating effect; these will be used to promote a state of mental alertness and concentration. Oils with low volatility will usually be used to promote a calm, peaceful state. These are obviously broad generalizations, however, and the same oil can both stimulate or calm, depending on the amount used.

How Does Aromatherapy Work?

Essential oils are inhaled, applied directly to the skin, or added to bath water. Aromatherapy is an accurate term in that an odor is always present, but it doesn't tell the whole story of the effects of these oils on the body and mind.

When an oil essence is inhaled, the presence of a particular odor is detected by the olfactory receptor cells, which contain cilia (tiny hairs). Information about the odor is processed by the olfactory bulb and is transmitted to the center of the brain. Electrochemical messages are then sent to the limbic system and the release of neurochemicals is triggered. These neurochemicals have a wide variety of effects. They may promote relaxation or stimulation; they may produce a sense of euphoria or they may act as sedatives. These messages are then transmitted to other areas of the body, which result in the gradual change in mood or the shift in energy or the sense of draining tension experienced by those using aromatherapy.

When an oil essence is applied to the skin (or dispersed in bath water), the molecules are absorbed through the hair follicles and the pores. They reach the bloodstream through the capillaries and circulate throughout the body. These oils act on organ systems, as well as on all the cells and body fluids. The mucous membranes are also affected by essential oils, which makes conditions of the lungs and nasal passages receptive to treatment with these substances, either through inhalation or by application on the skin in the form of a compress or a massage oil.

Essential oils are generally diluted in cold-pressed vegetable oils, known as "carrier oils." Emulsified oils mixed with water to form a lotion can also be used as carriers. (Animal or mineral oils are never used as carrier oils.) Nondiluted oils may actually harm the skin, so it is important to respect the powerful properties of these substances and use them carefully. The oils can be added to bath water, or in some cases, used in vaporizers in the home. Aromatherapists will also combine oils to form mixtures. Source books used by these practitioners contain hundreds of suggested combinations.

Some of the plants whose oils are used in aromatherapy are fairly common and the practitioners may undertake the extraction process themselves; other plants are more rare and the oils are purchased from specialty stores or through mail order sources.

The variety of oils used to treat dozens of conditions are too numerous to outline here, so we will list only a few to illustrate the range of possible formulations. For the most part, these oils are used based on anecdotal evidence and the experiences of practitioners; to date, the medicinal properties of the substances have not been tested in double-blind studies. Some, however, are used in well-known home remedies whose efficacy is generally accepted (i.e., oil of clove to relieve a toothache).

Eucalyptus oil is one of the more familiar substances used in aromatherapy. It has antiseptic properties and when inhaled, by adding it to hot bath water or by using a vaporizer, it may help prevent or treat common colds, sinusitis, bronchitis, and other respiratory complaints. It can also be applied to the skin in the form of compresses or as a massage oil, and it is said to relieve muscle and joint pain. It also acts as a stimulant to the circulatory system and may relieve cystitis. Eucalyptus promotes mental alertness, which explains its appeal as a cold remedy. It provides relief for the fatigue and drowsiness associated with cold symptoms that may be annoying and mildly debilitating, but not bad enough to force us to go to bed and stay there.

Rosemary is another well-known plant whose oil is used for dozens of health problems from headaches to indigestion. It is also said to regulate menstruation and promote healthy skin and hair. Rosemary oil is commonly used in formulations that promote mental clarity and those that relieve fatigue. Using it in a room inhaler, could, for example, help a student stay alert enough to keep on cramming for an exam or stimulate an office worker to concentrate and put in another hour or two at the desk. It is also used in inhalations to relieve respiratory symptoms.

Geranium oil is a general tonic used to relieve mental sluggishness or anxiety. When applied to the skin it can stimulate digestion and relieve a tendency to retain fluids, making it a common ingredient in formulations used to treat menstrual difficulties and menopause.

Juniper berries yield a high-quality oil that is used to relieve insomnia and other symptoms of stress. Rather than stimulating the mental processes, it will calm them. It can also be used as a tonic for sore muscles and serves as a useful bath oil when complete relaxation is the goal. Juniper berry oil also has diuretic properties and is said to help lower blood pressure.

Marjoram oil is also used in formulations that soothe the emotions and uplift the spirits. It also relieves muscle spasms and general aches and pains, which is why it is used in massage oils.

Clary sage oil relieves tension and promotes sleep, which is the reason it is not used when the person will be driving or is expected to stay awake. Its properties are also used for various menstrual complaints, including menstrual irregularity and swollen, tender breasts. It has antispasmodic effects and is used to relieve menstrual cramps. While it promotes relaxation it also is mentally uplifting and has a sweet, sensuous aroma, which some say has an aphrodisiac effect.

Peppermint oil is generally associated with digestion and is widely used to relieve stomach acidity, heartburn, motion sickness, and nausea. When adequately diluted, it also soothes itchy skin and minor inflammations. (If it's too concentrated, it may cause itchiness.)

Tea tree oil has antifungal and antibacterial properties and can be used in a variety of ways. A professional aromatherapist can suggest ways to use it as a mouthwash to relieve gum disease and sores in the mouth. It is used to relieve athlete's foot and other fungal infections and is sometimes suggested as an ingredient in a vaginal douche—probably because it can combat the overgrowth of yeast.

A few additional commonly used oils come from the following plants: fennel, lavender, garlic, onion, cypress, Roman chamomile, rose, sandalwood, bergamot, myrrh, lemon, orange, frankincense, patchouli, dill, caraway, basil, melissa, camphor, pennyroyal, violet, nutmeg, and cardamom. As you can see, some of these plants are used in cooking, perfumery, and in cosmetics. Many have made their way into the so-called "folk remedies" and even into ancient folklore.

All the above essential oils can have adverse effects if used incorrectly, used for extended periods of time, or used in concentrations too strong for the application. Pregnant and nursing women are also cautioned about using the oils without adequate information about their properties. Similarly, people with asthma, allergies, or chronic respiratory conditions should also exercise caution when first using the oils. Therefore, we recommend consulting a practitioner before trying aromatherapy formulations at home.

What Happens During a Visit to an Aromatherapist?

While it is possible to learn to use many aromatic formulations that you may already be using in the form of massage oil, a trained practitioner can assess your needs and provide you with high-quality therapeutic products. If you visit a practitioner who is trained only in aromatherapy, you will likely have a previous diagnosis and a treatment plan suggested by a health care provider. The aromatherapist will augment treatment with essential oils, matching the formulation to the condition for which you are being treated by other practitioners.

On the other hand, if you know you are generally in good health and want to use aromatherapy to help you cope with the mundane day-to-day stresses of life, an aromatherapist can provide you with formulations to inhale (perhaps while listening to a relaxation tape or meditating), to add to your bath, or to use during massage at home or to take to a professional massage therapist. Most aromatherapists can refer you to other alternative health care practitioners in your area if you need care that is outside of their expertise. Like all practitioners, they are concerned with general health issues, and you may be questioned about your diet, sleep habits, exercise program, and so forth. Some general recommendations might be made in these areas, because aromatherapy is part of the holistic health care world and you are viewed as a whole person.

If the practitioner is a massage therapist, the oil used will be chosen based on your reported physical and emotional health. For example, if you are recovering from an illness or are very tired, the oil will probably be different from that chosen if you have muscle spasms or a sports injury. While relaxation might be the goal one week, mental stimulation and emotional uplift might be the goal the next. Many massage therapists can sell these oils to you to use at home.

You may find that aromatherapy is suggested by an herbalist, naturopath, nutritionist, and so forth. (Many types of practitioners are currently incorporating aromatherapy into treatment and prevention programs.) If this is the case, aromatherapy formulations will probably be provided by the practitioner and changed as needed.

Is Aromatherapy Dangerous in Any Way?

When properly used, aromatherapy is probably one of the safest treatment methods in existence today. Any number of formulations can be tried without ill effects and no harm is done if they are ineffective. The obvious exceptions are for pregnant and nursing women and those with allergies, asthma, and other respiratory conditions. Certainly, some of the oils can be toxic if ingested or applied directly to the skin. Aromatherapy by itself should not be used to treat serious, life-threatening conditions. It can be used as an antidote for side effects of other treatments and medications, although we don't recommend doing this without consulting a practitioner. For the most part, aromatherapy is a pleasant addition to a treatment plan; it can promote general well-being and help relieve the tension and fatigue associated with the common stresses of life.

Generally speaking, the effects of aromatherapy are subtle. You may notice a slight change in mood or a temporary relief of mental fatigue, but aromatherapy is not like taking a drug with its attending dramatic effects. It can stimulate various body systems and may both relieve symptoms and play a role in preventing some common ailments. However, no qualified aromatherapist will claim that this treatment will always prevent or cure any illness. In addition, reaction to these oils, individually and in combination, varies from person to person and no one can absolutely predict how you will feel after using one or more essential oil.

How Do I Find a Qualified Aromatherapist?

Aromatherapy is not recognized as a treatment, meaning that there are no accredited schools or licensing procedures. In general, aromatherapy products are regulated as cosmetics and these formulations cannot be labeled with claims to cure any specific ailment. On the legal front, there are no laws preventing a person from suggesting aromatherapy formulations, and some practitioners are self-taught through books and manuals, many of which are widely available. In fact, most people could learn the basics from books and instruction manuals if they wanted to take the time to study the properties of the plants and experiment with the oils. However, since most of us are unlikely to do that, the best referral source is probably another alternative health care practitioner who you know well and trust.

Although not regulated, there are some well-established aromatherapy courses and a growing network of practitioners who have studied with experienced people. Some aromatherapy courses are primarily home-study programs. Others are a combination of home-study and seminars. These programs are privately operated and developed by practitioners, some of whom market aromatherapy products. They will generally provide referrals to those who have taken their courses. If the practitioner has another specialty, be sure to find out how he or she became knowledgeable about aromatherapy and how long it has been among this person's treatment tools.

The following is a list of resources, including course sponsors and associations.

National Association for Holistic Aromatherapy
P.O. Box 17622
Boulder, CO 80308

This is a small association of practitioners whose goal is to elevate professional standards. They offer information to their members and have a vehicle for referrals. They also publish a quarterly journal.

Jeanne Rose Aromatherapy
219 Carl Street
San Francisco, CA 94117
415/564–6337

Run by aromatherapist and author, Jeanne Rose, this company sponsors a home-study aromatherapy course.

Aromatherapy Seminars
1830 Robertson Boulevard
Suite 203
Los Angeles, CA 90035
310/838–6122

This group offers a certification course consisting of a five-day seminar and a home-study course. They also offer training for others to teach aromatherapy.

The New England Center for Aromatherapy
  60 Myrtle Street
  Suite 1
  Boston, MA 02114
  617/720–4585

Run by Jade Shutes and Elizabeth Gray, this center has a home-study course.

Smell and Taste Treatment and Research Foundation
  Water Tower Place
  845 North Michigan Avenue
  Suite 990W
  Chicago, IL 60611
  312/938–1047

Run by Alan Hirsch, M.D., this facility treats smell and taste disorders and conducts scientific research on olfaction using artificial smells. Olfaction and its role in weight control and loss of the ability to smell and its relationship to depression are examples of the type of work this center does.

Chapter Fourteen

Environmental Medicine

The new arena of environmental medicine has become the center of much controversy in the last fifteen years. While some people, including for a long time the allopathic medical community, tried to dismiss environmental causes of illness, evidence has mounted since the end of World War II that pollutants have caused and are causing damage to people and the environment. Recent Environmental Protection Agency (EPA) studies, for instance, concluded that deadly dioxin, a by-product of pesticides, herbicides, and incineration, as well as a number of industrial processes, is toxic in much lower doses than was previously thought and may be affecting fertility rates in men and women.

Considering the degradation the environment has undergone, it was perhaps inevitable that a specialty like environmental medicine would arise. The media has reported on people who, through various environmental exposures, have become the "canaries in the cage" of the 1990s. These people, through chemical exposures, have become hypersensitive to their environment. Some of these victims of environmental toxicity have what is known as multiple chemical sensitivity (MCS). They are allergic to, and in some cases have life-threatening episodes from, exposure to a range of environmental pollutants. Indeed, some have become so allergic to modern life that they have had to withdraw themselves from the world and live in remote, rural areas of the country where exposure to offending industrial substances is kept to a bare minimum. But these individuals represent only the most extreme cases of environmental sensitivity.

Understanding Environmental Illness

Environmental illness is a term coined in 1951 by Dr. Theron Randolph, a Harvard-trained physician and allergist. He saw that a range of synthetic products, from hair dyes to deodorants and perfumes, were causing allergic reactions in people. During the following decades, the list of substances that cause acute and severe reactions in people when exposed has grown. The list of allergens is long and varies with individual people. Dyes, perfumes, building materials, and a whole host of non-nature based substances are the culprits.

These offending substances are called allergens or antigens. The body's immune system reacts to foreign substances, such as bacteria and viruses by turning on an incredible array of body defenses. In people with allergic responses, the body does the same thing, by identifying certain foods, dyes, fumes, or toxins as foreign. "Allergy" has been the blanket word the medical profession generally uses to describe an abnormal response to substances such as pollen, dust, foods, chemicals, and drugs. The range of symptoms of traditional allergies run from runny noses and eyes to yeast infections and bronchial attacks. In the last two decades, however, a new range of disorders have been added to the list, including stomach, bladder, and lung problems, muscle and joint pain, nervous system malfunction, and in severe cases, even death.

A New Theory of Illness

Environmental medicine holds that much of what happens with someone who is experiencing a toxic reaction and who becomes environmentally ill has to do with the overloading of the body's natural defenses. Doctors who specialize in this field often say that the human body is like a rain barrel that can only hold so much water. When the body reaches the point where the barrel is past full, it overflows. The human body also cannot withstand a limitless amount of toxins from air, food, and water being put into it. When the biological limits of the body are reached, illness occurs. There can even be a cascading effect when one exposure creates sensitivities to other chemicals, as is believed to be the case with MCS.

Environmental doctors often talk in terms of "total load" when describing the array of allergens and toxins that a given person's bodily systems are fighting. Often the hormonal or endocrine system of the body is involved in the reaction. These major glands, including the thyroid, adrenals, thalamus, and pituitary, are many times thrown out of balance and send the wrong amount of hormone at the wrong time, when the body is under attack by an environmental stressor. In severe cases, imbalance turns into an immunological overload. The rain barrel is so full that a major, chronic breakdown in functioning occurs. Some practitioners believe that the skyrocketing rates of asthma in the last ten years and the rise in the number of certain auto-immune disorders, such as lupus and multiple sclerosis, are the end result of this chain of events.

The symptoms of environmental illness can include

- Running nose and hay fever-like symptoms can be reactions to pollen-type allergens, but can also be reactions to food products. Allergists and environmental doctors have a number of accurate tests for food and pollen-type allergies.
- Disorientation, dizziness, vertigo, and nausea can be a reaction to a number of environmental toxins, including chemicals in carpeting and office furniture that "outgas" (send out as an invisible vapor) solvents, plasticizers, and other noxious chemicals, like formaldehyde, that are known carcinogens.

- Headaches, including migraines, and general body aches, especially of the joints, can arise after exposure to herbicides, pesticides, and chemical building materials.
- Difficulty in breathing, concentrating, memory loss, and nerve disorders are some of the acute and potentially life-threatening symptoms that have been reported after exposure to pesticides, chemicals, and hazardous wastes.
- Chronic fatigue syndrome (CFS) is one of the classic clinical groups of symptoms of people who have had chemical or other environmental exposures. Sometimes CFS is a passing illness; other times the patient is forced to deal with the malady for months or years. Candida, the yeast-fungi infection, is sometimes a primary or contributing factor to CFS. This type of infection especially affects women. It can form in the vagina or intestines and then become generalized. Causes can include prolonged birth control pill use, too much sugar in the diet, or too many antibiotics taken over an extended period of time.

A number of factors can put a person at risk for environmental illness:

- **Exposure to toxic as well as nontoxic chemicals.** This runs the gamut from dyes, perfumes and food additives—such as nitrates, sulfites (used to preserve fruits and wine), and food colorings—to exposure to pesticides, herbicides, and other petrochemicals.
- **Poor nutrition**, such as unhealthy dieting and binge eating, can contribute to the development of allergies and illness.
- **Heredity** seems to play some role in allergic reactions. The ancestor who passed on the susceptibility to allergens may go back many generations and be unknown to you. People also change as they grow. Statistically, in childhood there are more boys than girls who have allergies, while in adulthood the numbers reverse themselves.

- **Stress** plays a role in allergies. This varies heavily from person to person, with some people able to withstand a greater degree of stress before symptoms occur.
- **Infection** as the result of bacterial or viral infection followed by sensitization is not uncommon. MCS has been found to occur after cases of mononucleosis, Lyme disease, and hepatitis, for instance.

Beyond Common Allergies

The Legacy of a Chemically Intensive World

Almost everything we use, from clothes and furniture to automobiles, are made with or processed with chemicals. Only a few of the more than sixty thousand synthetic chemicals used in industrial processes have ever been tested by the EPA for toxicity, hence only a very few are regulated in any way. While allergies to pollen, dust, molds, and danders are common, increasing numbers of people are proving susceptible to these human-made pollutants.

In the 1980s, the names Love Canal and Times Beach became historic markers of environmental damage. In 1993 and 1994, estrogen-mimicking compounds from herbicides, such as Kepone and PCBs, showed up in the body fat of mutated fish in the Great Lakes, as well as lakes in Florida. In dozens of other communities across the United States, from McFarland, California, to Woburn, Massachusetts, cancer clusters, bronchial diseases, and even birth defects have occurred near the sites of landfills and toxic dumps. These are the communities across America where the toxins of the twentieth century have come home to roost.

Multiple Chemical Sensitivity

The phenomenon of multiple chemical sensitivity (MCS) has grown steadily in the last twenty years as the total level of toxins in the environment has risen. The causes of MCS are not completely understood, but it appears that there is a high correlation between being exposed to toxins and having the body's immune system taxed beyond its limits. When this happens, health disorders often follow, from sinusitis, headaches, disorientation, and breathing problems to cell abnormalities and even statistical increases in cancer rates.

Usually there is an initial, triggering incident, where an allergen or toxin stresses the system. The body responds, and then responds further as an individual is exposed to more of the toxin or a wider variety of toxins. Suddenly the person is allergic to many substances. In other cases, a person may come down with mononucleosis or a form of viral hepatitis, or have a chemical-based exposure. Following the illness or initial exposure, the person becomes highly sensitized, with MCS often emerging at the same time.

Common complaints linked to MCS include, but are not limited to, rashes, chronic fatigue, depression, headaches, sinusitis, and nerve disorders. Everything, from the clothes you wear and the foods you eat to the building where you work or the materials in the car you drive, can suddenly be the cause of debilitating illness. The ability of people with MCS to work or drive a car can become impaired to the point where both activities are impossible. In the worst cases, people can even become allergic to their own homes.

Sick Building Syndrome

Prominent among the sources of pollutants and toxins that can cause environmental illness, including MCS, may be the building where you work. Sick building syndrome is the name given to this late–twentieth-century malady, which demonstrates the collision of large amounts of chemically enhanced building materials with large numbers of people working in an enclosed environment. This point of contact for environmental exposure has created devastating results for thousands of people. The syndrome, finally recognized after years of conjecture, has cost, by some estimates, fifteen to one hundred billion dollars a year in lost productivity in America.

The causes of sick building syndrome are the result of several factors. Building materials changed drastically after World War II and continued to become more chemically intensive through the 1950s, '60s, and '70s. More petrochemical-based products went into building construction, especially petrochemicals and formaldehyde-based products. Home insulation installers advertised that they could come to your house and fill your walls with liquid insulation laced with formaldehyde. Office furniture changed from being made of wood and steel to plastic and chemically treated wood composition materials that looked like wood and metal. New chemical glues were used to hold pressed furniture materials together. Other glues held down carpeting made of fiber material that itself was a product of the chemical process and had new and strange odors. The result was that the indoor air quality in the modern home and office building decreased dramatically. As these building materials "outgassed" their solvents, plasticizers, and other chemicals, the lungs and breathing systems of many people were simply unable to cope with this barrage of chemical stressors and the symptoms we spoke of earlier were sometimes the result.

At the same time, the energy crisis of the 1970s made the construction of buildings and homes much tighter in order to conserve energy. Windows became double-paned, doorways were redesigned, and vents were made to fit tighter and use less fresh air from the outside of a building. The office building especially became a closed environment. This meant that there was much less air exchange between the outside and the inside of a building than there had been previously. It meant that people inside buildings were breathing air that had greater concentrations of the petroleum-based chemicals that were increasingly more a part of curtains, walls, furniture, and insulation than ever before.

There are many examples across the United States of sick build-ings. A couple of famous examples will highlight the problem.

Downers Grove, Illinois

The disastrous situation at the DuPage County courthouse in suburban Chicago made headlines for over three years. Originally, in 1991 and 1992, hundreds of people were trans-ferred out of the new, $53-million facility after complaints of nausea, repeated vomiting, dizziness, and disorientation became common for people working in or visiting the building. The building stood empty for many months while carpeting and fur-niture were removed and ventilation ducts were inspected and rerouted. Initially, building materials were thought to be the sole cause of the problem.

In August 1994, it was discovered that the roof top ventila-tion system was so inadequately designed that chemical-laden air pulled out of the building for ventilation was immediately recycled back into the building as "fresh air," in essence forcing the people working inside the building to breathe noxious air. In this case, a combination of building materials and bad building design worked together to cause illness. A total of 140 people are now suing the builders after experiencing environmental illness. Forty people maintain that their health has been permanently damaged by their exposure at the county building.

Washington, D.C.

One of the great ironies of our national dependence on these chemically intensive building materials came to rest at the door of the Environmental Protection Agency in Washington, D.C. In 1988, after new building materials, including carpeting, had been installed throughout the national offices of the EPA, people began to get sick. Dizziness, nerve disorders, memory loss, vomiting, and acute allergies plagued hundreds of people. Eventually the entire building's carpeting, all twenty-seven thousand square yards, was pulled up, thrown away, and replaced. The glue that held the carpeting down was the prime suspect. The building became easier to work in after these changes. But still the problem has persisted for some people who have been chemically sensitized by the episode. Scores of people have been permanently stationed off-site and wear filter masks when they make brief forays into the building to pick up work or be paid.

Only in the last few years, with the recognition of sick building syndrome and a number of lawsuits, has the building industry begun to take heed. The home insulation foams containing formaldehyde have been taken off the market. Some office buildings and homes are now being constructed in part with less toxic or low-impact materials. Wool is now being used as carpet fiber in some high-end office buildings. In other instances, furniture made from nonchemical processes is also being used. Unfortunately, this change is slow and far from universal. The fast food restaurant, mall, or office you may be visiting is likely to still be mainly a product of chemical processes.

A Session with an Environmental Doctor

The American Academy of Environmental Medicine in Denver can help you locate a practitioner in environmental medicine if one is not readily available to you. We should mention that in the diagnostic stages, naturopaths, homeopaths, and traditional Chinese doctors also deal with environmental illness. Once you have located a physician and have an appointment, you will be asked to give a detailed environmental history. There may even be a request to keep an environmental diary to record what you eat and drink and what your living environments are like. Interviews and case history will be very important in getting a clear picture of your condition. In assessing what drugs, medications, foods, pollutants, or environmental chemicals to which you are exposed, the practitioner usually develops several likely suspects that may be causing your problem. Environmental doctors know that a number of underlying problems may be filling up your immunological rain barrel.

Blood and Fluids Testing

Many toxic chemicals are stored in the lipids or body fats of the body. Tests may be done to monitor the functioning of the kidney and liver to see how they are coping with bodily toxins. These tests will generally include tests of T-cell and B-cell lymphocytes and levels of immunoglobulin E (IgE) to judge the condition of your immune system. Additional tests may be performed on the blood to get a clearer picture of pesticides, herbicides, or volatile chemicals that may be in the bloodstream. Hydrocarbons, the chemicals from smokestacks and auto emissions, can also be measured. Hair analysis and urine tests can be performed to confirm the presence of heavy metals like cadmium and mercury.

Environmental Testing

This testing, as with the blood tests, can be done at a hospital or doctor's office. One or several of the following methods may be used to determine your environmental health.

1. You may be given an amount of an allergen under your skin—intracutaneously. A little red area the size of a mosquito bite will form, which is called a wheal. If an allergic response occurs to this challenge, the bite area (wheal) will usually grow within five to fifteen minutes. This type of skin test is used especially for pollens, animal danders, molds, foods, and dust.

2. You may be given a shot in the arm or have drops placed under your tongue to cause an allergic reaction. These substances are called excitants. These excitants can be food substances or environmental chemicals.

3. You may be treated with a tiny bit of allergen that is too small to produce a negative body reaction. This amount,

however, can be large enough to prevent a reaction and hence enable you to tolerate greater amounts of the substance in question, particularly if the offending substances is one that is not easily avoidable. This process is called neutralization and can also be part of your treatment program.

Treatments

Once your tests have been completed, your history looked into, and an evaluation done, treatments will be recommended. They will probably consist of some combination of the following.

Diet adjustment is often a key in healing the environmentally ill patient with food allergies. You may be asked to abstain from eating certain foods for a specified period of time. This could be three to five days. Food may also be introduced or reintroduced after a period of time. This is called rotation diet, or sometimes an elimination diet.

Hospitalization may be the course of action recommended for some people in acute or chronic situations. An environmental control program, as part of hospitalization, is not frequently recommended, but may be a necessary step to accurately assess your illness and provide relief. By putting a patient in a controlled environment, the environmental substances (such as clothes or furniture) in a person's life can be monitored very closely, and then added or subtracted from the living environment, one at a time. Diet can also be controlled and closely monitored. Air filtration systems as part of the clinic or hospital environment can filter out pollutants, danders, and pollens.

Complete environmental controls often requires water and air filters, and sometimes the use of negative ion generators. The selection of furnishings and cleaning materials, as well as building materials, where applicable, will be instituted to reduce or eliminate exposure to allergens and toxins.

Immunization or neutralization therapy involves allergens given to patients, in the form of shots or drops, to build their tolerance to various environmental stressors. It is generally used to find an optimal dose for you to control adverse responses from toxins and allergens. This may involve a maintenance program which, over time, increases your tolerance to the offending substance.

Rotary diversified diet may be used to keep certain food groups to a minimum that may be causing allergic problems, and balance the nutrients that the body is using.

Some Amazing Successes

While an environmental control program may sound draconian and the list of allergens that cause toxic reactions very long, there are some promising anecdotal stories. There is some hope for relief for some people. Changes in diet, as we mentioned, often can have a profoundly positive effect. Changes in clothing or household environment are other areas where people have taken charge and improved their quality of life without having to move to the desert or mountains. Air and water filters can also have positive effects on health when people are allergic to chlorine and other pollutants.

In the neutralization therapy we mentioned, doctors are now using drops placed under the tongue of patients to build tolerance to offending substances. These sublingual drops, in highly diluted form, contain the essence of the offending chemical within them. For people with sensitivities to such things as chlorine, formaldehyde (exposure to this toxin can come from a number of sources, as we said), and even the petrochemicals in car exhaust, relief has been found using drops with minute amounts of these toxins within them.

Some startling and positive results have been shown with patients able to stand much greater levels of exposure to the allergy-producing chemical in the outside world. Usually, though not always, a patient will have to take the drops for a long period of time on a maintenance program to treat the sensitivity. Nutrient therapy in the form of anti-oxidants, such as beta carotene, and including vitamins C and E, are now commonly recommended for MCS. This type of treatment has shown remarkable success in some people. In an even more recent development, people with MCS have responded well to the use of hydrogen peroxide given intravenously in diluted form. In this oxygen therapy symptoms disappear or are greatly reduced. This treatment, we should stress, is relatively new and much more work remains to be done in the area of MCS.

Precautions

Environmental medical treatments can provide the long-sought-after help that patients with MCS or more basic allergies have been trying to find. The lifestyle changes that are required for optimum health may be minor and easy to live with. Others may be more drastic and involve changing the clothes or car you own, or even, in rarer cases, where you live or work, in order to eliminate an environmental exposure. In most cases, most people can tolerate the treatments described above very well. People with severely compromised immune systems, such as those undergoing chemotherapy and people with AIDS, may want to approach the therapy with some caution as injections and testing with allergens is often part of the diagnostic process.

Environmental Medicine Resources

American Academy of Environmental Medicine
P.O. Box 16106
Denver CO 80216
303/622–9755
303/622–4224 (fax)

The academy certifies medical doctors and doctors of osteopathy in the specialty of environmental medicine. It has over five hundred members and can provide a list of practitioners in your area.

> Environmental Health Center
> 8345 Walnut Hill Lane
> Suite 205
> Dallas TX 75231
> 214/368–4132
> 214/691–8432 (fax)

The center deals with a wide range of environmental illnesses. It also has a detoxification unit capable of handling up to thirty people at a time.

> American Environmental Health Foundation
> 8345 Walnut Hill Lane, Suite 225
> Dallas, TX 75231
> 214/361–9515
> 214/691–8432 (fax)
> 800/428–2343

The foundation offers for sale a number of air and water filters, ecomasks, chemical-free clothes, and hypoallergenic vitamins, among other products.

> Naperville Holistic Health Center
> 1280 Iroquois Drive
> Suite 200
> Naperville, IL 60563
> 708/369–1220
> 708/369–1639 (fax)

This center has dealt with numerous cases of MCS as well as sick building syndrome.

Chapter Fifteen

An Array of Treatment Choices

Some therapies do not fit neatly into one philosophy or category, but they may have a place in many treatment programs. This chapter includes brief descriptions of therapies you may encounter as you search for alternative and complementary treatments for many conditions, including cancer. Referral sources and information for all the treatments are listed at the end of the chapter.

Chelation Therapy

Chelation therapy was created to remove toxic metals from the body. To physicians practicing it today, it also is a legitimate prevention and treatment tool for cardiovascular disease, some environmental illnesses, and other degenerative disorders such as scleroderma, lupus, and arthritis.

The word "chelation" derives from the Greek word "chele," meaning claw or bind. If you picture an agent circulating through the body, picking up other substances that bind to it, then you have a visual image of chelation therapy. Chelation uses a non-toxic agent (ethylene-diamine-tetra-acetate, or

EDTA); damaging substances are "trapped" by the EDTA and eliminated from the body through the kidneys.

EDTA's Many Uses

EDTA is a synthetic amino acid developed for the dye industry in Germany. It is a binding agent, in that calcium molecules become trapped by it, thus making it a way to remove calcium from hard water. From this industrial use, a few physicians reasoned that EDTA could help treat symptoms of metal toxicity. An American physician documented successful treatment of lead toxicity, and in the 1950s, the U.S. Navy began using EDTA to treat sailors exposed to lead-based paint who showed symptoms of toxicity. As it turned out, there were positive side effects of EDTA, which included improvement of symptoms linked with arthritis and hardening of the arteries (atherosclerosis).

Although the FDA approves EDTA solely for treating heavy metal toxicity, over one thousand U.S. physicians use it in chelation therapy for, among other things, an alternative to bypass surgery for heart disease. EDTA is the chelating—or binding— agent in the intravenous solution given to patients with problems related to cardiovascular disorders including hypertension, angina pain, difficulty breathing, and poor circulation in the legs (peripheral vascular disease). People with peripheral vascular disease often suffer leg cramps, and as the disease progresses, some patients develop ulcers or sores on their feet. Poor circulation slows the healing process and the sores can become gangrenous. Conventional treatment may include amputation, but chelation therapy can sometimes reverse the condition, allowing the patient to avoid surgery.

Circulation throughout the body improves because EDTA binds with calcium, which helps form plaque, the substance that clogs the arteries. As plaque decreases, more blood flows to the heart and all the blood vessels in the body. EDTA also moves calcium from the soft tissues of the body, where it doesn't belong, and redirects the calcium to the bones. Although there are other chelating agents (Vitamin C, for example), EDTA remains the primary agent in chelation solutions. There are also oral chelation agents, but they are not necessarily a substitute for intravenous treatments.

Allopathic or osteopathic physicians are the only practitioners qualified to do chelation treatment, although a nurse may monitor the treatment. The series of twenty to thirty treatments, each taking about three hours, is always done on an out-patient basis. A treatment regimen usually calls for two or three treatments a week. The solution is slowly introduced to your body through a vein while you relax in a reclining chair. Other than the initial needle prick, it is a painless procedure. The dosage of EDTA is individualized, based on your age and weight and other factors such as kidney function.

What Are the Benefits of Chelation Therapy?

Physicians who use chelation therapy programs have documented both subjective symptomatic relief and objective, measurable improvements. Studies show that chelation reduces arterial blockages, lowers blood pressure, and improves general circulation. Research also shows that although it isn't a cure, the therapy improves symptoms of diseases affecting bones, joints, and connective tissue. For example, people with arthritis report that pain and swelling in joints sometimes dramatically improves. There is also research suggesting that diabetics may benefit from chelation therapy, and some can significantly reduce their dosages of insulin. European studies are following chelation therapy as a cancer prevention regimen because the treatment removes free radicals from the body. Although there are no claims that it reverses the illness, research suggests that chelation therapy may slow the progress of Alzheimer's disease.

Are There Risks Associated with Chelation Treatment?

Pregnant women and patients with severe kidney disease are not candidates for chelation therapy. It was once thought that chelation damaged healthy kidneys, but over the forty or so years of use in many countries, this has been disproved. During treatment, patients may become weak or dizzy, usually because blood sugar levels drop. This isn't a serious side effect and should not deter you from seeking more information about chelation therapy.

Chelation Therapy in the Future

Chelation therapy remains controversial, despite the studies showing its benefits. Insurance companies and the U.S. government Medicare and Medicaid programs continue to respond to the pressure applied by the orthodox medical establishment and do not cover this treatment. The patent for EDTA has run out, so there is no financial incentive for drug companies to fund studies.

Proponents of chelation therapy believe that it represents a significant advance in low-risk, nonsurgical treatment for cardiovascular disease. The organization of physicians who use this therapy have done their own research and conclude that the patients who seek chelation therapy before their heart disease is advanced get the best results. In the future, chelation therapy may become a preventive regimen for many conditions, heart disease among them.

Colon Therapy

Colon therapy uses water to flush the colon and detoxify the lower intestine. The colon is a major organ for eliminating bodily wastes and we absorb nutrients into our bodies through the intestinal wall. There are several dozen varieties of bacteria and microflora in a healthy digestive tract. The balance of the bacteria and flora is maintained through a healthy diet, which promotes regular bowel movements and helps eliminate toxic substances from the body. But if harmful bacteria, fungi, viruses, parasites, and impacted feces accumulate, a condition called "bowel toxemia" may result. Bowel toxemia leads to impaired immunity because, as toxins enter the bloodstream through the colon, the lymphatic system, the kidneys, and the liver become overburdened. Colon cleansing removes the toxic build-up and helps restore proper functioning of the gastrointestinal (GI) tract.

Colon therapy has been used in Europe since the nineteenth century and became popular in this country in the early years of this century. It is still associated with European health spas and with naturopathic physicians and other alternative practitioners in this country. It is used in many detoxification programs, including fasting regimens and treatments for environmental medicine. Naturopaths learn to perform colon therapy in their medical schools and other practitioners are trained and certified by professional associations.

In a typical colon therapy session, twenty to thirty gallons of unfiltered water circulate through the colon, dislodging fecal material from the folds of the entire colon. (The colon is usually about fifteen feet long.) The practitioner inserts an applicator into the anus and releases the water slowly over a period of thirty to forty minutes. This is a painless, if not completely comfortable, procedure and some patients report feeling refreshed and energetic. To get full benefit, more than one session may be needed.

What Are the Benefits and Risks of Colon Therapy?

Besides the direct benefits to the entire GI tract, colon therapy simulates your immune system and helps detoxify the blood. It may be recommended as one part of your treatment for allergies and chemical sensitivity. Colon cleansing is routinely used to treat chronic constipation and bloating. Skin conditions, headaches, fatigue, indigestion, and many other conditions may improve following one or more treatments.

You should not use colon therapy if you have intestinal conditions such as diverticulitis, ulcerative colitis, Crohn's disease, severe hemorrhoids, or if you have reason to believe that you have benign or malignant tumors in your colon. The treatment room and equipment must be sterile and the tubing and applicator should be disposable. Fecal matter can carry disease, so ask the practitioner what procedures he or she follows to maintain the sterility of the facility.

Bach Flower Remedies

Edward Bach was a British physician and bacteriologist who became disenchanted with orthodox medicine and turned to homeopathy. Bach practiced from the early years of this century until he died in the 1930s. He eventually became convinced that emotional states cause disease, and he developed his remedies to treat these states of mind instead of physical symptoms. Later, he became more mystical than scientific and based his flower remedies on their power to cleanse the personality and realign it with the soul. In other words, he believed that illness resulted when our deepest self—or soul—is at odds with our personality.

For the most part, Bach developed his flower remedies intuitively, believing that he could sense the properties of the particular plant. He isolated and defined emotional states in very specific ways and treated them with one of the thirty-eight remedies he developed. For example, holly treats one variety or form of over-sensitivity (jealousy and suspicion), while walnut treats another variety (over-sensitivity to outside influences occurring during major life changes). Rock rose is given for terror or panic, one of Bach's varieties of fear, and aspen treats fear of the unknown or anxiety.

The remedies come in liquid concentrate form. To use the remedy, you place two or three drops in a glass of water or juice and sip it slowly. Bach believed the power inherent in the flowers transfers to the water or juice, making it part of the remedy. The best-known of the remedies is "rescue remedy," and is a combination of five flower remedies used for severe stress and emotional shock.

Some homeopaths, naturopaths, nutritionists, herbalists, and aromatherapists use flower remedies, which may or may not be exact replicas of the original Bach formulas. The Bach remedies and other flower essences are available over the counter in many natural food stores, but it is best to ask a practitioner to tell you how and when to use them. To date, there are no known risks involved with using the flower remedies as directed.

Iridology

Iridology is based on the assumption that our eyes can provide information upon which a trained person can assess general health and diagnose illness. In addition, the iris, the most important part of the eye in iridology, reveals what illnesses we have had in the past and what conditions we could be vulnerable to developing in the future.

An iridologist "maps" the iris by dividing it into segments, each section representing an organ or a bodily function. The practitioner detects disorders by noting discolored or dull areas and markings; the texture of the iris, which can appear coarse or smooth, also provides information. In general, the left side of the iris provides a map of the left side of the body; the right side of the iris corresponds to the right side of body. The brain and the glands of the upper body are represented on the top of the iris and the lower organs and feet correspond to the lower portion. Other organs are represented within three zones of the iris.

Iridology is a diagnostic specialty within many alternative therapy practices. It is a painless, noninvasive procedure, sometimes used to confirm a diagnosis. The original way of creating the map of the eye involved using a magnifying glass and bright light. Nowadays, practitioners are more likely to use a specialized camera to take a picture of the eye. The photograph is enlarged into a slide so the patient sees exactly what a practitioner means when he or she makes a diagnosis based on an irregularity in the iris.

What Are the Benefits and Risks of Iridology?

Iridology is sometimes used to confirm diagnoses of illnesses and conditions that could have many causes. For example, while chemical sensitivities are often subtle, the eye may reveal toxicity in the gastrointestinal system and a weakness in the lymphatic system, both of which may confirm the practitioner's initial impression that the patient is suffering from environmentally induced symptoms. Treatment can be monitored by how the patient feels, but also by the changes in the eyes. Similarly, the appearance of the eye changes during an acute infection. When the eye's appearance returns to normal, the practitioner knows the infection is gone.

There are no known dangers associated with iridology, and it may be a useful alternative to x-rays or blood tests in some situations. We don't recommend relying on iridology as the sole diagnostic tool to evaluate any illness or condition.

Unconventional Dentistry

Also known as biological dentistry, this school or branch of dentistry promotes using nontoxic dental restoration materials. Some of these dentists take additional training in nutrition and homeopathy and incorporate this information into their practices.

These unconventional dentists are perhaps best known for their concern about the toxic effects of mercury fillings (amalgams). But their concerns also include a wider understanding of the ways that dental problems can affect general health. For example, according to biological dentistry, an infection under and around a tooth may not cause obvious problems and, because they usually aren't detected by x-rays, you may be unaware that the infection exists. But the bacteria are slowly affecting the entire body, which forces the immune system to overwork to maintain health.

Mercury is the most harmful of the metals used for dental fillings and many biological dentists remove them from their patients' teeth. (Mercury is the primary metal in "silver" fillings, which are usually no more 25 percent silver.) Mercury and other metals eventually leak and trace amounts make their way into the bloodstream, causing symptoms of metal toxicity. There is still no ideal replacement for these fillings, but biological dentists substitute a combination of less toxic metals to construct a filling.

Biological dentistry is concerned with total dental and oral health from the most common fillings and root canals to fluoridation and effects of electrogalvanism (the electricity our fillings generate). These dentists may prescribe homeopathic remedies for dental emergencies, such as an abscess or a severe toothache. Some dentists use oral acupuncture to treat pain, sensitive teeth, and periodontal problems.

What Are the Benefits and Risks of Biological Dentistry?

Critics of this new approach to dental health accuse its proponents of making serious issues out of insignificant problems. The American Dental Association (ADA) has not approved many techniques used by unconventional dentists, nor has it acknowledged that mercury-based fillings are harmful in any way. However, if you are being treated by an alternative practitioner for environmental illness, allergies, and so forth, he or she may recommend that you include this newer form of dental care in your treatment plan. In addition, these practitioners can use many sophisticated diagnostic techniques to find out how dental problems may be affecting your health. For the most part, biological dentistry, while sometimes expensive, doesn't have any significant health risks.

Developmental Optometry

Also known as behavioral optometry, this specialty is concerned with how the brain works with the eyes in processing and organizing what we see. It is an important therapy because children are sometimes diagnosed with learning disabilities when they actually have a developmental vision disorder. For example, children with impaired visual functioning, as opposed to impaired sight, may not be able to concentrate on a reading assignment or they may confuse words and numbers. These children may also appear clumsy or careless. This problem isn't necessarily outgrown and some adults operate with a perceptual handicap.

Conventional optometrists correct a patient's sight and prescribe compensating lenses, designed to give the person 20/20 vision. Behavioral optometrists use behavioral lenses and visual exercises to train the eyes and the brain to work together. The treatment is also used with people who are victims of head trauma, brain tumors, and strokes. According to behavioral optometrists, adults and children can develop problems with visual organization as a result of emotional stress or trauma.

This therapy is available only from specially trained optometrists. Conventional practitioners may tell you that it is not a proven or even a valid treatment. However, if you or your child has unexplained visual or perceptual difficulties, this therapy is worth exploring.

Alternative or Complementary Cancer Treatments

Unfortunately, much discussion about unconventional approaches to cancer treatment is still bitter and acrimonious. In our country, there are standard treatment protocols and experimental drugs and surgery are for the most part monitored within the well-established academic medical centers. In many other countries, where unconventional therapies were never pushed off the table, so to speak, more than one legitimate approach to cancer treatment exists.

Causes, treatments, and potential prevention measures are openly debated in many European countries and Japan. In the United States, however, we are just beginning to bring some alternative or complementary treatments to the public arena. The public's demand for the freedom to use unorthodox treatments has sparked a new level of debate.

In this country, the rancor over alternative cancer treatments was for decades fed by the arrogant attitudes often present on both sides of the debate. On one hand, the orthodox medical establishment labeled just about everything not included in its treatment protocols as quackery and the practitioners using them as charlatans. On the other hand, some advocates of alternative treatments called conventional treatments the "poison, slash, and burn," methods, and the conventional physicians advocating them were characterized as uncaring brutes.

Pharmaceutical companies must shoulder a share of the blame, as they have not supported extensive clinical trials using common, inexpensive substances that cannot be patented. We are now at a crossroads, where patients and practitioners are searching for a middle ground. While it is true that some physicians do not support their patients' searches for alternative treatments, many are willing to work together to find a group of treatments that offer patients greater physical and psychological well-being.

The therapies listed below are a sample of many available complementary treatments; some are often used with conventional treatments. Others are truly alternative in that they are sometimes substitutes for conventional chemotherapy, surgery, or radiation. You can get information about the treatments from the resources listed at the end of the chapter. In addition, many professionals consider the body/mind therapies discussed in Chapter 8 appropriate complementary cancer treatments.

The Gerson Diet

Long before the arrival of the macrobiotic diet as a complementary cancer therapy, the German-trained physician Max Gerson was treating patients with diet and attempting to get the medical establishment to listen to him. In the 1920s, he treated his first cancer patient using a special diet, which he continued using after emigrating to the United States in the 1930s. He began publishing reports of his promising findings in the 1940s, but was attacked by the American Medical Association, which, at that time, did not welcome nutritional approaches to prevent or cure cancer. (Gerson became especially unpopular for his claim that patients who received no treatment for cancer lived longer than those who submitted to the available conventional treatments.)

Gerson believed that toxins in the body cause cancer, and he theorized that tumor growth could be stopped through intense detoxification treatment. He also believed that the long-term presence of toxins interfered with normal cell metabolism. Today, the Gerson diet still consists of large quantities of raw fruit and vegetable juices, which are rich in potassium but low in sodium. Patients currently using Gerson's diet take supplements providing such things as Vitamin C, thyroid extract, and digestive enzymes. Other Gerson treatments include ozone therapy, hydrogen peroxide, and live cell therapy. Gerson's coffee enema, used to accelerate liver detoxification, has always been ridiculed and controversial, but it remains part of the treatment. Although there is an in-patient treatment center in Mexico, it is possible to use many elements of the Gerson diet at home.

European studies suggest that as a complementary treatment the Gerson diet has much to offer. British and Austrian studies noted that even patients with very advanced cancer felt relatively well and needed little or no pain medication. They also experienced fewer side effects of chemotherapy. The Gerson Institute has documented stories of patients whose cancers have been in remission for twenty years or more; some of their patients have never had a recurrence of their disease. (Opponents say that there are always some patients who fully recover, even when the odds against them are great. Therefore, they claim, the Gerson patients are among this exceptional group and would have recovered with conventional treatment.) The institute continues its own research and remains a major player in alternative and complementary cancer treatments.

The Nutritional Approach

In addition to vegetarian and macrobiotic diets (see Chapter 8), nutritional supplements are components of immunotherapy in that certain nutrients boost the immune system and enable the body to resist or fight the cancer. Taking large doses of the antioxidant nutrients and trace minerals, such as germanium-132, is currently recommended as a complementary cancer therapy.

Organic germanium stimulates production of interferon, which in turn stimulates the body's production of natural killer (NK) cells. In the 1960s, a Japanese scientist synthesized a form of organic germanium (Ge-132) and discovered that many plants (e.g., ginseng, aloe, and garlic) traditionally used in healing contain germanium. Patients using nutritional therapies usually take very high doses of nutrients before, during, and after other treatments. Therefore, a nutritionist or a practitioner with training in nutrition science should monitor nutritional treatment.

Shark Cartilage

Unlike bones and muscles, cartilage tissue is avascular, meaning that it does not contain blood vessels. This is important, because solid tumors need new blood vessels to grow. The medical name for the process by which a network of blood vessels forms in a tumor is angiogenesis. Researchers have shown that shark cartilage appears to inhibit angiogenesis, and therefore, tumors cannot continue to grow.

Bovine cartilage also has antiangiogenesis properties, but mammals have only small amounts of cartilage in their bodies. A shark's skeleton, however, is entirely composed of cartilage.

Shark cartilage is a rich source of calcium and phosphorus and currently is classified as a food supplement, making it available in natural food stores and through mail order suppliers.

In Cuba, a small clinical trial using shark cartilage with twenty-seven cancer patients—all considered terminal cases—brought encouraging results. Nearly every patient's condition improved, with no significant side effects or toxic reactions to the cartilage. In some patients the size of the tumors were significantly reduced; other patients became cancer-free. Other human and animal studies suggest that shark cartilage shows promise in preventing the spread of cancer (metastasis) because of its anti angiogenesis properties.

I. William Lane, Ph.D., co-author (with Linda Comac) of *Sharks Don't Get Cancer*, pioneered rectally administered shark cartilage treatment with a small group of cancer patients. Some patients with advanced cancer received high doses of shark cartilage as their only treatment. Preliminary results of Lane's work are encouraging, but much more research is needed before this treatment will be accepted by the medical establishment. If you mention shark cartilage to your oncologist, he or she is likely to tell you that it is nothing more than "voodoo" treatment. However, this attitude has not stopped many cancer patients from using shark cartilage on their own, often as a complementary treatment.

There is no question that preliminary research with shark cartilage holds great promise for treating many types of cancer and other conditions such as arthritis and scleroderma. If you choose to investigate further, we recommend that you read Lane and Comac's book and talk with a health care provider who believes in trying unconventional cancer treatments. Currently, some homeopaths, naturopaths, chiropractors, and osteopaths are probably the best sources of information. They can advise you about dosages and brands (quality varies among brands) or refer you to a holistic cancer center where you can get more information.

Hydrogen Peroxide

You undoubtedly know that hydrogen peroxide is a common antibacterial substance. But it may eventually find its way into conventional treatment for various kinds of cancer. Many published studies indicate that hydrogen peroxide can enhance the effectiveness of other cancer treatments, particularly radiation therapy. While it isn't an illegal treatment, it's not approved by either the AMA or the FDA.

Hydrogen peroxide is the simplest and the least expensive of the oxygen therapies. Cancer cells thrive in an environment that is low in oxygen, while normal cells thrive in an oxygen-rich environment. Ozone therapy and hyperbaric oxygen therapy are methods that use oxygen in various forms to promote wound healing and to enhance cell metabolism. Oxygen therapies are more widely known—and respected—in Russia and Germany than in the United States. These therapies are rarely used alone, but are a component of treatment plans for many illnesses, including cancer.

Intravenous hydrogen peroxide treatment is used at some alternative treatment centers. It is an older, unconventional cancer treatment, considered safe when used under controlled conditions. However, you should *never* use the hydrogen peroxide available in grocery and drug stores to treat any serious illness, including cancer. While practitioners sometimes recommend oral doses of hydrogen peroxide, it is *not* a "home remedy." We recommend discussing the benefits of this and other oxygen treatments with alternative health care practitioners who can guide you to researchers or clinicians who know how to use these therapies safely.

Alternative "Chemotherapy"

Many substances used in chemotherapy put great stress on the body's healthy tissues. However, some chemical compounds exist that work in a variety of ways to fight primary tumor growth and metastasis. While detailed discussion is outside the scope of this book, you can find information about these chemicals in many books about alternative cancer treatments and through the centers that use them. These chemical agents, each of which has a different action in the body, include the following.

Hydrazine sulfate. This compound does not kill cancer cells directly, but through a complex biochemical process it can deprive tumors of energy needed to grow. It also helps fight cachexia, which is the medical term for the weight loss and weakness affecting many cancer patients. There is significant controversy about the effectiveness of this compound, and the FDA has not approved it. Some alternative cancer treatment centers outside the United States use it.

Clodronate. This compound is used to treat bone cancer, but is not available in the United States. It is approved in other countries and appears to prevent loss of calcium from the bones affected by cancer. Proponents say that while it is not a cure for bone cancer, it greatly improves patients' quality of life, prevents or slows metastasis, and may result in long-term remission of the disease.

Amygdalin (laetrile). This is probably the best-known of all the controversial alternative cancer treatments, but practitioners in many countries use it and continue to report positive results. Amygdalin occurs in some plants and is part of a group of substances called nitrilosides, meaning they contain cyanide. Amygdalin, also known as vitamin B17 and laetrile, is a concentrated form of the substance. Proponents say that it is not toxic to normal cells but it does destroy cancer cells; opponents claim that it lacks specific anticancer properties and offers false hope to cancer patients. This controversy continues worldwide, but in any case, you should never attempt to use laetrile on your own because it can be dangerous when taken improperly. The alternative cancer clinics that use laetrile do so in combination with other treatments.

Antineoplastons. Stanislaw Burzynski, M.D., Ph.D., developed a different type of anticancer agent, one that makes use of a specialized biochemical system in the body that may change or reprogram cancer cells rather than destroy them. The therapy he developed involves using protein compounds that occur naturally in the body. Burzynski isolated and synthesized these compounds in the blood and urine, and developed nontoxic cancer agents currently used and studied in many countries. These substances are not approved by the FDA nor are the treatments used in Burzynski's clinic (located in Houston, Texas) reimbursed by insurance companies. However, Burzynski and others continue using antineoplastons, and the compounds do not appear to interfere with conventional chemotherapy.

Plant Therapies

Many different plants may have anticancer properties when used alone or in groups. Some common plants used as complementary cancer treatments include mistletoe, a plant studied and used in Europe; pau d'arco, the name of a tea made from the bark of a South American tree; chaparral, a desert shrub found in the Southwestern United States; and Juzentaihoto (JT-48 or JTT), one of many Chinese herbs used in cancer treatment.

We mention these herbs because they may reduce the side effects of conventional chemotherapy and strengthen the immune system. Some researchers believe that these and other herbs show promise in preventing cancer from developing in the first place, and in slowing tumor growth and preventing metastasis. Some herbalists, homeopaths, naturopaths, chiropractors, nutritionists, and physicians can tell you how to use these herbs correctly. Some alternative cancer treatment centers also use these herbs in their protocols.

Sources of Information and Referrals

Note: Some of the therapies described in this chapter are used by a variety of health care practitioners, whose associations are listed elsewhere in this book. In addition, the cancer treatment organizations listed below represent only a tiny sample of resources for cancer patients. However, at the end of this book, the reading list includes books devoted entirely to unconventional cancer treatment. Many of them include lists of associations, research services, practitioners, and treatment centers in North America.

American Board of Chelation Therapy
70 West Huron Street
Chicago, IL 60610
800/356–2228

This organization provides a list of physicians certified to do chelation therapy, and it has established the standard protocol for the treatment in this country.

American College of Advancement in Medicine
P.O. Box 3427
Laguna Hills, CA 92654
714/583–7666

This college provides a directory of its members, who use chelation therapy and other unconventional treatments.

American Association of Naturopathic Physicians
2366 Eastlake Avenue
Suite 322
Seattle, WA 98102
206/323–7610

This association provides referrals to naturopathic physicians who do colon therapy.

Environmental Dental Association
   9974 Scripps Ranch Boulevard, #36
   San Diego, CA 92131
   800/388–8124

This association provides a referral service and information about biological dentistry.

DAMS
   6025 Osuna Boulevard, N.E.
   Suite B
   Albuquerque, NM 87109
   505/888–0111

DAMS stands for Dental Amalgam Syndrome, and is an organization that helps those who suffer from mercury toxicity.

Optometric Extension Program
   1921 East Carnegie
   Suite L
   Santa Ana, CA 92705
   800/424–8070

This program offers information about developmental optometry and has a referral service.

The Gerson Institute
   P.O. Box
   Bonita, CA 91908

You can write to the institute to request information about the Gerson diet and the treatment center.

The Bio-Oxidative Medicine Foundation
   P.O. Box 895951
   Oklahoma City, OK 73189
   405/478–4266

This foundation publishes a newsletter about oxygen therapies.

The Burzynski Clinic
   12000 Richmond Avenue
   Suite 260
   Houston, TX 77082
   713/597–0111

You can receive information about antineoplaston therapy by calling Burzynski's clinic.

Chapter Sixteen

Maverick Doctors

M any traditionally trained physicians are jumping on the
alternative medicine bandwagon, no longer believing that
many unconventional therapies are radical or even unusual. We
call these physicians "mavericks," because they influence their
colleagues and are changing health care delivery in this country
for the better. These physicians have had to put up with ridicule,
criticism, and even legal action taken against them by members
of the medical establishment.

Criticism and skepticism continue, but the public is increasingly suspicious of doctors who casually dismiss their innova-
tive colleagues as unscientific or even unethical. Indeed, the
public flocks to alternative practitioners and to physicians who
incorporate some unconventional treatments into their practices.
Today's sophisticated medical consumers are interested in prevention, not only to avoid unnecessary suffering, but also to
control the rising costs of health care.

Maverick Organizations

A few organizations represent physicians who search for new
ways to combine their valuable training in orthodox medicine

with ideas about holistic health care. The American Holistic Medical Association (AHMA), founded in 1978, is one example. Its membership is open to allopathic and osteopathic physicians and medical students with an interest in the holistic trends in medical practice. The AHMA sponsors conferences, publishes a journal, and has a referral network. It also supplies information about many complementary and alternative treatments, believing that patients have a right to choose treatments they believe are appropriate for them. The organization also supports insurance reimbursement for many alternative therapies.

The American College for Advancement in Medicine (ACAM) represents doctors using nutritional therapies and chelation. ACAM holds conferences, issues reports about current research, establishes protocols for chelation therapy, and provides referrals to their members. This organization also works for changes in insurance reimbursement policies.

These groups help maverick doctors stand together against harassment. Medical boards in some states have tried to prohibit allopathic and osteopathic doctors from using herbs, chelation therapy, homeopathic remedies, or nutrition as primary treatments. These attempts are legal, because state licensing boards, for better and for worse, establish accepted standards of care. The insurance industry is involved because it pays only for treatments that conform to these standards.

The pharmaceutical industry shares part of the blame for discouraging inexpensive treatments, because profits are dependent on developing and patenting new drugs. The Food and Drug Administration does not allow the producers of nutritional or herbal supplements to state what conditions or illnesses are effectively treated with these agents. The battle between advocates of natural and inexpensive therapeutic agents and the drug companies wages on, and there isn't likely to be a solution anytime soon.

Meanwhile, however, consumers have growing numbers of advocates among the conventional health care world, making it more difficult for the medical establishment to prevail in every controversy. Consumers are increasingly aware that some treatments that helped them may come under attack at any time, and they are joining forces with others to guarantee the public freedom of choice in health care.

Individual Mavericks

We could have profiled any number of individual practitioners in this chapter, because the list of maverick doctors is long—and growing. We might have chosen physicians such as Susan Lark or Michelle Harrison, both of whom pioneered a holistic approach to treating PMS. These physicians began using primarily nutrition and lifestyle changes (and sometimes natural progesterone) when the conventional treatment largely consisted of prescribing diuretics and referring patients to mental health professionals. (Many types of alternative practitioners were already using a variety of therapies to successfully treat PMS, but few conventional physicians believed in them or referred patients to these practitioners.)

We could have chosen Jonathan Wright, M.D., who uses many nutritional remedies in his Tahoma Clinic, in Kent, Washington. Because he has written books and columns read by the lay public, he is well known to health-conscious people. When in 1992 FDA agents (accompanied by armed local police officers) raided his clinic, his patients and many readers were shocked. Wright is an internationally respected physician, but nevertheless, FDA agents ransacked his office and seized everything from his postage stamps to his payroll data, along with his supply of nutritional products. At this time, a grand jury investigation of his practice is underway, but no charges have been filed.

We could have chosen Christine Northrup, a gynecologist who opened a unique women's health care center in Maine. Her center has earned a national reputation for its holistic approach to women's health, and body/mind medicine is integral to her practice. Women come from all over the country to get second (or third or fourth) opinions about persistent gynecological problems, which can sometimes be successfully treated with simple nutritional or herbal formulas. Northrup is vocal about social problems that affect women's health, and she and her staff help patients deal with the effects of physical and sexual abuse, which she believes continue to damage women long after the incidents of abuse have stopped. Believing that the society's attitudes about women and their bodily functions can contribute to health problems, Northrup works with women to help them overcome negative body image. In short, Northrup's biggest contribution might be her ability to empower women to take control of their own health care.

Other choices would include two physicians, Bernie Siegel, who was once copresident (with Christine Northrup) of the AHMA, and O. Carl Simonton, both of whom played a role in revolutionizing cancer treatment. They did this by introducing body/mind therapies to conventional cancer treatment regimens. One could say that Simonton created visualization as a complementary treatment for cancer, and Siegel, through his popular writing, made sure the world knew that there was more to offer cancer patients than surgery, radiation therapy, and chemotherapy. Many conventional physicians now recommend guided imagery, support groups, art therapy, massage, and meditation to their cancer patients. Patients with AIDS, multiple sclerosis, and other serious diseases also may find their physicians approving of these complementary treatments.

There are hundreds of physicians who we could legitimately call mavericks. The two whose work we chose to discuss in detail each introduced integrated and holistic treatment programs into the conventional health care world. Deepak Chopra, an American physician originally from India, is at least in part responsible for both the growth of Ayurvedic medicine and for sparking the intense public interest in the basic issues of why and how we become ill. The other physician whose work we will discuss is Dean Ornish, who developed a noninvasive approach to treating heart disease. Ornish's program was once criticized, but it has been shown to be so effective that many insurance companies now pay for this treatment.

Deepak Chopra and Ayurvedic Medicine

Were it not for Chopra, many Americans would never have heard about Ayurveda, the ancient philosophy of life, health, and healing that comes to us from India. Although Chopra is a conventionally trained physician with a specialty in endocrinology, he is best known for his involvement in the body/mind medicine movement in this country. Through his popular books, Chopra offers the public a unique view of health and illness, and in particular, the reasons we get sick and how we participate in creating health as well as illness.

The roots of Ayurveda are as ancient as traditional Chinese medicine, and include a system of explaining and illustrating the universe and everything in it. The word "Ayurveda" literally means the science or knowledge of life. It's also similar to Chinese medicine; it holds all living things are composed of elements and energies, which must be in perfect balance to maintain a naturally healthy state.

Ayurvedic medicine does not accept the idea that we "catch" a cold because a particular virus is traveling through the air and we happen to inhale it. The condition of the host is more important than the disease agent in determining whether a person becomes ill or stays well. Our belief in a disease and its consequences play a vital role in our ability to maintain health or recover from an illness.

In his books, Chopra illustrates this principle when he discusses the changes patients experience when they are diagnosed with a serious illness, such as cancer. Before being told they have the illness, they may feel well and live normally. But as soon as the diagnosis is confirmed, they become sick, often reporting symptoms they didn't have only a short time before. Chopra talks about people who have died shortly after learning they had cancer, when it was obvious they had lived with the disease in their bodies for many years. Of course, Western physicians know that this phenomenon exists, but until recently, scientists haven't probed into the mystery of the way the mind communicates information to the body.

Chopra, using principles of Ayurvedic medicine as a starting point, believes that we often become identified with a disease. The formerly well patients heard the word "cancer" and began to identify with being seriously ill. Our minds communicate thoughts and beliefs to every cell in our bodies, and like Pavlov's dogs, we respond by exhibiting symptoms that our minds associate with the disease. Chopra might argue that if a person doesn't know that cancer is a dreaded disease, linked with eventual and almost certain death, he or she might not have symptoms at all. This is an extreme example of what Chopra sometimes calls "bodymind," but it applies to many other life situations, too.

If, for example, we dislike a certain food, we will have a physical reaction if someone tries to pressure us to eat it. Our minds communicate the dislike and the psychological discomfort and the physical response will continue until our thoughts transmit the information that the "threat" is over.

The Ayurvedic Body Types or Doshas

In this philosophy of health care, a person's body type determines—or defines—his or her basic constitution. Our body type helps the Ayurvedic physician diagnose and treat us as individuals. Our individual constitutions are determined by *doshas*, also called metabolic body types. We are all a combination of the three doshas, which are linked with specific energies and organ systems and are present in every life form. The preponderance of one type of energy over another is what determines our constitution and influences our personality.

The descriptions following are very brief. In reality, the doshas are only one part of a very complex system of principles that guide the entire universe, the natural world, human consciousness—and the food we eat. Chopra speaks of the doshas as psychophysiological body types that are the key to biochemical individuality.

The *kapha* type of person tends to be overweight and generally moves slowly, sleeps soundly, and has a good-natured personality. These are the people who don't get angry very often, are tolerant of others, but who also may procrastinate. Their digestion is usually slow and when out of balance, kapha people are vulnerable to clinical obesity and high cholesterol levels. Unfortunately, these individuals don't necessarily have bodies that fit the media image of the ideal physique, so they might think they're fat when their weight is actually ideal for them.

The *vata* type of person is intuitive and quick. He or she is usually thin and may be moody but energetic and enthusiastic, a life-of-the-party sort of person. The unbalanced vata type may become anxious or nervous and seek help for chronic anxiety disorders. Unlike the kapha type, the vata person may not sleep well when this energy is out of balance.

The *pitta* type usually has a medium build, neither too thin or too heavy. These are intense people who love order above all else. Intelligent and warm, they also may have bad tempers and be quick to erupt. Often perfectionists, they tend to have disorders of the digestive tract such as ulcers and hemorrhoids.

Like many other systems we've described in this book, Ayurvedic medicine bases treatment on restoring balance and harmony. We become ill, at least in part, because our doshas are out of balance. Our metabolic type may be hereditary, but this means only that under certain conditions, the person may be vulnerable to certain diseases or conditions. The doshas are part of a system designed to keep us well and should not be viewed as a kind of negative fate. Our environment has great influence on our ability to stay well, regardless of our constitution, and part of Ayurvedic treatment is achieving dosha balance under any conditions.

According to Chopra, once we understand our unique constitution, we can take steps to stay balanced and alter diet and lifestyle to correct tendencies that may be damaging. For example, while drinking coffee in the morning might suit a kapha person, it is not good for a pitta type. A vegetarian diet that emphasizes raw foods might suit a pitta person, but a vata type might thrive on heartier fare and should eat raw food sparingly.

In Ayurvedic philosophy, our body's natural—and spontaneous—intelligence attempts to keep us physically, emotionally, and spiritually well. External influences, such as psychological stress or poor eating habits, can disrupt this balance. The seasons represent dosha qualities, too, and influence the other doshas. During the winter, the kapha characteristics dominate, and the kapha person may be vulnerable to colds or flu, but the coming of spring promotes a return to balance.

Ayurvedic Diagnosis and Treatment

Diagnostic techniques share some similar principles with Chinese medicine. The doshas have corresponding pulses, and the Ayurvedic physician evaluates the quality of a patient's vata, pitta, and kapha pulses. Six pulses can be detected on each wrist, giving the physician clues about current strengths and weaknesses in the body's organ systems. The tongue is examined to find imbalances in the body and, for example, a white, coated tongue may suggests that kapha is disturbed and out of balance. An Ayurvedic physician examines the color and clarity of the urine, because it provides information about disturbances in one of the doshas.

Just as dietary advice varies because of biochemical individuality, treatments vary as well. In most cases, internal detoxifying and cleansing using combinations of herbs, fasting, and oil massage are combined with changes in the diet that balance the doshas. Mental and spiritual healing techniques include yoga, sound and light therapies, breathing exercises, and meditation.

Most conditions and diseases can be treated with Ayurvedic medicine, sometimes in conjunction with Western therapies. Dr. Chopra has made a unique contribution because, although he uses Ayurveda in his work, he recognizes that it may be one of many systems that help patients. The patient's receptiveness is the most important element in any healing philosophy, because if the mind has either confidence and belief or fear and doubt, every cell in the body knows it.

Chopra encourages patients to look within and understand that they are much more than a collection of atoms and molecules. Meditation is an integral part of Ayurvedic treatment, but it is also part of prevention and maintaining optimal health. Meditation is a vehicle by which we can come to a deeper understanding of our nature, and, over time, become less identified with disease and illness. Even desperately ill people will, at some point during regular meditative practice, discover the place in consciousness that is not sick. Experiencing this place can then help people move beyond the notion that they have become their disease.

Ayurvedic therapy is available in many towns and cities in the United States, and other alternative practitioners are incorporating its philosophy into their practices. There is no inherent danger in any of the treatments recommended and our only caution is that you explore all your options before committing to any treatment that excludes conventional therapy.

Deepak Chopra has written about all aspects of health and healing and because of his Western training is able to explain esoteric Eastern ideas in language many of us can understand. This ability is perhaps his greatest contribution to the current drive to explore body/mind issues and reach a deeper understanding of our human experience.

Dean Ornish

Dean Ornish "borrows" techniques from many philosophies. While it shouldn't seem unusual for a doctor to recommend a radical change in diet, regular meditation, and yoga as treatments for heart disease, it has taken years for the integrated program Ornish created to be accepted by the orthodox medical world. Today, even though some insurance companies pay for the cost of his treatment program and many of his colleagues respect his work, some conventional doctors continue to claim that the program is too difficult to comply with and has little value anyway.

When Ornish began his research, there were no other controlled studies (in the United States) underway to find out if therapies other than drugs or surgery could reverse heart disease. But Ornish believed that the available therapies were not the miracle cures the medical establishment claimed they were. The widely used drug and surgical techniques may work, at least some of the time, in a "mechanical" way, but they don't begin to touch the underlying causes of heart disease. In addition, even bypass surgery is only a temporary fix, and not everyone responds well to either drugs or surgery. Some patients' heart disease actually becomes worse after these treatments.

While still a medical student Ornish examined the professional literature and discovered that stress, diet, lack of exercise, smoking, and so forth had been established as risk factors. Lifestyle changes such as lowering cholesterol in the diet, stress management, and the benefits of not smoking were studied and documented, but only in isolation from other factors. These lifestyle issues were well-established prevention factors. But no one had yet designed a study that included all the lifestyle interventions. Ornish also wanted to see if some key lifestyle changes that could prevent the disease also could reverse its progress.

Ornish took a year off from medical school to explore his idea that heart disease could be reversed with a program designed around nonmedical intervention. His first study was small by medical standards and included only ten people, all of whom had previously diagnosed heart disease. Some had incapacitating chest pain upon even mild exertion, and many were unable to take care of themselves.

This and subsequent studies used high-tech diagnostic tools to measure patients' progress. All ten participants reported feeling better in a matter of a few days and after thirty days, they were objectively better. Subjectively, many hadn't felt so good in years. Cholesterol levels had dropped, and some patients could stop taking drugs to lower their blood pressure. Perhaps most important, coronary blood flow also significantly improved. Encouraged by his results, Ornish took another year off from medical school to design a larger study, one that had a control group comprised of patients undergoing "usual and customary" treatment. Again the patients using his diet and lifestyle approach improved dramatically and showed measurable signs that their diagnosed heart disease was reversing. The patients in the control group either stayed the same or became worse during the thirty-day period. These results seemed almost too good to be true, and instead of embracing them, many conventional physicians simply refused to believe that they were possible.

One criticism that still persists is that no one knows which, if any, factor is the important one and holds the key to reversing the disease. Ornish and his supporters say that all the changes are probably important, but since nothing in his program is harmful, this objection to his work doesn't hold up.

Ornish, who went on to complete his medical training, describes the initial studies in *Dr. Dean Ornish's Program for Reversing Heart Disease,* a book offering valuable information for the lay reader. The scientific information is both well-documented and reassuring, and the description of Ornish's struggle to have his program accepted by cardiologists is an eye opener. Today, however, some insurance companies will pay for a twenty-four- or thirty-day stay at a treatment center using Ornish's program. Over the long haul, this treatment is far less expensive than drugs or surgery and it shows lasting results.

Not to be confused with a quick fix, Ornish's program requires that patients take responsibility for their health. In fact, early critics claimed that Ornish's approach couldn't work because people would refuse to eat a vegetarian diet and most would think that learning to meditate and doing yoga was weird. (Apparently, Westerners respond more positively to these techniques if they are called stress management tools, rather than ancient practices.)

Ornish concedes that his program depends on patients' willingness to continue a self-care program. But he argues that it makes no sense to refuse to study methods that by definition are inexpensive, safe, noninvasive, and effective because some doctors speculate that many patients can't or won't comply. Why not, he maintains, begin working with willing people and then attempt to motivate others as results continue to show how effective this program is?

The "Opening Your Heart" Program

Ornish was influenced by others who explore mind/body therapies, and he concluded that changing diet alone is not enough to produce significant reversal of heart disease. Simply telling patients to manage their stress better and take a walk a few times a week is also insufficient advice. Patients need ways to integrate these changes into their lives and understand that they have a better chance of getting better if they change the way they think and live.

One reason Ornish named his program "Opening Your Heart" is that he links emotional well-being with a person's ability to reverse heart disease. Ornish found that some of his early study participants lacked emotional intimacy in their lives, and it was a new experience for them to get the support of a peer group that meets regularly in a relaxed and intimate setting. He initially thought that the group meetings would provide time to explain the program and give patients instructions. But as the participants began to talk about their lives and their feelings,

Ornish realized that these meetings had much therapeutic value. Emotional isolation is one of those "difficult to measure" risk factors, but Ornish believes that healing the body cannot be separated from healing the mind and spirit.

The program's stress management component includes yoga stretches, progressive relaxation techniques, breathing exercises, meditation, and guided imagery. Participants who go to an "Opening Your Heart" center do these exercises daily, but Ornish stresses that these can be done at home. They form a sound stress management program for anyone and may help prevent the onset of heart disease. For those of us who are still well, the advice and training that patients receive during a stay at a treatment center is freely available in Ornish's books and through the work of many alternative and conventional practitioners.

In addition, the program advocates a vegetarian, low-fat diet. The prevention diet is a bit less strict than the diet patients use to reverse heart disease. (A diet this low in fat is not recommended for children.) Another component of the program includes helping patients find strategies for handling addictions, such as cigarette smoking, which is a significant risk factor for heart disease. Walking is the recommended exercise and Ornish believes that taking regular one-hour or half-hour walks several times a week is sufficient for maintaining a healthy heart.

The Opening Your Heart program is adaptable to people with special needs (such as diabetes) or physical disabilities. Even those who had diagnosed heart disease for many years may benefit from the program. As we've seen, the basic program can benefit just about any adult.

A Look at the Future

As we have said, these two doctors represent a much larger movement within conventional health care. Alternative health care practitioners and unconventional physicians show us that it is possible to develop valuable partnerships in health care. Some day, we will probably look back at the decades dominated by technological medicine as a stage we grew out of. Certainly, the maverick doctors have a valuable role in leading us to the next stage, which we hope will be characterized by a spirit of cooperation among all health care professionals.

Sources of Information

American Holistic Medical Association
  4101 Lake Boone Trail
  Suite 201
  Raleigh, NC 27607
  919/787–5181

AHMA supplies an information packet to anyone who requests it. Associate memberships are available to alternative practitioners and to lay persons interested in holistic health.

The American College of Advancement in Medicine
  P.O. Box 3427
  Laguna Hills, CA 92654
  714/583–7666

ACAM has a referral service and will send information to you about its work if you enclose a self-addressed, stamped envelope with your letter.

American Preventive Medical Association
  459 Walker Road
  Great Falls, VA 22066
  800/230–2762

This association's members include medical doctors and other alternative practitioners dedicated to ensuring that a variety of effective treatments are legally available to the public. Their widely distributed newsletter is called *Health and Healing*.

Citizens for Health
P.O. Box 1195
Tacoma, WA 98401
800/357–2211
206/922–2457

This is an organization of citizens interested in the rights of health care consumers. They study legislative issues and support freedom of choice legislation on both state and national levels. It has chapters in all fifty states and publishes a newsletter.

American School of Ayurvedic Sciences
10025 Northeast Fourth Street
Bellevue, WA 98004
206/453–8022

This is a college that provides Ayurvedic training for doctors and alternative health care practitioners. Lay people are also welcome to take courses.

The College of Maharishi Ayur-Veda Health Center
P.O. Box 282
Fairfield, IA 52556
800/248–9050

This center trains practitioners and also offers referrals to treatment centers that use Ayurveda.

Preventive Medicine Research Institute
900 Broadway
Suite 1
Sausalito, CA 94965
415/332–2525
Life Choice: 800/328–3738

This institute provides information about Dean Ornish's program to prevent and treat heart disease. It provides referrals to medical centers that offer his specific program. Life Choice is the company that sells Dr. Ornish's books, tapes, and other educational materials.

A Reading List

The books and resources listed here represent a tiny fraction of the available material about alternative therapies. We have chosen these few because they provide comprehensive information and are readily available through conventional channels such as bookstores, health food markets, or mail order catalogs. Many of the books described below contain reading lists and information about sources of additional information, products, and services. Generally speaking, these are complex books about complex topics and space allows us to describe them only in brief.

In addition to these books, we also recommend that you ask health care providers and professional associations to recommend material that further explains their philosophies and treatment methods. Some organizations listed at the end of each chapter have catalogs of books and audio and videotapes.

General Information

World Medicine: The East West Guide to Healing Your Body, Tom Monte and the Editors of *EastWest Natural Health* (Jeremy P. Tarcher/Perigee, 1993).

Covering six different health care philosophies, this book provides information about the way conditions affecting various organ systems are treated by each school of healing.

Alternative Medicine: The Definitive Guide, compiled by the Burton Goldberg Group (Future Medicine Publishing, 1993).

This is an extensive book (1068 pages) that includes explanations of alternative therapies plus a lengthy guide to using various treatments for specific illnesses.

Health and Healing, Andrew Weil (Houghton Mifflin, 1988).

This is a classic book about the philosophy of health and includes valuable discussions of the history of the politics of medical care. Weil brings his perspective as an unconventional physician to information about alternative health care and body/mind medicine.

Chiropractic and Osteopathy

Today's Health Alternative, Raquel Martin (America West Publishers, 1992).

Written for the lay public, this book provides an overview of chiropractic treatment and the development of the philosophy.

Osteopathic Medicine: An American Reformation, George Northup (American Osteopathic Association, 1987).

Available through the professional association (see Chapter 2), this book provides an explanation of osteopathic treatment and its history in the United States.

Osteopathic Self-Treatment, Leon Chaitow (Thorsons, 1990).

This book explains both in-office and self-care osteopathic treatment.

Energy Therapies and Body Work

Hands-On Healing, Editors of *Prevention* Magazine (Rodale, 1989).

This volume covers many areas of the new medicine, including many anecdotal asides.

Herbalism

Herbal Healing for Women, Rosemary Gladstar (Fireside, 1993).

This is an excellent volume for women in particular and the public in general. The herbal knowledge is thorough and deep.

The Herbalist newsletter of the American Herbalists Guild in Soquel, California.

A good starting point for people interested in learning more about herbalism (address at the end of Chapter 9).

Natural Health, Natural Medicine, Andrew Weil (Houghton Mifflin, 1990).

A range of health problems are discussed and natural medicines recommended.

Homeopathy

Everybody's Guide to Homeopathic Medicines, Stephen Cummings and Dana Ullman (Jeremy P. Tarcher/Perigree, 1991).

This book explains the philosophy of homeopathy and explains treatments for common conditions and illnesses. Dana Ullman has also written other books about homeopathy.

The Family Guide to Homeopathy: Symptoms and Natural Solutions,
Andrew Lockie (Prentice Hall, 1993).

This is a guide to treating a variety of conditions with homeopathic remedies, nutritional supplements, and diet.

Massage

Acupressure's Potent Points, Michael Reed Gach (Acupressure Institute, 1994).

An excellent book on how to relieve dozens of ailments from skin problems to insomnia.

Massage for Common Ailments, Sara Thomas (Fireside, 1988).

A basic massage book, highlighting individual complaints and how they can be addressed. It also has a basic shiatsu routine.

Naturopathy

Encyclopedia of Natural Medicine, Michael Murray and Joseph Pizzorno (Prima Publishing, 1991).

Written by two naturopathic physicians, this is a comprehensive guide to this healing philosophy and its array of treatments.

Natural Alternatives to Over-the-Counter and Prescription Drugs, Michael Murray (William Morrow, 1994).

The author provides extensive information about natural remedies for common illnesses and conditions.

Nutrition and Diet

Prescription for Nutritional Healing, James F. Balch and Phyllis A. Balch (Avery Publishing Group, 1990).

A practical and comprehensive book, it explains the role of individual nutrients in human health and provides advice for using nutritional supplements and diet to treat specific conditions.

Dr. Wright's Guide to Healing with Nutrition, Jonathan Wright (Keats Publishing, 1990).

Dr. Wright uses case studies to discuss the ways nutrition can heal many conditions.

Foods that Heal, Bernard Jensen (Avery, 1993).

This book explains the therapeutic value of certain foods and how to incorporate them into a health care plan.

A Guide to the Food Pyramid, Shirleigh Moog (The Crossing Press, 1993).

The author explains the recent change from the four basic food groups guide to healthful eating to the new pyramid format with its emphasis on a diet low in fat and rich in complex carbohydrates. The book includes many recipes.

Orthomolecular Nutrition (Revised), Abram Hoffer and Morton Walker (Keats Publishing, 1978).

This book gives an overview of orthomolecular medicine and discusses the role of specific nutrients in medical and psychiatric treatment.

The Cancer Prevention Diet, Michio Kushi (St. Martin's Press, 1983).

The author is a well-known macrobiotic teacher and the book discusses the ways in which a macrobiotic diet can both prevent and help to heal cancer.

A Natural Approach to Diabetes and Hypoglycemia, Michio Kushi (Japan Publications, 1985).

This is one of the many books by Kushi on macrobiotic living. It explains the philosophy in a language lay people can understand.

Healing for Everyone, Evarts Loomis (DeVorss and Co., 1975).

This book recounts the author's research and clinical experience with fasting programs.

Fasting Signs and Symptoms: A Clinical Guide, Trevor K. Salloum (Naturopathic Press, 1992).

Detailed and precise, this book is written as a guide to fasting as a health care treatment.

Mind/Body Therapies

Full Catastrophe Living: Using the Wisdom of Your Body and Mind to Face Stress, Pain, and Illness, Jon Kabat-Zinn (Delta, 1990).

This is a self-help book that tells readers how they can benefit from meditation. The goal is to use the mind to create wellbeing during the ups and downs of everyday life.

Minding the Body, Mending the Mind, Joan Borysenko (Bantam Books, 1988).

Written for a lay audience and considered a classic in the field, this is both a practical and philosophical book that discusses body/mind healing techniques.

Healing Yourself: A Step-by-Step Program for Better Health through Imagery, Martin Rossman (Mentor, 1986).

This is a basic primer about using guided imagery in physical and emotional healing.

Beyond the Relaxation Response, Herbert Benson (Putnam/ Berkley, 1993).

This is a follow-up to his popular book, *The Relaxation Response,* and continues the discussion of meditation and its positive value for stress reduction and healing.

How To Meditate, Lawrence LaShan (Bantam, 1974).

This is one of the classic books on various kinds of meditation and the benefits of regular practice.

Hypnotherapy, Dave Elman (Westwood, 1984).

Detailed and somewhat technical, this book provides extensive information about the clinical applications of hypnosis.

Why Me? Harnessing the Healing Power of the Human Spirit, Patricia Norris and Garrett Porter (Stillpoint, 1985).

A patient describes using biofeedback over many years of her cancer treatment.

Movement Therapies

The Complete Illustrated Book of Yoga, Swami Vishnudevananda (Harmony Books, 1980).

A well-known book that describes the practice of yoga, it includes information about postures, meditation, and the spiritual path of yoga practitioners.

Richard Hittleman's Yoga: 28 Day Exercise Plan, Richard Hittleman (Workman, 1969).

A classic for those beginning a yoga program. Each day's instruction includes a new posture and a mental theme.

The Yoga Back Book, Stella Weller (HarperCollins, 1993).

This book emphasizes stretches and postures that promote a strong, healthy back.

Complete Tai Chi: The Definitive Guide to Physical and Emotional Self Improvement, Master Alfred Huang (Charles E. Tuttle Company, 1993).

This is a detailed instructional manual with many photographs, making it especially useful for beginners.

The Complete System of Self-Healing: Internal Exercises, Stephen Chang (Tao Publishing, 1986).

This is a clear description of qigong exercises and philosophy. It includes illustrations and a guide to begin daily practice.

The Self-Applied Health Enhancement Methods, Roger Jahnke (Health Action Books, 1989).

This book explains qigong in simple terms that Westerners can understand, and offers advice for starting regular practice.

Light and Sound Therapies

Light: Medicine of the Future, Jacob Liberman (Bear and Co., 1991).

This book provides an overview of the history and future of light therapy as a treatment for many disorders.

Health and Light, John Ott (Devin-Adair, 1988).

The author explains his ideas about the effects of artificial and natural light on human health. He discusses early research and the development of light as a therapy.

Healing with Color and Light, Theo Gimbel (Fireside, 1994).

This is a complete self-help guide to using color to improve well-being. It covers the concepts of auras and chakras.

Sound Health, Steven Halpern (Harper and Row, 1985).

Using research from many fields, this book explains the way sound and music affect all aspects of human life.

The Conscious Ear, Alfred Tomatis (Staton Hill Books, 1991).

The author discusses his research using sound therapy to treat learning disabilities.

Mind, Music, and Imagery, Stephanie Merritt (Plume Press, 1990).

In addition to exploring the role of music and sound in human life, the author offers exercises for stress reduction and to enhance specific functions such as memory.

Aromatherapy

The Aromatherapy Book: Applications and Inhalations, Jeanne Rose (Herbal Studies Course and North Atlantic Books, 1992).

This is a comprehensive guide to aromatherapy, including its philosophy, descriptions of essential oils, and instructions for using scents at home.

Aromatherapy for Common Ailments, Shirley Price (Fireside, 1991).

This book offers information about using aromatherapy at home as a treatment for a variety of ailments.

Chelation Therapy

The Healing Powers of Chelation Therapy, John P. Trowbridge, M.D. and Morton Walker (New Way of Life, Inc., 1992).

This book explains chelation therapy in easy-to-understand terms. Some chelation doctors give it to their patients prior to treatment.

Colon Therapy

Colon Health: Key to a Vibrant Life, Norman Walker (Norwalk Press, 1979).

In addition to describing colonics, this book provides information about finding a qualified therapist.

Bach Flower Remedies

Handbook on the Bach Flower Remedies, Phillip Chancellor (Keats, 1971).

This book, written for a lay audience, teaches readers how to use Bach Flower Remedies.

Bach Flower Therapy, Mechthild Scheffer (Inner Traditions, 1987).

The remedies are explained in depth and the reader can learn how to use them in a self-help program.

Alternative Cancer Treatments

Alternatives in Cancer Therapies: The Complete Guide to Non-traditional Treatments, Ross Pelton and Lee Overholser (Fireside, 1994).

The authors describe many different alternative cancer treatments, providing background and current information about efficacy. There is also a list of clinics and other resources.

Choices in Healing, Michael Lerner (MIT Press, 1994).

This is a comprehensive book about complementary cancer therapies. It provides extensive lists of resources and a glossary.

Double Vision: An East West Collaboration for Healing, Alexandra Dundas Todd (Wesleyan Press, 1994).

The author tells a personal story about her son's recovery from cancer and her family's search for complementary treatments. It includes information about using such treatments as diet and imagery.

The Healing Path: A Soul Approach to Illness, Marc Ian Barasch (Penguin, 1993).

The author recounts his experiences as a cancer survivor and the personal challenges and transformation he encountered during his journey to healing. He also explores societal attitudes about illness.

"Maverick" Doctors

Dr. Dean Ornish's Program for Reversing Heart Disease, Dean Ornish (Ballantine Books, 1990).

Ornish explains his unconventional program and offers advice to readers about starting it on their own. It includes background information about Ornish's early research projects and gives advice about meditation, exercise, and diet (including recipes).

Creating Health, Deepak Chopra (Houghton Mifflin, 1987).

One of many of Chopra's books, it provides an overview of his beliefs about mind/body medicine.

Quantum Healing: Exploring the Frontiers of Mind/Body Medicine, Deepak Chopra (Bantam Books, 1990).

Dr. Chopra expands his body/mind philosophy and relates the ideas of Ayurvedic medicine to quantum mechanics.

Ayurvedic Healing, David Frawley (Morson Publishing, 1990).

This is a detailed book about Ayurvedic philosophy and healing methods.

A Life of Balance, Maya Tiwari (Healing Arts Press, 1995).

The author provides a complete guide to Ayurvedic body types and nutrition and includes recipes.

A Different Kind of Healing: Why Mainstream Doctors Are Embracing Alternative Medicine, Oscar Janiger and Philip Goldberg (Jeremy P. Tarcher, 1994).

Using case studies to illustrate, the authors discuss the movement among conventionally trained physicians to use alternative therapies.